Merry Christmas Sionnie
Love Chelsea
2013

Campbell's Kitchen COOKBOOK

Publications
International, Ltd.

Pictured on the front cover (clockwise from top left) Super Simple Nacho Pasta *(page 240)*, Chicken Tortilla Soup *(page 173)*, Weekday Pot Roast & Vegetables *(page 149)*, and Chicken Sorrento *(page 92)*.

Pictured on the back cover (top to bottom): Easy Asian-Style Chicken & Rice *(page 60)*, Bacon Potato Chowder *(page 164)* and Slow Cooker Mole-Style Pulled Pork *(page 266)*.

Pictured on cover flap (front to back): Chicken Fajitas *(page 125)* and Classic Tuna Noodle Casserole *(page 161)*.

Microwave Cooking: Microwave ovens vary in wattage. Use the cooking times as guidelines and check for doneness before adding more time.

Preparation/Cooking Times: Preparation times are based on the approximate amount of time required to assemble the recipe before cooking, baking, chilling or serving. These times include preparation steps such as measuring, chopping, and mixing. The fact that some preparations and cooking can be done simultaneously is taken into account. Preparation of optional ingredients and serving suggestions is not included.

Visit the *Campbell's* Kitchen Facebook® page for daily recipe posts plus ideas and inspiration from our community of fans. And if you want to take Campbell's Kitchen with you, check out our apps designed for mobile devices.

contents

introduction **4**

quick & easy dishes **24**

budget-friendly meals **62**

family favorites **108**

comfort classics **158**

best of the season **188**

kids' top picks **222**

creative & different ideas **248**

parties & entertaining **286**

index **315**

cooking basics

If you're looking for delicious, easy-to-follow recipes your friends and family will rave about, then this cookbook from *Campbell's* Kitchen could very well become one of your most trusted kitchen companions! Whether you're looking for a quick and easy supper, an entrée for a special celebration, or something that the kids around your table will love as much as the grownups, you can solve nearly any dinner dilemma right here!

Packed from cover to cover with test kitchen-perfected recipes featuring ingredients from *Campbell's*®, *Swanson*®, *Pace*®, *Prego*®, *Pepperidge Farm*® and *V8*®—brands you know and trust—this cookbook is also a terrific source for tips and techniques to help make your time in the kitchen easier and more enjoyable.

And if you like what you see here, then definitely check out **www.campbellskitchen.com**, where you can search hundreds more fantastic recipes, save them to your own online recipe box, and get seasonal tips, holiday menu ideas, and so much more. With *Campbell's* Kitchen by your side, it's easy to discover delicious!

Campbell's **Kitchen Team**

tools & gadgets

There seems to be a tool or gadget out there for every cooking task imaginable. But just a few basic pieces of equipment will make your life in the kitchen easier. We've cut through the clutter and come up with a list of the tools and gadgets every kitchen should have.

The Basics

■ ***Box grater:***
Four-sided stainless steel grater with rubber base for stability.

■ ***Can opener:***
Whatever you choose, make sure it's sturdy and has a smooth operating mechanism.

■ ***Citrus reamer:*** A wooden or metal lemon reamer with a large, easy-to-grip handle.

■ ***Colander/strainer:*** For pasta and vegetables, you'll want a large stainless steel colander with two handles; a medium-size fine-mesh strainer is great for removing seeds from fresh lemon juice, straining small amounts of sauces, and for dusting powdered sugar over desserts.

■ ***Cutting boards:*** While wooden and composite boards are equally safe, the lighter composites are becoming quite popular. They're reasonably maintenance free and are dishwasher-safe.

■ ***Electric hand mixer:*** A basic three-speed model is sufficient for most mixing jobs—cookie dough, cake batter, mashing potatoes, etc.

■ ***Glass 2-cup liquid measuring cup.***

■ ***Instant-read thermometer:*** Digital models are relatively inexpensive and work well; dial-style are even less expensive and are fairly accurate.

■ ***Ladle:*** You only need two—a 2-ounce for cooking, and a 6-ounce for soup.

■ ***Large spoon:*** Wooden styles will prevent scratching your pans. A tight-grained wood, like olive or maple, won't absorb flavors.

■ ***Nesting mixing bowls:*** Stainless steel bowls with slip-resistant bases are wonderful, but glass bowls are good too.

■ ***Peeler:*** Choose either a standard "scraper-" style peeler or a "Y" peeler with a comfortable ergonomic handle. It's worth spending a little money on a good peeler because it's used so often in the kitchen—don't skimp here.

■ ***Rolling pin:*** Choose a maple or ash wooden pin with handles. It should be easy to roll and not too heavy.

■ ***Rubber spatula:*** Silicone is best since it can withstand temperatures up to 900°F. Some are designed so that the rubber spatula head can be removed from the wooden handle and go straight into the dishwasher for easy cleanup.

■ ***Stainless steel dry measuring cups and spoons:*** Having a couple of sets of both cups and spoons come in very handy.

■ ***Tongs:*** One 9-inch pair and one 12-inch pair, stainless steel with non-slip handles, lockable for easy storage. The long pair can double for grill duty.

- **Turner:** The best turner, hands down, is a slotted turner, also called a fish turner. Flexible and easy to control, it acts as an extension of your hand.

- **Whisk:** You only need one, a French whisk (otherwise known as an egg or sauce whisk). It can handle everything from whipping cream to smoothing out sauces.

Extra Splurges

- **Food processor:** If you do a lot of chopping, slicing, shredding, or puréeing, a food processor is a great tool to have. It's also great for making and kneading dough in no time.

- **Stick blender:** Also called an immersion blender, these hand-held tools store easily, are a snap to clean and allow you to blend and purée foods in the same pot they're cooked in. Stick blenders are also great for milkshakes, smoothies and for frothing milk for coffee.

Knife Drawer Essentials

In our opinion, a couple of good-quality knives will make cooking much more enjoyable and efficient, and when properly cared for will last for years, making them one of the best kitchen investments you can make. Here's what you need to know when looking for quality knives:

- A high-carbon steel blade—extremely durable, it will not rust and can be sharpened easily.

- Knife blades come either forged or stamped. Forged blades are usually better quality and will last longer, but if they're not in your budget, stamped knives are fine. They're thinner and lighter weight but can cut meat, vegetables and fish just as well as heavy-duty forged knives.

- The most important characteristic of any knife is how it feels when you hold it. Grip the handle to see if it has a weight and shape that suits your hand.

- The type of handle you choose is a personal preference. Molded plastic handles are sturdy but tend to be slippery when wet or oily. Wood handles are great looking but require a little maintenance to keep them in good shape. To help prevent a slippery grip, wrap a few rubber bands around the knife handle—it'll make the knife easier to hold on to if the handle is wet or greasy.

Which knives do I need?

Ultimately, you really need just 2 knives in your kitchen:

- **Chef's knife:** Used for a variety of tasks, including chopping, mincing, and slicing, a chef's knife is the most versatile kitchen knife. It has a pointed tip and a wide, curved blade that allows the knife to rock back and forth. An 8-inch blade is usually the most comfortable size for most people.

- **Paring knife:** Usually 3 to 4 inches long (including the handle) with a pointed tip, paring knives are perfect for simple tasks like cutting and peeling fruits and vegetables.

If you'd like to add more knives and tools to your collection, these are good options:

- **Boning knife:** The narrow, rigid blade of a boning knife is specially designed to pierce meat and work around the contours of bones.

- **Utility knife:** The blade of a utility knife is shaped like a paring knife but is longer (usually 4 to 7 inches), making this tool useful for anything from slicing to mincing to trimming meat.

- **Kitchen shears:** You won't believe how often you'll find yourself reaching for a pair of kitchen shears. Helpful for cutting a whole chicken into pieces, snipping fresh herbs, and, of course, opening packages.

- **Santoku knife:** This Japanese-style chef's knife can perform all the same tasks as a chef's knife, but the blade has a less pronounced curve, allowing it to double as a meat slicer.

- **Serrated knife:** Indispensable for slicing bread but also great for cutting rind from melons and pineapple.

Cleaning & Care

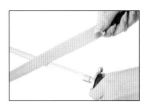

Always wash knives by hand in warm water and mild soap, wipe dry and return them to the knife drawer or block. Never put them in the dishwasher. The harsh detergent and drying cycle will dull the blade and destroy the finish.

Quality knives need to be sharpened for top performance. A cooking store can help you find a sharpening specialist in your area. Or, purchase a sharpening steel and keep them up yourself.

Pots & Pans

Like knives, a few carefully selected, high-quality pots and pans will last you a lifetime.

Look for triple-ply construction, tight-fitting lids, and oven-safe, riveted handles. Triple-ply means there are 3 layers of metal— one that conducts heat well, like aluminum or copper, sandwiched between 2 layers of another metal chosen mainly for its looks, durability, or usefulness. A nonstick interior is up to you, but it's nice to have at least 1 or 2 sauté pans with a nonstick surface, especially for cooking eggs.

The Basics

- **Frying pans:** One 8- and one 10-inch slope-sided pan. Classically speaking, frying pans don't have lids, but some manufacturers include them. The 8-inch pan is just the right size for omelets.

- **Saucepan:** Straight-sided deep pan good for boiling vegetables, grains, and sauces.

- **Saucier:** A slope-sided saucepan. Since sauciers have no corners, stirring is a snap, making this a perfect pan for preparing classic risotto. Depending on the size of your family, a 3- or 4-quart should be fine.

- **Sauté pan:** A straight-sided shallow pan with a lid. A large, 14-inch sauté pan is best, making it perfect for slow-simmered dishes, sauces, and braises.

- **Stockpot:** A 12-quart (or larger) stockpot is handy for soups, stews, chilies, pasta, corn on the cob, and other big batches of food. A heavy-bottomed pot is essential for minimizing scorching.

Extra Splurges

- **Double boiler:** A double boiler is a 2-part double-decker pot. The bottom pot holds water while the second pot rests snugly on top. Double boilers are used to cook delicate sauces and melt chocolate: the heat generated from the simmering water in the bottom pan is more gentle than direct heat from a stovetop burner and reduces the risk of scorching.

- **Dutch oven:** Similar to a stockpot, a Dutch oven should be heavy and have a tight-fitting lid for long, slow braises in the oven. Dutch ovens can also be used for cooking pasta and boiling ears of corn.

Cookware & Bakeware

You'll get a lot of mileage out of a few choice pieces of bakeware:

The Basics

- **Baking pans and casserole dishes:** Generally speaking, casseroles are usually deeper than baking pans and are often round or oval. Some have handles and most come with tight-fitting lids. They are measured by volume. Baking pans, on the other hand, are usually no more than 2 inches  deep and are measured from inside edge to inside edge. The following are our suggested pieces, with the most standard sizes in bold.

Baking Pans	Casserole Dishes
8×8-inch square	**1½ quart**
9×9-inch square	**2½ quart**
9×13-inch rectangle	

tip *If a casserole dish's volume is not marked, pour pre-measured cups of water into the pan until the water reaches the rim.*

- **Baking sheets:** Whether or not the sheet has a rimmed side or is insulated is less of a factor than color—lighter colored pans will give you the best results.

- **Muffin pan:** A heavy-gauge nonstick 12-muffin pan is best. And it's not just for muffins—it also comes in handy for hors d'oeuvres and side dishes.
- **Roasting pan:** A 13×16-inch triple-ply (or "clad") stainless roasting pan with riveted handles and nonstick interior. Make sure it comes with a rack.

If you like to bake, add these to the list:

- **Bread pan:** 9×5×3-inch, glass or metal. Glass will help you keep an eye on how brown the crust of bread gets.
- **Cake pans:** 8- or 9-inch rounds. A light-colored interior will help keep crusts from getting too dark.
- **Pie pans:** 9-inch. Glass helps you gauge how the crust is browning.
- **Ramekins:** 7-ounce dishes are perfect for individual soufflés or crème brûlées.

Extra Splurges

- **Silicone muffin pans:** Sugary muffins, individual quiches, and cheesecakes slip right out of these rubber-like baking pans.
- **Springform pan:** A straight-sided pan (2 to 3 inches high) that has a detachable bottom so cakes, tortes, and cheesecakes can be removed easily.

Is it Done?

Recipes always give you a general idea of how long a dish should cook. But there are so many variables in the kitchen, it helps to have additional clues. Here are some helpful hints:

Meats

For safety purposes, the USDA recommends cooking foods to the following internal temperatures:

- **Beef, veal, and lamb steaks or roasts:** 145°F.
- **Fish:** 145°F.
- **Pork steaks, chops or roasts:** 145°F.
- **Ground beef, pork, veal or lamb:** 160°F.
- **Egg dishes (quiche, etc.):** 160°F.
- **Turkey, chicken and duck (whole, pieces, or ground):** 165°F.

An instant-read thermometer will help ensure that your meats are properly heated through and cooked to perfection every time.

Baked Goods

Baked goods such as cakes and brownies are done when they spring back when lightly pressed in the center, begin to pull away from the sides of the pan, or when a toothpick or skewer inserted in the center comes out clean. Breads are done when the loaf sounds hollow when tapped and reaches an internal temperature of 200°F. to 210°F. when an instant-read thermometer is inserted in the bottom of the loaf.

Vegetables

Most vegetables are "done" when you like the texture—either crisp and crunchy, soft and tender, or someplace in between. Because of that, the only way to determine whether or not vegetables are cooked properly is to taste them as they cook.

Some vegetables, however, must be cooked until tender. Potatoes, squash, beets and root vegetables, like turnips, should be cooked until they're soft through and through, with no hint of crunch. Test by either tasting or by inserting a knife tip into the vegetable: the knife shouldn't meet with any resistance.

Pasta, Beans & Rice

Dried pasta should be cooked until tender but not mushy. Many Italian recipes call for pasta to be "al dente," which means "to the tooth"—tender yet still with a bit of "bite." Like vegetables, the only way to see if pasta is cooked to the proper stage is to bite into it. If it's still white at the core, give it another minute, then test again. Dried beans should also be cooked until tender with no sign of chalkiness, and again, the best way to find that out is to taste. Taste test several beans before deciding whether or not to cook them any further—they can cook somewhat unevenly. Most varieties of rice are done when tender but not mushy or soggy, and there shouldn't be any crunch. Rice is easy to overcook, though, so sample the rice after its initial cooking and if it's still chewy, let it stand, covered, for a few minutes—residual steam should be enough to cook it through.

The Prepared Pantry

Keeping a well-stocked pantry is smart—it minimizes last-minute trips to the grocery store, and allows you to put a good dinner on the table even when time is tight. To help you identify what's really

essential, we've created a list of pantry basics at the Campbell's Kitchen website, **www.campbellskitchen.com**. There you'll find our suggestions for stocking your pantry based on the type of cook you are: *Starting Out, Comfortable in the Kitchen,* or a *Seasoned Chef.* With a supply of basic ingredients on hand, you can always be assured that a good meal is never far away!

Cook from the Pantry

With a well-stocked pantry, creative and scrumptious dinners are literally at your fingertips. Unleash the power of your pantry with these inspirational ideas.

Pasta

Pasta is a great foundation for delicious dinners. Short pastas, such as bow ties or corkscrews, are great for skillet dishes or adding to soups. If you have orzo, a rice-shaped pasta, serve it as a side dish in place of rice, or toss it with an assortment of fresh vegetables (cucumber, tomatoes, bell pepper, etc.), your favorite vinaigrette and canned tuna, chicken or leftover roast pork or beef for a new take on pasta salad! (*Flavor tip: Boil pasta in* Swanson® *broth instead of water.*)

Egg noodles are the ultimate speedy side dish. Toss hot noodles with a tablespoon or two of olive oil or butter, Parmesan cheese and chopped fresh herbs for a side that goes with anything! Or, add frozen mixed vegetables to the noodle water during the last minute or two of cooking, drain then toss everything with canned chicken or tuna and a touch of Parmesan for a quick dinner. Egg noodles are also a must-have ingredient for family-favorite casseroles and skillets.

Rice & Grains

An assortment of rice and grains are great for unique side dishes. Here are a few ways to use them:

- Five minutes is all the time it takes to make couscous, a perfect accompaniment to saucy stews. (For deeper flavor, make couscous with *Swanson®* broth instead of water.)

- Polenta is a great stand-in for pasta or mashed potatoes and cooks fairly quickly. It's also a delicious hot cereal with fresh or dried fruit, nuts and milk.

- For adventuresome eaters, quinoa and bulgur make nutritious side dishes, and are terrific foundations for grain salads.

Beans & Legumes

Canned beans and dried lentils provide several delicious, quick-to-make options.

- Canned beans give you a head start on great soup or chili, but they're also good for quesadillas, skillets and salads. Unexpected guests drop in? Make a quick, delicious dip for snacking by puréeing black beans or chickpeas with garlic and a splash of *Swanson®* broth. Serve as a dip with assorted *Pepperidge Farm®* crackers and fresh vegetables.

- Brown lentils are also wonderful additions to soup or stew and, when paired with rice, make a great-tasting side dish. For something super-quick and different, toss cooked, drained lentils while they're warm with any prepared vinaigrette you have on hand (or lemon juice and olive oil), a handful of your favorite fresh herb (parsley and thyme are outstanding) and sprinkle with crumbled feta or blue cheese.

Staples

Canned and jarred staple ingredients are the hub of any pantry, and you'll find yourself turning to them for all kinds of cooking solutions.

- A container or two of *Swanson®* Chicken or Beef stock or broth is a must for making soups and stews, but it's also great as a base for a quick pan sauce for sautéed meats.

- *Campbell's®* Condensed soups are great for everything from meatloaf to enchiladas and side dishes, but you can also use them in salads and dips.

- *Swanson®* Chunk Chicken Breast is excellent for quick sandwiches, pasta salads, skillets or baked dishes.

- Prepared *Prego®* sauces are great on pasta, of course, but you can also use them on pizza, to simmer pork chops or bake chicken.

- A jar of *Pace®* Chunky salsa or Picante sauce is a must for tacos or burritos, but it also makes a zesty simmer sauce for chicken and chops or as a marinade for steaks. You can also use it in pasta dishes and stir-fries.

- Other staples to have on hand include olives, artichoke hearts, roasted red peppers, mushrooms and capers—add them to pasta, sandwiches, pizzas or salads. Canned vegetables, like green beans and corn, are quick and easy ways to boost the veggie power of soups and stews, and fruit (pineapple chunks, peaches, mandarin oranges, etc.) can be added to skillets, meat sauces and salads. And while peanut butter is a given for sandwiches, it also adds a delicious savory dimension to salad dressings, stir-fries and soups.

Herbs & Spices

A sprinkle or two of a favorite dried herb or spice blend can add another flavor angle to practically everything you cook. Of course, you can buy any number of spice blends at the store, but try making your own combos with the herbs and spices you already have on hand. Here are some suggestions:

- *BBQ seasoning:* Blend equal parts brown sugar, paprika, garlic powder and onion powder together; add black pepper and cayenne to taste. Sprinkle it on chicken breasts, steaks or chops before grilling, or use it to enhance purchased BBQ sauce.

- *Cajun seasoning:* Stir together equal parts paprika, onion powder, garlic powder and dried thyme; add black and white peppers and cayenne to taste. Add to jambalaya or gumbo, or use to season fish fillets.

- *Italian seasoning:* Mix together equal parts dried basil, oregano, marjoram, thyme and sage. Use on fresh vegetables, to season rice, or rub on steak or chicken before cooking.

- *Jerk seasoning:* Mix onion powder, dried thyme, ground allspice and cinnamon together in equal parts; add black pepper and cayenne to taste (classic jerk seasoning is very spicy). Use it on everything from soups to steaks for a spicy Caribbean twist.

- *Taco seasoning:* A blend of equal parts onion powder, garlic powder and ground cumin; add chili powder to taste. Use in chili, to season taco meat or season fajitas.

Dry Goods

Of course, every pantry should have a supply of flour and sugar on hand, but here are a few more suggestions for dry goods:

- A box of baking mix (for pancakes, biscuits, etc.)

- An assortment of instant puddings (for speedy desserts)

- Flour or corn tortillas (for extended storage, keep them in the freezer)

- Cocoa powder, semi-sweet chocolate chips, baking soda, baking powder and cornstarch for baking recipes and desserts

Smart Swaps

One advantage to cooking at home is that you have control over what goes into the dishes. With a little bit of experimentation, you'll discover that you can make smart swaps to lower fat and calories without sacrificing flavor. This chart can help you trim down your favorite recipes (note that not all substitutions will work for all dishes):

Ingredient	Substitution
Bacon	Turkey bacon, Canadian bacon, smoked turkey or prosciutto
Butter or oil (baking)	Applesauce (substitute only half the amount of butter or oil called for with applesauce; use butter or oil for the other half or the baked goods may turn out tough and chewy)
Cream cheese	Neufchâtel-style cream cheese (one-third less fat)
Enriched white pasta	Whole wheat pasta
Evaporated milk	Evaporated skim milk; low-fat or nonfat mayonnaise; or plain low-fat yogurt combined with low-fat cottage cheese
Full-fat cheese	Low-fat, skim or nonfat cheese
One egg (to thicken)	One tablespoon flour
One egg yolk	One egg white
Red wine	An equal amount of cranberry juice with a touch of red wine vinegar
Ricotta cheese	Low-fat or nonfat cottage cheese (purée in a food processor or blender before using), or low-fat or nonfat ricotta cheese
Sour cream	Plain low-fat yogurt, or ½ cup cottage cheese blended with 1½ teaspoons lemon juice, or low- or nonfat sour cream
Whipped cream	Chilled, whipped evaporated skim milk or nondairy whipped topping
White flour (baking)	Whole wheat flour (substitute up to half the amount of white flour called for in a recipe with whole wheat; use white flour for the other half or the baked goods may turn out heavy and dense)
White rice	Brown rice
White wine or beer	An equal amount of apple juice or *Swanson*® Chicken broth with a touch of apple cider vinegar
Whole egg	Two egg whites or ½ cup egg product
Whole milk	Skim, 1%, or 2% milk

cooking techniques

Sautéing, Pan-Frying & Stir-Frying

Sautéing

■ *What is it?* A dry-heat cooking method (that is, no liquid is involved) where food is cooked, tossed, or stirred over medium-high heat in a small amount of oil. Similar  to stir-frying, it can be used to cook a wide range of foods including vegetables, meats, and seafood.

■ *Equipment:* To properly sauté, choose a heavy frying or sauté pan—one with sloped sides is helpful because it's easier to toss the foods as they cook. But a pan with straight sides works fine too. Whatever pan you use must be large enough for the amount of food you'll be sautéing. If the pan is crowded, things will just steam.

■ *How to Sauté:* Heat the pan over medium-high, then add oil and swirl to coat the bottom. Add the ingredients and toss or stir frequently until cooked.

Pan-Frying

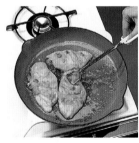

■ *What is it?* Pan-frying is similar to sautéing and stir-frying in that it also involves cooking in a pan or skillet on top of the stove. However, pan-frying is most often used to cook larger cuts of meat like chicken breasts or pork chops, and generally requires more fat (although not so much that it completely covers the food—that's deep-frying). Pan-frying is also used to cook breaded items (chicken, shrimp, etc.) because it helps create a crunchy coating on the surface of the food.

■ *Equipment:* Choose a frying or sauté pan large enough to hold whatever you're cooking without crowding—in a crowded pan food doesn't brown well and, in the case of anything breaded or coated, could become greasy. Also, make sure the pan is fairly heavy to ensure a controlled, consistent temperature—lightweight pans tend to have hot and cool spots which result in uneven browning.

■ *How to Pan-Fry:* Add vegetable oil to the pan to come about ¼ inch up the sides. Gradually heat it over medium-high until it's 350°F. to

360°F.—cooler temperatures will make foods greasy; hotter will cause them to burn. Add food and pan-fry until golden on one side then turn it over and fry on the second side until golden and cooked through.

Stir-Frying

- **What is it?** Stir-frying is related to frying and sautéing but the biggest difference is the amount of heat required—you need a lot of it to stir-fry correctly. This intense heat quickly cooks the ingredients, retaining much of the vegetables' colors while caramelizing the meat and intensifying its flavor. The technique gets its name because as you fry, you "stir" everything constantly so nothing dries out.

- **Equipment:** The classic stir-fry pan is a wok. Its unique deep bowl shape is ideal for this technique because it allows for intense heat on the bottom for browning and searing, while the pan's gently curved sides, which are naturally cooler, act as a buffer and help prevent the ingredients from overcooking or scorching—just push them up the sides to bring their temperature down. And a wok's wide top allows steam to rapidly escape from the stir-fry so vegetables don't wilt. No wok? No problem. A 10- to 12-inch sauté pan does a good job too. Just be sure the pan is big enough to hold ingredients without crowding. And for the best heat retention, it should be made out of heavy-duty stainless steel or cast iron.

- **Ingredients:** Once you've got your wok or pan, you need to think about the ingredients. Because the cooking process is so fast, it's essential that everything is "in its place" (French cooks call this

mise en place) before you turn the burner on. Do all cutting, slicing, dicing, and measuring first so they're organized and ready when you need them. The following five categories are typical to most stir-fries:

Aromatics: Aromatics, like garlic and ginger, add intense flavor to stir-fries. Other aromatics include lemongrass, dried orange peel, whole star anise, and dried chiles. In general, aromatics should be minced so they infuse the stir-fry with flavor, but leave dried peel, chiles, and spices whole so you can remove them before serving.

Meats: For the fastest cooking, meats should be sliced as thinly as possible. To make the job easier, freeze the meat for 20 to 30 minutes before slicing to firm it up a bit. But never try to slice rock-solid meat—the knife blade slips very easily and can be dangerous. When slicing, always cut the meat against the grain (that is, across the muscle fibers) to make it tender, and be sure the pieces are bite-size.

Oils: Peanut oil is the best oil for stir-frying, but other options include canola, safflower, and corn oil. Nutty-tasting toasted sesame oil (also called Asian sesame oil) is sometimes drizzled over the stir-fries before serving but it shouldn't be used for frying itself.

Sauces: You can buy prepared stir-fry sauces and simply pour them over cooked meat and vegetables, but you'll get better flavor if you make a sauce using a handful of pantry items. Start with a cup or so of *Swanson*® stock or broth, a teaspoon or two of cornstarch to thicken the sauce, then add any of the following Asian condiments to round out the flavor: soy sauce, hoisin, oyster sauce, chili sauce, or fish sauce. You can also try orange or pineapple juice to add sweetness or prepared curry pastes for herbal dimension and spicy heat.

Vegetables: Most stir-fry vegetables can be classified as slow-cooking (carrots, broccoli, cauliflower), medium-cooking (bell peppers, celery, mushrooms), and fast-cooking (bean sprouts, spinach, green onions). Because of that, the vegetables must be grouped according to their classification (all slow-cooking in one bowl, medium-cooking in another, etc.) so they can be added to the stir-fry in stages depending on the cooking time required. And, like meat, cut the vegetables into bite-size pieces so they're easy to eat and cook as quickly as possible.

■ *How to Stir-Fry:* To start stir-frying, preheat the wok or pan over medium-high heat for 5 minutes. It's ready when you can feel heat radiating from it when you hold your hand over the pan. Drizzle in the oil, then add the aromatics to the hot oil and listen for the sizzle. No sizzle? The pan isn't hot enough. And if, during the course of stir-frying, you don't hear sizzling, the pan is overcrowded and too cool. Cook the aromatics just until fragrant, about 30 seconds, then add the prepared meat. During cooking, stir the meat and look for browning in the pan indicating that you're achieving proper caramelization. But watch for burning and scorching too, adding a little more oil or a splash of *Swanson*® stock or broth, if necessary. Once the meat is cooked, transfer it to a plate and return the pan to the burner. Drizzle in more oil, wait for it to get hot then stir-fry the slow-cooking vegetables until they're tender-crisp; add any medium-cooking vegetables after about 3 or 4 minutes. Then finally, return the meat to the pan along with any fast-cooking vegetables and the sauce. Simmer, stirring to blend, until the sauce thickens and coats everything.

Get more information on sautéing, pan-frying and stir-frying at the Campbell's Kitchen website, **www.campbellskitchen.com**.

Braising & Slow Cooking

Braising

■ *What is it?* Braising is a slow, low heat cooking method where meats and vegetables are cooked in a small amount of liquid. It's ideal for cooking tough, inexpensive  cuts of meat (such as brisket and pork shoulder) until they're melt-in-your-mouth tender, but can be done with quicker cooking cuts like chicken breasts as well.

■ *Equipment:* Really, the only piece of equipment required for braising is a heavy-duty Dutch oven, sauté pan or stockpot with a tight-fitting lid. A good choice is one made of cast iron—the even and consistent heat conduction and retention of cast iron make it ideal for braising. But a heavy-duty stainless steel pot or sauté pan works great, too, as does your slow cooker!

A tight-fitting lid is critical—it keeps steam inside the pot for more even cooking and moisture retention. If the lid isn't as tight as it should be, wrap the base with heavy-duty aluminum foil (keep the handle exposed so you can remove the lid easily), pressing down on the lid firmly to mold it to the edge of the pot for an air-tight seal.

A pot full of ingredients can be heavy so make sure the pot's handles are sturdy and safe. And be sure that the handle material is ovenproof—plastic and wood won't hold up to the prolonged cooking times of braising.

■ *Ingredients:* While you can braise just about anything, the technique is best for tenderizing large, tough cuts of meat and fibrous vegetables through low, slow cooking. These three categories of ingredients are most commonly used in braised dishes:

Liquids: All liquids function the same way in a braise, but flavored liquids deliver more punch— *Swanson*® stock or broth, wine, beer, fruit or vegetable juices, even *Pace*® Picante sauce can provide a terrific flavor foundation to the sauce. Don't be afraid to combine different liquids for a more complex taste.

Meats: The best cuts for braised dishes include beef short ribs, brisket and chuck roast; pork shoulder and spareribs; lamb shanks and shoulder; turkey legs, chicken thighs and drumsticks. Leaner meats, such as pork tenderloin and chicken breasts may also be braised but should be cooked for much shorter periods of time so they don't dry out and turn tough. Keep in mind, though, that the sauce may not be as rich and flavorful with shorter cooking times.

Vegetables: Aromatic vegetables, like onions, carrots and celery, are used to flavor most braises. Because they turn mushy and dull-looking over the long braising time, you may want to add more vegetables during the last 30 to 40 minutes of braising for a fresh hit of flavor. Potatoes and root vegetables, like rutabaga and turnips, may also be added to the braise in the last 30 to 40 minutes.

■ **How to Braise:** Braising can be divided into three steps: browning the meat, deglazing the pan and braising. Browning creates deep, rich color on the meat and also helps render out some of the fat.

The next step, deglazing, helps loosen the bits of food stuck to the bottom of the pan after browning. These bits are called fond, and they're loaded with flavor which will become the foundation for building a delicious sauce. To deglaze, transfer the browned meat to a plate

then add liquid (*Swanson*® stock or broth, wine or juice) to the hot pan, scraping the fond loose with a wooden spoon so it blends into the liquid.

For the final braising step, return the browned meat to the pan along with any vegetables and aromatics called for in the recipe, preferably in a single layer, adding more liquid to submerge everything about halfway. Cover the pan with a tight-fitting lid (a steamy environment inside the pot is key to keeping the meat moist) then let it all simmer, either on top of the stove or in the oven until the meat is cooked through and very tender—time will vary depending on the type of meat being braised.

Slow Cooking

■ **What is it?** The only difference between slow cooking and braising is that slow cooking occurs in an appliance made especially for the job—a covered ceramic or stainless steel crock which sits inside an electrical unit that surrounds the crock with gentle heat. Like braising, slow cooking is especially good for tougher cuts of meat like brisket or pork shoulder where they can simmer until fork-tender. But it's also perfectly suited for soups, stews and other all-in-one dishes. And entrées aren't the only thing that can be prepared in a slow cooker— it's also great for side dishes, even cakes! Be sure to check the Campbell's Kitchen website, **www.campbellskitchen.com**, for literally hundreds of outstanding slow cooker recipes and tips!

■ **Equipment:** The popularity of slow cooking has created a wide variety of options when it comes to buying a slow cooker. Think about these things when you set out to buy a slow cooker for your kitchen.

Slow cookers come in a variety of sizes ranging from about 1½ quarts up to 7 quarts or more. For most families, a cooker in the 5- to 6-quart range works fine. You want a model with a removable ceramic or stainless steel insert for easy cleaning, and it should have sturdy handles for safe moving from the cooker to the table. And if the insert can be used on the stove or in the oven to brown meats, all the better, but it's not a must-have feature (note that traditional ceramic-style crocks are not safe for stovetop browning). The manufacturer's instructions will tell you if your slow cooker insert is capable of stovetop browning.

A programmable timer is a nice feature if you won't be around to turn the slow cooker on yourself. Timers also allow you to program the cooker so it adjusts to the warm setting after the recipe is done. This helps prevent overcooking the dish.

Check for a tight-fitting lid. This is critical to the success of recipes as well as an indication of the quality of construction.

Most slow cookers have heating elements in the bottom, but high-quality models have elements wrapped around in the body as well. Appliances with this feature are usually more expensive than bottom-only elements, but heat surrounding the insert tends to cook the food inside more evenly.

■ **Slow Cooker Safety:** Although slow cookers are known for being easy to use and don't require advanced technical skills, there are some important things to keep in mind whenever you use yours.

Never put frozen food in the slow cooker. Frozen foods (especially meats which take a long time to defrost) reduce the temperature inside the slow cooker and expose foods to dangerous temperatures for longer periods of time.

For the best results, don't fill the crock more than two-thirds full, and avoid removing the lid during cooking—each time you do, the temperature in the cooker goes down and it can take 10 minutes for the temperature to return to normal.

If you do need to remove the lid during cooking, raise it carefully and away from you. During cooking, steam collects in the slow cooker, condenses on the lid, and can drip hot water onto hands and arms. To help eliminate some of the condensation on the lid and help absorb moisture, place a few paper towels between the lid and the slow cooker during cooking.

During cooking, the temperature of the contents in the slow cooker should be between 170°F. and 280°F. Temperatures lower than 170°F. encourage bacterial growth, so use an instant-read thermometer to check food as it simmers. If the temperature is below 170°F. and the cooker is at its highest setting, purchase a new slow cooker (finish cooking the recipe on top of the stove in a saucepot or in the oven in an ovenproof vessel).

Never place a hot ceramic insert on a cold countertop or in the fridge. Extreme temperature swings could cause the crock to crack or break.

You'll find great recipes and tips for braising and slow-cooking at Campbell's Kitchen, **www.campbellskitchen.com**.

Poaching, Boiling & Steaming

Poaching

■ **What is it?** Poaching is a gentle moist-heat cooking method used to simmer foods (fish, chicken breasts, eggs, fruit) in hot (not boiling) liquid until cooked. Water is often used but its flavor is typically enhanced with *Swanson*® stock or broth, wine, juice or vinegar, as well as vegetables (carrot, onion, celery), citrus (lemon, lime, orange), herbs and spices.

■ *Equipment:* Choose a lidded sauté pan large enough to hold the food in a single layer without crowding.

■ *How to Poach:* Add liquid to come about halfway up the sides of the pan (don't overfill: the liquid will rise when food is added) as well as any vegetables, citrus, or herbs for flavor, then cover the pan and bring the liquid to a simmer over medium-high heat. When small bubbles begin to rise and just break the surface (usually at 140°F. to 180°F.; use an instant-read thermometer to check), gently slip the food into the pan and cover with the lid. Let the liquid come back up to a bare simmer over medium-high (the liquid's temperature will drop as soon as the food is added) then adjust the heat to medium or medium-low.

Keep the liquid gently simmering (not boiling) until the food is cooked through. When poaching fish or chicken, take the pan off the heat when the food is nearly but not quite cooked through and let stand, covered, in the poaching liquid for 2 to 3 minutes before serving—the residual heat of the liquid will finish cooking it. Fruit can be poached until still slightly firm then cooled and chilled in the liquid. For best results poach fruit that is a bit under-ripe; test poached fruit for doneness by inserting the tip of a paring knife. If it resists slightly, it's done. And don't toss that poaching liquid! If it's not too strongly flavored (taste it first, especially if you've poached fish or shrimp), use it as a base for a sauce or add it to soups or stews.

Boiling

■ *What is it?* More intense than poaching, boiling is a technique where foods are cooked in rapidly bubbling liquid, most often water. It's generally

best for items that can withstand the high heat (212°F.) and agitation of rapidly moving water— potatoes, pasta, rice, hearty greens (kale, turnip greens, collards), carrots, broccoli, cauliflower and beets, to name a few.

■ *Equipment:* A pot, Dutch oven or stockpot big enough so that food moves freely in the rapidly boiling liquid.

■ *How to Boil:* Fill the pot with water (but not so much that the pot overflows when food is added), cover and bring to a rapid boil over high heat. Add the food, return the water to a boil (the temperature will drop as soon as food is added and will stop boiling) and cook to desired doneness. As soon as the food is done, drain it from the water to prevent overcooking. To stop the cooking quickly, run cold water over the food or plunge into an ice water bath (this is called blanching).

---

tip *When boiling pasta, do not rinse it after draining—that washes off the starch on the surface of the pasta which is what helps sauces cling.*

Steaming

■ *What is it?* Here foods are cooked by steam generated from boiling water. Since there's no direct contact with water, steaming is the perfect technique to use when you want foods

to retain their shape, texture, and bright color without becoming water-logged or soggy; it's also great for retaining vitamins and minerals. Even some baked goods (cakes, puddings, custards, etc.) can be steamed.

- **Equipment:** Steaming requires a pot with a lid and a steam basket insert that fits inside the pot. Collapsible baskets can often be found in the housewares aisle of grocery stores; bamboo baskets commonly used in Asian cooking are usually stocked in Asian markets and cookware stores. In a pinch, a metal colander can double as a steam basket as well.

- **How to Steam:** Fit the basket inside a pot then fill the pot with water to within an inch of the bottom of the basket (the water shouldn't touch the basket). Cover the pot and bring the water to a boil over high heat until steam forms. Carefully remove the lid (lift the lid away from your face to avoid being scalded by the escaping steam) and arrange the food loosely in the basket—steam should circulate freely inside the pot. Cover and cook to desired doneness, taking care not to remove the lid too often since that drops the temperature inside the pot.

Steaming times will vary depending on what and how much is being cooked and how "cooked" you want the food to be. Green beans, broccoli and asparagus could take anywhere from 3 to 8 minutes, while fish fillets and chicken breasts may take up to 20 minutes depending on thickness. And very dense items, such as beets, could take up to an hour depending on their size. Don't forget to check the water level in the pot periodically and add more water when the level is low.

Roasting & Grilling

Roasting

- **What is it?** Roasting is a dry-heat cooking method (which means there's no water involved) where meats, poultry, fish or vegetables are cooked in the oven. To prepare meat for roasting, season it simply with salt and pepper or, for more flavor, spice rubs, or herb pastes. Before seasoning, remove excess surface fat from the meat, but not all of it: the fat will melt and baste the meat during roasting.

---

tips *Depending on the cut of meat, roasts, especially beef, pork or lamb, may be tied so they hold their shape and cook evenly. Leave the strings on during cooking—you'll trim them off before serving.*

If you're roasting a chicken, it's often best to split the bird for faster, more even cooking. To split a chicken, use kitchen shears to cut down both sides of the backbone. With the backbone removed, flatten the bird out slightly, season both sides with salt and pepper, then roast skin side up.

When roasting large cuts of meat or a whole chicken, create a flavorful roasting "rack" by building a grid in the bottom of the roasting pan with stalks of celery, whole carrots and thick slices of onion. The vegetables will flavor the pan drippings, making for delicious gravy.

- **Equipment:** When it comes to cooking methods, roasting is about as easy as it gets. If you have an oven and a rimmed baking sheet, you can roast! Take it a step further with a roasting rack and pan. The rack sits inside the roasting pan, elevating the meat so air can circulate around it, helping speed the cooking process. However, the most essential item for successful roasting is an instant-read thermometer. It's really the only way to accurately determine progress during cooking.

■ **Is it done?** Since roasts are different shapes and sizes, cooking times will vary. Because of that, you'll need to rely on an instant-read thermometer to give you an idea of progress. Begin checking the temperature about halfway through the cooking time specified in the recipe. Insert the thermometer stem into the thickest part of the meat, avoiding bone (if present), which will give an inaccurate reading. For chicken and turkey, check the thigh—this dark meat area takes longer to cook than the breast meat. (With poultry, white meat and dark meat are considered properly cooked at different temperatures: 150°F. for white meat, 180°F. for dark.) And keep in mind that once you pull the roast out of the oven and let it rest before carving, the internal temperature will rise 5 to 10 degrees. So pull the roast from the oven once it's 5 to 10 degrees away from being "done."

tips *After the roast or chicken comes out of the oven, let it rest for 10 minutes before carving. Why? During cooking, juices concentrate toward the center of the meat. This "downtime" allows juices to redistribute throughout the meat, keeping it moist and juicy. Early carving just causes the juices to just leak onto the cutting board.*
To safely transfer a roasted chicken or turkey to a cutting board, insert a sturdy metal skewer or the handle of a long wooden spoon through the cavity and use it to lift and move the bird. For more roasting tips and recipes, go

to the Campbell's Kitchen website, **www.campbellskitchen.com**.

Grilling

■ **What is it?** Grilling is a technique where foods are cooked on a grate suspended directly over a heat source. It's usually fueled by charcoal, wood or propane, creating temperatures hot enough to sear and char.

Grilling is typically a very fast cooking method, but adjusting the heat source so one side of the grill is hotter than the other is one way to control the heat's intensity. This is called two-zone grilling, and it's ideal for large items that can take a while to cook, like a whole chicken or roasts, as well as more delicate things like quesadillas that can burn quickly over an intense flame.

Don't confuse grilling with barbecuing. Although the term "barbecuing" has morphed to mean cooking outdoors on a grill, it's actually a much slower cooking method where the heat source is away from, not directly underneath the food. Wood smoke is also typically used in barbecuing to impart flavor, and barbecued items are often basted with sauce during cooking.

tips *Most recipes are meant to be cooked with the lid closed. This helps keep heat inside the grill for faster, more even cooking.*

Entrées aren't the only thing that taste great on the grill—think about grilling halved heads of romaine lettuce for salad, pineapple or peaches for dessert, even pizza!

Charcoal vs. Gas

If you're a year-round griller, you may want to invest in a **gas grill.** Easy to start, clean and store, gas models can be ready to use in as little as 15 minutes

(charcoal grills can take up to 45 minutes to preheat). Plus, gas grills are fairly clean to operate—no need to wait until the coals burn out before storing, and no ashes to clean out after each grilling session. They come in a range of sizes and price points, starting at around $150 for pretty basic (and small) models, increasing in price along with size and the amenities offered. Look for a model that has a grilling surface large enough to handle your needs with at least 2 burners underneath. Two burners not only help prevent hot spots, but also give you the option to use indirect heat (see "Direct vs. Indirect Grilling"). The best burners are cast out of heat-retaining brass, but stainless steel burners also work well. Other bells-and-whistle accessories, like built-in thermometers, rotisseries, and stovetop-like burners, may seem like a good idea, but think seriously about whether or not you'd use them enough to make it worth spending the extra money.

A charcoal grill might be your best bet if price is your primary consideration and you only grill during the summer; a quality model usually costs around $125. Charcoal grills can do everything gas grills can, but require a little more attention with regards to preheating, cool down, and cleanup.

Direct vs. Indirect Grilling
Types of Grilling

There are 2 types of grilling methods—direct heat and indirect heat. Neither has anything to do with what kind of grill you use, but rather how you use it. Both methods work on gas and charcoal grills.

- *Direct grilling:* Hot and fast, this is the method most of us are familiar with. In essence, food is cooked directly over the fire. That's it! Steaks, burgers, hot dogs, brats, fish fillets, shrimp and scallops are just some items that work well with this method.

  Two-zone grilling: One way you can control the heat and speed of direct grilling is to set up a fire with two "levels"—one side is very hot and the other is medium-low. This technique which is great for thick (2 inches or more) steaks, chops or fillets, and is worth mastering. Start the food out briefly on the hot side to sear for color and flavor then move it to the cooler side for longer, more even cooking.

tips *For charcoal grills, charcoal briquets are just fine. Made of char and wood, these uniformly shaped briquets are easy to work with, burn for a long time, and are available everywhere.*

More experienced grillers sometimes use lump hardwood charcoal because it burns hotter and without the chemical fumes and aromas of composite briquets. Find lump hardwood charcoal at specialty grill stores and some home improvement stores.

If you're a gas griller, it's always a good idea to keep a spare tank of propane on hand so you never find yourself with an empty tank, half-cooked burgers on the grill, and hungry guests!

*Looking to expand and enhance your grilling tool collection? We've got suggestions! Just go to the Campbell's Kitchen site, **www.campbellskitchen.com,** for more information.*

■ *Indirect grilling:* Much slower and gentler than direct grilling, this cooking method is a bit like oven-roasting—heat surrounds food instead of searing and cooks it from the bottom. Indirect grilling is perfect for value cuts like pork shoulder, large roasts, and poultry that require longer cooking times. To grill indirectly, one side of the grill is the primary heat source; the other side is unlit or without coals underneath. Food goes over the side without the fire then the grill lid is closed and the food is left to cook virtually undisturbed, much like roasting in an oven. This method results in meats that are beautifully browned and amazingly moist; plus, it's extremely forgiving. You don't have to tend to the fire every minute to prevent dinner from going up in flames.

10 Rules for Good Grilling

■ *Preheat:* You wouldn't bake in a cold oven, so don't expect to get a good sear on a cold grill. For gas models, light as instructed in the owner's manual then turn on both burners to high and close the lid. Preheat gas grills for at least 15 minutes then adjust the temperature according to the recipe instructions. With charcoal grills, you want the coals to burn until they're ashy and gray, about 45 minutes.

■ *Clean:* A clean grill grate is essential. It prevents off-flavors, keeps sooty residue from forming on foods, and helps prevent sticking. Once the grate is hot, use a wire-bristled grill brush to scrape it thoroughly.

■ *No stick:* After brushing the grill clean, use a long-handled brush to lightly coat the hot grate with vegetable oil. This will help prevent food from sticking during grilling.

■ *Keep flammable items away:* If your grill has side shelves for storage, keep flammable items, like lighters, lighter fluid, pressurized cans and alcohol, off of them.

■ *No stabbing or piercing:* Jabbing your steak to turn it over just sends the juices to the bottom of the grill. You want to keep juices inside the steak, so use tongs or a spatula to turn foods over.

■ *Trim the fat:* Trimming excess fat from meat not only shaves a few calories, but it also prevents flare-ups during cooking. Fat around the edges of meat adds no flavor so it's best to remove it—it's the fat and marbling in the meat that delivers the flavor.

■ *No sugar until the end:* Sugary glazes, marinades and sauces tend to burn if exposed to too much or long periods of heat. Caramelization (where sugars are heated to the point that they turn brown) adds color and flavor, but too much translates to scorched food. Because of that, apply sauces and glazes toward the end of the grilling process to prevent burning.

■ *Keep it covered:* Regardless of whether you're using a charcoal or gas grill, it'll work best when it's covered so it retains heat. Unless noted, all grilling should be done with the cover on.

■ *Pay attention:* Grilling and barbecuing need constant tending to ensure safety as well as perfectly cooked food. Vigilance also keeps flare-ups in check.

■ *Resting:* After grilling, let the meat rest 10 minutes or so before carving or slicing. During cooking, interior juices constantly move away from the heat source and ultimately concentrate in the center of the meat. Cut into a steak straight off the grill, and all the juices would leak onto the cutting board, causing the meat to turn dry. Use this "time out" to do any last minute salad tossing or table setting.

For important grilling safety rules, tips on food safety and guidelines for determining doneness in grilled foods, be sure to check out all the information on the Campbell's Kitchen website, **www.campbellskitchen.com**.

quick & easy dishes

Recipes surprisingly fast, thus requiring less time making dinner and more time enjoying it.

chicken pizza muffins

prep 10 minutes | **broil** 3 minutes | **makes** 4 servings

4 **English muffins, split and toasted**

½ **cup Prego® Chunky Garden Combination Italian Sauce**

2 **cans (4.5 ounces *each*) Swanson® Premium White Chunk Chicken Breast in Water, drained**

¼ **cup shredded part-skim mozzarella cheese Crushed red pepper *or* dried oregano leaves**

1. Place the muffins on a rack in a broiler pan. Spread **about 1 tablespoon** Italian sauce on **each** muffin half. Divide the chicken and cheese among the muffin halves. Sprinkle with the crushed red pepper.

2. Broil 4 inches from the heat for 3 minutes or until the cheese is melted.

5 hints for busy cooks

Spend more time enjoying dinner than making it with these five helpful hints.

■ *Prep ahead.* Take a few minutes on a weekend to prepare vegetables, like onions, carrots, celery and bell peppers, then package them in separate containers or bags. They'll come in handy during the week when making soups, stews, stir-fries and chilies.

■ *Buy a rotisserie chicken.* A 2- to 3-pound chicken will yield about 4 cups of shredded meat. Most recipes call for 2 cups—freeze or chill the remaining meat to use in another meal.

■ *Wash and spin-dry lettuces then store in plastic bags lined with paper towels.* You won't believe how long lettuce will stay crisp this way.

■ *Make your own vinaigrettes and salad dressings.* It requires a little up-front work, but homemade vinaigrettes are a simple way to add a huge flavor boost to your meal—you'll be dressing those crisp greens with outstanding flavor all week!

■ *Buy fresh fruits in season—they'll be at the peak of flavor and reasonably priced.* Freeze them for fresh flavor year-round.

2-step skillet chicken broccoli divan

prep 10 minutes | **cook** 15 minutes | **makes** 4 servings

1 **tablespoon butter**

4 **skinless, boneless chicken breast halves (about 1 pound), cut into 1-inch pieces**

3 **cups fresh *or* frozen broccoli florets**

1 **can (10¾ ounces) Campbell's® Condensed Cream of Chicken Soup (Regular *or* 98% Fat Free)**

½ **cup milk**

½ **cup shredded Cheddar cheese**

1. Heat the butter in a 10-inch skillet over medium-high heat. Add the chicken and cook until well browned, stirring often.

2. Stir the broccoli, soup and milk in the skillet. Reduce the heat to low. Cover and cook for 5 minutes or until the chicken is cooked through. Sprinkle with the cheese.

tip *Try this recipe with Campbell's® Cream of Mushroom Soup **and** shredded Swiss cheese.*

broccoli con queso

prep 10 minutes | **cook** 5 minutes | **makes** 6 servings

1 cup Pace® Mexican
    Four Cheese Salsa
    con Queso
1 pound broccoli, cut into
    spears, cooked and
    drained

In a 1-quart saucepan over low heat, heat the salsa. Serve over the broccoli.

glazed pork chops

prep 5 minutes | **cook** 25 minutes | **makes** 6 servings

2 tablespoons cornstarch
½ cup water
1 tablespoon butter
6 bone-in pork chops, ¾-inch thick (about 2 pounds)
1 can (10½ ounces) Campbell's® Condensed French Onion Soup
2 tablespoons packed brown sugar

1. Stir the cornstarch and water in a small bowl with a fork.

2. Heat the butter in a 12-inch skillet over medium heat. Add the chops and cook until they're well browned on both sides.

3. Stir the soup and brown sugar in the skillet and heat to a boil. Reduce the heat to low. Cover and cook for 10 minutes or until the chops are cooked through.

4. Remove the chops from the skillet. Cover and keep warm. Stir the cornstarch mixture in the skillet. Cook and stir until mixture boils and thickens. Serve the sauce over the chops.

beef & pasta

prep 5 minutes | **cook** 25 minutes | **makes** 4 servings

- ¾ **pound ground beef (85% lean)**
- 1¾ **cups Swanson® Vegetable Broth (Regular *or* Certified Organic)**
- 1 **tablespoon Worcestershire sauce**
- ½ **teaspoon dried oregano leaves, crushed**
- ½ **teaspoon garlic powder**
- 1 **can (about 8 ounces) stewed tomatoes**
- 1½ **cups *uncooked* medium tube-shaped (ziti) *or* corkscrew-shaped (rotini) pasta**

1. Cook the beef in a 10-inch skillet over medium-high heat until it's well browned, stirring often to separate the meat. Pour off any fat.

2. Stir the broth, Worcestershire, oregano, garlic powder and tomatoes in the skillet and heat to a boil. Stir in the pasta. Reduce the heat to low. Cover and cook for 10 minutes, stirring often. **Uncover.**

3. Cook for 5 minutes or until the pasta is tender.

tuna & pasta cheddar melt

- 1 can (10½ ounces) Campbell's® Condensed Chicken Broth
- 1 soup can water
- 3 cups *uncooked* corkscrew-shaped pasta (rotini)
- 1 can (10¾ ounces) Campbell's® Condensed Cream of Mushroom Soup (Regular *or* 98% Fat Free)
- 1 cup milk
- 1 can (about 6 ounces) tuna, drained and flaked
- 1 cup shredded Cheddar cheese (about 4 ounces)
- 2 tablespoons Italian-seasoned dry bread crumbs
- 2 teaspoons butter, melted

1. Heat the broth and water in a 12-inch skillet over medium-high heat to a boil. Stir in the pasta. Reduce the heat to medium. Cook until the pasta is tender, stirring often. Do not drain.

2. Stir the soup, milk and tuna in the skillet. Top with the cheese. Stir the bread crumbs and butter in a small bowl. Sprinkle over the tuna mixture. Cook until the cheese is melted.

20-minute turkey & rice

prep 10 minutes | **cook** 10 minutes | **makes** 4 servings

1   can (10¾ ounces) Campbell's® Condensed Cream of Chicken Soup
       (Regular *or* 98% Fat Free)

1½ cups water

¼   teaspoon paprika

¼   teaspoon ground black pepper

2   cups *uncooked* instant white rice

2   cups cubed cooked turkey

2   cups cooked vegetable combination (carrots, green beans, peas)

Heat the soup, water, paprika and black pepper in a 10-inch skillet over medium-high heat to a boil. Stir in the rice, turkey and vegetables. Reduce the heat to low. Cook for 5 minutes or until the rice is tender.

beef taco skillet

- 1 **pound ground beef**
- 1 **can (10¾ ounces) Campbell's® Condensed Tomato Soup (Regular *or* Healthy Request®)**
- ½ **cup Pace® Picante Sauce**
- ½ **cup water**
- 6 **flour tortillas (6-inch), cut into 1-inch pieces**
- ½ **cup shredded Cheddar cheese**

1. Cook the beef in a 10-inch skillet over medium-high heat until well browned, stirring often to separate the meat. Pour off any fat.

2. Stir the soup, picante sauce, water and tortillas in the skillet and heat to a boil. Reduce the heat to low. Cook for 5 minutes. Stir the beef mixture. Top with the cheese.

Creamy Mexican Fiesta: Stir in ½ *cup* sour cream with the soup.

Ranchero Style: Use corn tortillas instead of flour tortillas and shredded Mexican cheese blend instead of Cheddar.

baked pork chops & gravy

prep 10 minutes I **bake** 20 minutes I **makes** 6 servings

- 1 **egg, beaten**
- 2 **tablespoons water**
- 6 **boneless pork chops, ¾-inch thick (about 1½ pounds)**
- 2 **tablespoons all-purpose flour**
- 1½ **cups Pepperidge Farm® Herb Seasoned Stuffing, crushed**
- 1 **can (10½ ounces) Campbell's® Turkey Gravy**

1. Beat the egg and water in a shallow dish with a fork or whisk. Coat the pork with the flour. Dip the pork into the egg mixture. Coat with the stuffing. Place the pork onto a baking sheet.

2. Bake at 400°F. for 20 minutes or until the pork is cooked through.

3. Heat the gravy in a 1-quart saucepan over medium heat until it's hot and bubbling. Serve the gravy with the pork.

broccoli & garlic penne pasta

prep 20 minutes I **cook** 10 minutes I **makes** 4 servings

- 1 cup Swanson® Chicken Broth (Regular, Natural Goodness® **or** Certified Organic)
- ½ teaspoon dried basil leaves, crushed
- ⅛ teaspoon ground black pepper
- 2 cloves garlic, minced
- 3 cups broccoli florets
- 4½ cups penne pasta, cooked and drained
- 1 tablespoon lemon juice
- 2 tablespoons grated Parmesan cheese

1. Heat the broth, basil, black pepper, garlic and broccoli in a 10-inch skillet over medium heat to a boil. Reduce the heat to low. Cover and cook until the broccoli is tender-crisp.

2. Add the pasta and lemon juice and toss to coat. Sprinkle the pasta mixture with the cheese.

creamy pesto chicken & bow ties

prep 10 minutes **I cook** 20 minutes **I makes** 4 servings

- 2 **tablespoons butter**
- 1¼ **pounds skinless, boneless chicken breast halves, cut into cubes**
- 1 **can (10¾ ounces) Campbell's® Condensed Cream of Chicken Soup (Regular *or* 98% Fat Free)**
- ½ **cup milk**
- ½ **cup prepared pesto sauce**
- 3 **cups bow tie pasta (farfalle), cooked and drained**

1. Heat the butter in a 10-inch skillet over medium-high heat. Add the chicken and cook until it's well browned, stirring often.

2. Stir the soup, milk and pesto sauce in the skillet and heat to a boil. Reduce the heat to low. Cook for 5 minutes or until the chicken is cooked through. Stir in the pasta and cook until the mixture is hot and bubbling.

fish & vegetable skillet

prep 15 minutes | **cook** 15 minutes | **makes** 4 servings

- ¼ **cup water**
- 2 **tablespoons dry white wine (optional)**
- ½ **teaspoon dried thyme leaves, crushed**
  Generous dash ground black pepper
- 1 **large carrot, cut into matchstick-thin strips (about 1 cup)**
- 2 **stalks celery, cut into matchstick-thin strips (about 1⅓ cups)**
- 1 **small onion, chopped (about ¼ cup)**
- 1 **can (10¾ ounces) Campbell's® Condensed Cream of Mushroom Soup**
  (Regular, 98% Fat Free or Healthy Request®)
- 4 **firm white fish fillets (cod, haddock or halibut) (about 1 pound)**

1. Heat the water, wine, thyme, black pepper, carrot, celery and onion in a 10-inch skillet over medium-high heat to a boil. Reduce the heat to low. Cover and cook for 5 minutes or until the vegetables are tender-crisp.

2. Stir the soup in the skillet. Top with the fish. Cover and cook for 5 minutes or until the fish flakes easily when tested with a fork.

chicken and bean burritos

1 **tablespoon vegetable oil**

1 **medium onion, chopped (about ½ cup)**

⅛ **teaspoon garlic powder**

1 **can (11½ ounces) Campbell's® Condensed Bean with Bacon Soup**

¾ **cup Pace® Picante Sauce**

2 **cans (4.5 ounces *each*) Swanson® Premium White Chunk Chicken Breast in Water, drained**

8 **flour tortillas (8-inch), warmed**

1. Heat the oil in a 10-inch skillet over medium heat. Add the onion and garlic powder and cook until the onion is tender.

2. Stir the soup, picante sauce and chicken in the skillet. Cook until the chicken mixture is hot and bubbling.

3. Spoon **about** ⅓ **cup** chicken mixture down the center of **each** tortilla. Fold up the sides of the tortillas around the filling then fold up the ends to enclose the filling.

classic beef stroganoff

prep 20 minutes **|** **cook** 20 minutes **|** **makes** 4 servings

- 1 **boneless beef sirloin steak, ¾-inch thick, cut into 2-inch pieces**
   Cracked black pepper
- 1 **tablespoon vegetable oil**
- 1 **medium onion, finely chopped (about ½ cup)**
- 1 **can (10¾ ounces) Campbell's® Condensed Cream of Mushroom Soup (Regular *or* 98% Fat Free)**
- ½ **cup water**
- ¼ **cup dry sherry (optional)**
- 1 **tablespoon tomato paste**
- ¼ **cup plain yogurt**
   Hot cooked medium egg noodles
   Chopped fresh parsley

1. Season the beef with the black pepper.

2. Heat the oil in a 10-inch skillet over medium-high heat. Add the beef and cook until it's well browned, stirring often. Remove the beef from the skillet. Pour off any fat.

3. Reduce the heat to medium. Add the onion and cook until tender.

4. Stir in the soup, water, sherry, if desired, and tomato paste and heat to a boil. Return the beef to the skillet and cook until the beef is cooked through. Remove the skillet from the heat. Stir in the yogurt. Serve the beef mixture over the noodles and sprinkle with the parsley.

beefy enchilada skillet

prep 5 minutes I **cook** 15 minutes I **makes** 4 servings

1 **pound ground beef**
1 **jar (17.5 ounces) Pace® Picante Sauce**
8 **corn tortillas (6-inch), cut into 1-inch squares**
1 **cup shredded Cheddar cheese (about 4 ounces)**
   Sour cream
   Chopped green onions

1. Cook the beef in a 10-inch skillet over medium-high heat until it's well browned, stirring often to separate the meat. Pour off any fat.

2. Stir the picante sauce, tortillas and **half** of the cheese in the skillet and heat to a boil. Reduce the heat to low. Cover and cook for 5 minutes or until it's hot and bubbling.

3. Top with the remaining cheese. Serve with sour cream and green onions.

quick & easy dinner nachos supreme

prep 10 minutes | **cook** 15 minutes | **makes** 4 servings

 1 **pound ground beef**
 1 **package (about 1 ounce) taco seasoning mix**
 1 **can (10¾ ounces) Campbell's® Condensed Tomato Soup**
1½ **cups water**
1½ **cups *uncooked* instant white rice**
    Pace® Chunky Salsa
    Shredded Cheddar cheese
    Shredded lettuce
    Tortilla chips

1. Cook the beef and taco seasoning in a 10-inch skillet until the beef is well browned, stirring often to separate the meat. Pour off any fat.

2. Stir the soup, water and rice in the skillet and heat to a boil. Reduce the heat to low. Cover and cook for 5 minutes or until the rice is tender.

3. Top with the salsa, cheese and lettuce. Serve with the tortilla chips for dipping.

french onion burgers

prep 5 minutes | **cook** 20 minutes | **makes** 4 servings

- **1 pound ground beef**
- **1 can (10½ ounces) Campbell's® Condensed French Onion Soup**
- **4 slices cheese**
- **4 Pepperidge Farm® Sandwich Buns with Sesame Seeds, split**

1. Shape the beef into **4** (½-inch-thick) burgers.

2. Heat a 10-inch skillet over medium-high heat. Add the burgers and cook until well browned on both sides. Remove the burgers from the skillet. Pour off any fat.

3. Stir the soup in the skillet and heat to a boil. Return the burgers to the skillet. Reduce the heat to low. Cover and cook for 5 minutes or until desired doneness. Top the burgers with the cheese and cook until the cheese is melted. Serve the burgers on the buns with the soup mixture for dipping.

tip You can also serve these burgers in a bowl atop a mound of hot mashed potatoes with some of the soup mixture poured over.

shortcut stuffed peppers

prep 10 minutes | **cook** 10 minutes | **makes** 4 servings

- 1½ **pounds ground beef**
- 1 **can (10¾ ounces) Campbell's® Condensed Tomato Soup**
- 1 **cup *uncooked* instant white rice**
- 2 **teaspoons garlic powder**
- ½ **teaspoon ground black pepper**
- 2 **large green peppers, cut in half lengthwise and seeded**

1. Mix the beef, soup, rice, garlic powder and black pepper in a large bowl.

2. Place the pepper halves, cut-side up, into an 8×8-inch microwavable baking dish. Divide the beef mixture among the pepper halves (the pepper halves will be very full).

3. Cover and microwave on HIGH for 10 minutes or until the beef mixture is cooked through.

tip *The shortcut is in the cooking— arrange the peppers in a glass dish in a circle for the most effective cooking in the microwave.*

quick & easy chicken quesadillas

prep 15 minutes I **cook** 15 minutes I **bake** 5 minutes I **makes** 8 servings

- 4 skinless, boneless chicken breast halves (about 1 pound), cut into cubes
- 1 can (10¾ ounces) Campbell's® Condensed Cream of Chicken Soup (Regular *or* 98% Fat Free)
- ½ cup Pace® Picante Sauce
- ½ cup shredded Monterey Jack cheese
- 1 teaspoon chili powder
- 8 flour tortillas (8-inch), warmed

1. Heat the oven to 425°F.

2. Cook the chicken in a 10-inch nonstick skillet over medium-high heat until well browned and cooked through, stirring often. Stir in the soup, picante sauce, cheese and chili powder and cook until the mixture is hot and bubbling.

3. Place the tortillas onto **2** baking sheets. Spread **about** ⅓ **cup** chicken mixture on **half** of **each** tortilla to within ½ inch of the edge. Brush the edges of the tortillas with water. Fold the tortillas over the filling and press the edges to seal.

4. Bake for 5 minutes or until the filling is hot. Cut the quesadillas into wedges.

crunchy no-fry chicken

prep 10 minutes | **bake** 20 minutes | **makes** 4 servings

¾ **cup finely crushed corn flakes**

½ **teaspoon garlic powder**

⅛ **teaspoon ground black pepper**

⅛ **teaspoon ground red pepper**

4 **skinless, boneless chicken breast halves (about 1 pound)**

¼ **cup Swanson® Chicken Stock**

1. Heat the oven to 400°F.

2. Stir the corn flakes, garlic powder, black pepper and red pepper in a shallow medium bowl.

3. Dip the chicken into the stock. Coat with the corn flake mixture. Place the chicken onto a baking sheet.

4. Bake for 20 minutes or until the chicken is cooked through.

fiesta chicken & rice wraps

prep 15 minutes | **cook** 5 minutes | **stand** 5 minutes | **makes** 4 servings

- 1 **can (10¾ ounces) Campbell's® Cream of Chicken Soup (Regular *or* Certified Organic)**
- 1 **cup Pace® Picante Sauce**
- ½ **cup water**
- 1 **cup *uncooked* instant white rice**
- 2 **cups cubed cooked chicken**
- 4 **flour tortillas (10-inch), warmed**

1. Heat the soup, picante sauce and water in a 2-quart saucepan over medium heat to a boil, stirring occasionally.

2. Stir the rice and chicken in the saucepan. Cover and remove the saucepan from the heat. Let stand for 5 minutes.

3. Spoon **about 1 cup** chicken mixture down center of **each** tortilla. Fold tortilla around the chicken mixture.

tip For *2 cups* cubed cooked chicken, cook *1 pound* skinless, boneless chicken breasts *or* thighs, cubed, in a 3-quart saucepan in *4 cups* boiling water over medium heat for 5 minutes or until chicken is cooked through.

turkey & avocado sandwiches

prep 10 minutes | **makes** 4 servings

- 4 **leaves lettuce**
- 8 **thin slices deli turkey breast (about 8 ounces)**
- ½ **peeled pitted avocado, cut into 8 slices**
- 8 **slices Pepperidge Farm® Whole Grain 15 Grain Bread, toasted**
- 2 **tablespoons Pace® Chunky Salsa**

Divide the lettuce, turkey and avocado among 4 bread slices. Top **each** with 1½ **teaspoons** salsa and the remaining bread slices.

salsa chicken soup

prep 5 minutes | **cook** 25 minutes | **makes** 4 servings

- 3½ **cups Swanson® Chicken Broth (Regular, Natural Goodness® *or* Certified Organic)**
- ½ **cup *uncooked* regular long-grain white rice**
- 1 **can (16 ounces) Campbell's® Pork and Beans**
- ½ **cup Pace® Chunky Salsa**
- 1 **cup cubed cooked chicken**

1. Heat the broth in a 2-quart saucepan over medium-high heat to a boil. Stir the rice in the saucepan. Reduce the heat to low. Cover and cook for 20 minutes or until rice is done.

2. Stir the beans, salsa and chicken in the saucepan and heat through.

skillet pork chops florentine

prep 5 minutes | **cook** 30 minutes | **makes** 6 servings

2 tablespoons olive *or* vegetable oil

6 boneless pork chops, ¾-inch thick (about 1½ pounds)

1 medium onion, thinly sliced (about ½ cup)

1 jar (24 ounces) Prego® Marinara Italian Sauce

1 package (10 ounces) frozen leaf spinach, thawed and well drained

4 ounces shredded mozzarella cheese (about 1 cup)

1. Heat **1 tablespoon** of the oil in a 12-inch skillet over medium-high heat. Add the pork chops and cook until the chops are well browned on both sides. Remove the pork chops and set them aside.

2. Reduce the heat to medium and add the remaining oil. Add the onion. Cook and stir until the onion is tender-crisp.

3. Stir the Italian sauce and spinach into the skillet and heat to a boil. Return the pork chops to the skillet and reduce the heat to low. Cover and cook until the chops are cooked through. Sprinkle with the cheese.

tip *To thaw spinach, microwave on HIGH for 3 minutes, breaking apart with a fork halfway through heating.*

quick chicken parmesan

prep 5 minutes **|** **bake** 25 minutes **|** **makes** 4 servings

- **4 skinless, boneless chicken breast halves (about 1 pound)**
- **2 cups Prego® Traditional Italian Sauce *or* Fresh Mushroom Italian Sauce**
- **2 ounces shredded mozzarella cheese (about ½ cup)**
- **2 tablespoons grated Parmesan cheese**
- **½ of a 16-ounce package spaghetti, cooked and drained (about 4 cups)**

1. Place the chicken in a 2-quart shallow baking dish. Top the chicken with the Italian sauce. Sprinkle with the mozzarella cheese and Parmesan cheese.

2. Bake at 400°F. for 25 minutes or until cooked through. Serve with the spaghetti.

grilled swordfish steaks with citrus salsa

prep 20 minutes | **grill** 10 minutes | **makes** 4 servings

- ¾ cup Pace® Picante Sauce
- 1 teaspoon grated orange zest
- 2 tablespoons orange juice
- 1 tablespoon chopped fresh cilantro leaves
- 1 cup coarsely chopped orange
- 1 medium tomato, chopped (about 1 cup)
- 2 green onions, sliced (about ¼ cup)
- 4 swordfish steaks, 1–inch thick (about 1½ pounds)

1. Stir the picante sauce, orange zest, orange juice and cilantro in a medium bowl. Reserve ½ **cup** to baste the fish. For the salsa, add the orange, tomato and onions to the remaining picante sauce mixture. Set the salsa aside.

2. Lightly oil the grill rack and heat the grill to medium. Grill the fish for 10 minutes or until it's cooked though, turning the fish over once during grilling and brushing often with the reserved picante sauce mixture. Discard the remaining picante sauce mixture.

3. Serve the fish with the citrus salsa.

lighter chicken cheesesteaks

prep 10 minutes | **cook** 20 minutes | **makes** 2 servings

Vegetable cooking spray
1 **medium onion, sliced (about ½ cup)**
1 **tablespoon water**
2 **portions frozen chicken sandwich steaks**
2 **slices fat-free American pasteurized process cheese product**
4 **slices Pepperidge Farm® 100% Natural 100% Whole Wheat Bread**
Sliced hot cherry pepper

1. Spray a 10-inch skillet with the cooking spray and heat over medium heat for 1 minute. Add the onion and water. Cover and cook for 5 minutes or until the onion is tender. Remove the onion from the skillet and keep warm.

2. Increase the heat to medium-high. Add the sandwich steaks and cook until they're well browned and cooked through. Top with the cheese and cook until the cheese is melted.

3. Divide the steak mixture between **2** bread slices. Top with the onions, hot peppers and remaining bread slices.

pork with mushroom dijon sauce

prep 10 minutes | **cook** 30 minutes | **makes** 4 servings

- 4 **boneless pork chops, ¾-inch thick (about 1 pound)**
- ½ **teaspoon lemon pepper seasoning**
- 1 **tablespoon vegetable oil**
- 1 **cup sliced mushrooms (about 3 ounces)**
- 1 **can (10¾ ounces) Campbell's® Condensed Cream of Mushroom Soup (Regular *or* 98% Fat Free)**
- ¼ **cup milk**
- 2 **tablespoons Chablis *or* other dry white wine**
- 1 **tablespoon Dijon-style mustard**

1. Season the pork with the lemon pepper.

2. Heat the oil in a 10-inch skillet over medium-high heat. Add the pork and cook until it's well browned on both sides. Remove the pork from the skillet.

3. Add the mushrooms to the skillet. Reduce the heat to medium. Cook until the mushrooms are tender, stirring occasionally.

4. Stir the soup, milk, wine and mustard in the skillet and heat to a boil. Return the pork to the skillet. Reduce the heat to low. Cover and cook for 10 minutes or until the pork is cooked through.

smothered pork chops

prep 10 minutes I **cook** 25 minutes I **makes** 6 servings

- 2 **tablespoons cornstarch**
- 1¾ **cups Swanson® Beef Stock**
- ¼ **teaspoon ground black pepper**
   Vegetable cooking spray
- 6 **bone-in pork chops, ½-inch thick (about 1½ pounds)**
- 1 **large onion, sliced (about 1 cup)**

1. Stir the cornstarch, stock and black pepper in a small bowl until the mixture is smooth.

2. Spray a 12-inch skillet with the cooking spray and heat over medium-high heat for 1 minute. Add the pork and cook for 5 minutes or until it's well browned on both sides. Remove the pork from the skillet. Remove the skillet from the heat.

3. Reduce the heat to medium. Spray the skillet with the cooking spray and heat for 1 minute. Add the onion and cook until it's tender-crisp, stirring occasionally.

4. Stir the stock mixture in the skillet. Cook and stir until the mixture boils and thickens. Return the pork to the skillet. Reduce the heat to low. Cover and cook for 5 minutes or until the pork is cooked through.

one-dish beef stroganoff

prep 15 minutes I **cook** 20 minutes I **makes** 4 servings

- 1 tablespoon vegetable oil
- 1 boneless beef sirloin steak, ¾-inch thick (about 1 pound), cut into thin strips
- 1 medium onion, chopped (about ½ cup)
- 3 cloves garlic, minced
- 1 teaspoon dried parsley flakes
- 1¾ cups Swanson® Beef Stock
- 2 cups sliced mushrooms (about 6 ounces)
- 3 cups *uncooked* medium egg noodles
- ½ cup sour cream
  Chopped fresh parsley

1. Heat the oil in a 12-inch nonstick skillet over medium-high heat. Add the beef and cook until it's well browned, stirring often. Add the onion, garlic and parsley and cook until the onion is tender-crisp.

2. Stir the stock and mushrooms in the skillet and heat to a boil. Stir in the noodles. Reduce the heat to low. Cover and cook for 10 minutes or until the noodles are tender.

3. Stir the sour cream in the skillet and cook until the mixture is hot and bubbling. Sprinkle with the parsley.

chicken tetrazzini

prep 20 minutes | **cook** 5 minutes | **makes** 4 servings

1 can (10¾ ounces) Campbell's® Condensed Cream of Mushroom Soup
   (Regular *or* 98% Fat Free)

¾ cup water

½ cup grated Parmesan cheese

2 tablespoons chopped fresh parsley *or* 2 teaspoons dried parsley flakes

¼ cup chopped red pepper *or* pimiento (optional)

½ package (8 ounces) spaghetti, cooked and drained

2 cans (4.5 ounces *each*) Swanson® Premium White Chunk Chicken Breast in Water, drained

Heat the soup, water, cheese, parsley, pepper, if desired, spaghetti and chicken in a 2-quart saucepan over medium heat until the mixture is hot and bubbling.

south of the border chicken & bean burritos

prep 10 minutes | **cook** 15 minutes | **makes** 6 servings

- 1 **tablespoon vegetable oil**
- 1½ **pounds skinless, boneless chicken breasts, cut into strips***
- 1 **jar (14 ounces) Pace® Picante Sauce**
- 1 **can (about 15 ounces) pinto beans *or* black beans, rinsed and drained**
- 6 **flour tortillas (10-inch), warmed**
  Shredded Cheddar cheese
  Guacamole
  Chopped tomato

*Or use 1½ pounds boneless pork chops or roast, cut into strips.

1. Heat the oil in a 10-inch skillet over medium-high heat. Add the chicken and cook until it's browned, stirring often.

2. Stir the picante sauce and beans in the skillet and heat to a boil. Reduce the heat to low and cook for 5 minutes.

3. Divide the chicken mixture and cheese among the tortillas. Top with the guacamole and tomatoes, if desired. Fold sides of tortilla over filling and then fold up ends to enclose the filling.

simple seasoned ravioli

prep 5 minutes I **cook** 15 minutes I **makes** 2 servings

1¾ cups Swanson® Chicken Broth (Regular, Natural Goodness® *or* Certified Organic)
  1 tablespoon drained canned diced tomatoes
  1 teaspoon grated Parmesan cheese
  ½ teaspoon Italian seasoning, crushed
  ¼ teaspoon garlic powder
  1 package (16 ounces) frozen cheese-filled mini ravioli

1. Heat the broth, tomatoes, cheese, Italian seasoning and garlic powder in a 3-quart saucepan over medium-high heat to a boil.

2. Stir the ravioli in the saucepan. Reduce the heat to low. Cook for 10 minutes or until the ravioli is tender, stirring often.

quick barbecued beef sandwiches

prep 10 minutes | **cook** 20 minutes | **makes** 12 servings

- 1 **tablespoon vegetable oil**
- 1 **medium onion, chopped (about ½ cup)**
- 1 **can (26 ounces) Campbell's® Condensed Tomato Soup**
- ¼ **cup water**
- 2 **tablespoons packed brown sugar**
- 2 **tablespoons vinegar**
- 1 **tablespoon Worcestershire sauce**
- 1½ **pounds thinly sliced deli roast beef**
- 12 **Pepperidge Farm® Classic Sandwich Buns with Sesame Seeds, split and toasted**

1. Heat the oil in a 4-quart saucepot over medium heat. Add the onion and cook until tender, stirring occasionally.

2. Stir the soup, water, brown sugar, vinegar and Worcestershire in the saucepot and heat to a boil. Reduce the heat to low. Cook for 5 minutes. Add the beef to the saucepot and and cook until the mixture is hot and bubbling. Divide the beef and sauce among the buns.

shortcut chicken cordon bleu

prep 10 minutes | **cook** 20 minutes | **makes** 4 servings

- 1 **tablespoon butter**
- 4 **skinless, boneless chicken breast halves (about 1 pound)**
- 1 **can (10¾ ounces) Campbell's® Condensed Cream of Chicken Soup (Regular *or* 98% Fat Free)**
- 2 **tablespoons water**
- 2 **tablespoons Chablis *or* other dry white wine**
- ½ **cup shredded Swiss cheese**
- ½ **cup chopped cooked ham**
- 4 **cups medium egg noodles, cooked and drained**

1. Heat the butter in a 10-inch skillet over medium–high heat. Add the chicken and cook for 10 minutes or until well browned on both sides.

2. Stir the soup, water, wine, cheese and ham in the skillet and heat to a boil. Reduce the heat to low. Cover and cook for 5 minutes or until the chicken is cooked through. Serve the chicken and sauce with the noodles.

layered pasta, veggie & cheese skillet

prep 20 minutes I **cook** 10 minutes I **makes** 4 servings

1   **jar (24 ounces) Prego® Veggie Smart® Chunky & Savory Italian Sauce**

1   **cup water**

1¼ **cups part skim ricotta cheese**

½   **cup grated Parmesan cheese**

1   **egg, beaten**

½   **of a 6-ounce package fresh baby spinach *or* arugula, coarsely chopped (about 4 cups)**

3   **cups trumpet-shaped pasta (campanelle), cooked and drained (about 4 cups)**

1. Stir the Italian sauce and water in a medium bowl. Stir the ricotta cheese, ⅓ **cup** Parmesan cheese, egg and spinach in a medium bowl.

2. Layer **1 cup** Italian sauce mixture, **half** the pasta and **half** the cheese mixture in a 12-inch skillet. Repeat the layers. Top with the remaining sauce mixture and the remaining Parmesan cheese. Cover the skillet.

3. Cook over medium heat for 10 minutes or until the mixture is hot.

easy asian-style chicken & rice

prep 5 minutes I **cook** 20 minutes I **makes** 4 servings

- 1 tablespoon vegetable oil
- 4 skinless, boneless chicken breast halves (about 1 pound)
- 1 can (10¾ ounces) Campbell's® Condensed Golden Mushroom Soup
- 1½ cups water
- 1 package (1.25 ounces) teriyaki seasoning mix
- 1 bag (16 ounces) frozen stir-fry vegetables
- 1½ cups *uncooked* instant white rice

1. Heat the oil in a 10-inch skillet over medium-high heat. Add the chicken and cook until well browned on both sides. Remove the chicken from the skillet.

2. Stir the soup, water, seasoning mix and vegetables in the skillet and heat to a boil. Stir in the rice. Return the chicken to the skillet. Reduce the heat to low. Cover and cook for 5 minutes or until the chicken is cooked through and the rice is tender.

beef teriyaki

prep 10 minutes I **cook** 15 minutes I **makes** 4 servings

- 2 **tablespoons cornstarch**
- 1¾ **cups Swanson® Beef Stock**
- 2 **tablespoons soy sauce**
- 1 **tablespoon packed brown sugar**
- ½ **teaspoon garlic powder**
- 1 **boneless beef sirloin steak**
- 4 **cups fresh *or* frozen broccoli florets**
  Hot cooked rice

1. Stir the cornstarch, stock, soy sauce, brown sugar and garlic powder in a small bowl until the mixture is smooth.

2. Stir-fry the beef in a 10-inch nonstick skillet over medium-high heat until it's well browned, stirring often. Pour off any fat.

3. Add the broccoli to the skillet and cook for 1 minute. Stir in the cornstarch mixture. Cook and stir until the mixture boils and thickens. Serve the beef mixture over the rice.

tip *To make slicing easier, freeze the beef for 1 hour before slicing.*

quick skillet ziti

prep 5 minutes I **cook** 20 minutes I **makes** 4 servings

- 1 **pound ground beef**
- 1 **jar (24 ounces) Prego® Traditional Italian Sauce *or* Marinara Italian Sauce**
- 5 **cups tube-shaped pasta (ziti), cooked and drained**
  Grated Parmesan cheese

1. Cook the beef in a 10-inch skillet until it's well browned, stirring often to separate the meat. Pour off any fat.

2. Stir the Italian sauce and pasta in the skillet and heat through. Sprinkle with the cheese.

budget-friendly
meals

Planning and savvy shopping

help make great meals.

chicken seasoned rice and vegetable casserole

prep 5 minutes | **bake** 1 hour | **makes** 6 servings

1   can (10¾ ounces) Campbell's® Condensed Cream of Mushroom Soup
     (Regular *or* 98% Fat Free)
1   cup water
1   package (6 ounces) seasoned long-grain and wild rice mix
1   bag (16 ounces) frozen vegetable combination (broccoli, carrots, water chestnuts)
1   cup shredded Cheddar cheese (about 4 ounces)
6   skinless, boneless chicken breast halves (about 1½ pounds)
     Paprika

1. Stir the soup, water, rice and seasoning packet, vegetables and **half** of the cheese in a 3-quart shallow baking dish. Top with the chicken. Sprinkle the chicken with the paprika. Cover the baking dish.

2. Bake at 375°F. for 1 hour or until the chicken is cooked through and the rice is tender. Uncover the dish and sprinkle with the remaining cheese.

shopping & saving

With a little planning and savvy shopping, great meals really are just a few dollars away. If you follow just two or three of these tips each week at the grocery store, you'll be amazed at how much money you'll save.

- *Meat cuts, like pork shoulder and chuck roast, are often less expensive than steaks or chops.* They require low, slow cooking methods (think stews and braises), but result in great-tasting, inexpensive dinners that don't require much hands-on work.
- *Learn to cut up whole chickens.* It's cheaper than buying precut chicken, and the technique isn't hard at all.
- *Try cutting meat into thin slices before serving.* Visually, this gives the impression of volume on the plate.
- *Clip coupons,* but buy only what you might use, not just what's on sale.

creamy chicken quesadillas

prep 15 minutes I **bake** 10 minutes I **makes** 4 servings

- 1 can (10¾ ounces) Campbell's® Condensed Cream of Chicken Soup (Regular **or** 98% Fat Free)
- 1 cup shredded Cheddar cheese (about 4 ounces)
- 1 jalapeño pepper, seeded and finely chopped (optional)
- 2 cans (4.5 ounces **each**) Swanson® Premium White Chunk Chicken Breast in Water, drained
- 8 flour tortillas (8-inch)
  Pace® Chunky Salsa
  Sour cream

1. Heat the oven to 400° F. Stir the soup, ½ **cup** cheese, pepper, if desired, and chicken in a medium bowl.

2. Place the tortillas onto **2** baking sheets. Spread ¼ **cup** chicken mixture on **half** of **each** tortilla to within ½ inch of the edge. Brush the edges of the tortillas with water. Fold the tortillas over the filling and press the edges to seal.

3. Bake for 10 minutes or until the filling is hot. Sprinkle with the remaining cheese. Serve with salsa and sour cream.

tip *Substitute* ***1½ cups*** *chopped cooked chicken for the Swanson® Chicken.*

cheddar broccoli frittata

prep 10 minutes I **cook** 15 minutes I **makes** 4 servings

6   eggs

1   can (10¾ ounces) Campbell's® Condensed Broccoli Cheese Soup (Regular *or* 98% Fat Free)

¼   cup milk

⅛   teaspoon ground black pepper

1   tablespoon butter

2   cups sliced mushrooms (about 6 ounces)

1   large onion, chopped (about 1 cup)

1   small zucchini, sliced (about 1 cup)

¼   cup shredded Cheddar cheese

1   green onion, chopped (about 2 tablespoons)

1. Beat the eggs, soup, milk and black pepper in a medium bowl with a fork or whisk.

2. Heat the butter in a 12-inch ovenproof nonstick skillet over medium heat. Add the mushrooms, onion and zucchini and cook until tender. Stir in the egg mixture. Reduce the heat to low. Cook for 5 minutes or until the eggs are set but still moist.

3. Heat the broiler. Sprinkle the cheese over the egg mixture. Broil the frittata with the top 4 inches from the heat for 2 minutes or until the top is golden brown. Sprinkle with the green onion.

easy taco tamale pie

prep 15 minutes I **bake** 25 minutes I **makes** 4 servings

- 1 **pound ground beef**
- 1 **can (16 ounces) whole kernel corn, undrained**
- 1 **jar (16 ounces) Pace® Picante Sauce**
- ½ **cup shredded Cheddar cheese**
- 1 **box (about 8 ounces) corn muffin mix**

1. Heat the oven to 375°F. Cook the beef in a 10-inch skillet over medium-high heat until it's well browned, stirring often to separate the meat. Pour off any fat.

2. Stir the corn with liquid, picante sauce and cheese in the skillet. Spoon the beef mixture into a 2-quart shallow baking dish. Mix the corn muffin mix according to the package directions. Drop the batter by spoonfuls on top of the beef mixture.

3. Bake for 25 minutes or until the topping is golden brown.

cheesy taco meatloaf

prep 10 minutes │ **bake** 1 hour 5 minutes │ **makes** 8 servings

- 2 **pounds ground beef**
- 1 **jar (16 ounces) Pace® Picante Sauce**
- 1 **cup crushed tortilla chips**
- ½ **cup shredded Cheddar cheese**

1. Thoroughly mix the beef, ⅔ **cup** picante sauce and tortilla chips in a large bowl. Place the beef mixture into a 3-quart shallow baking pan and shape into an 8×4-inch loaf.

2. Bake at 350°F. for 1 hour or until the meatloaf is cooked through.

3. Sprinkle the meatloaf with the cheese. Bake for 5 minutes or until the cheese is melted. Heat the remaining picante sauce in a 1-quart saucepan over medium heat to a boil. Serve the sauce with the meatloaf.

beef 'n' bean bake

prep 10 minutes │ **bake** 30 minutes │ **makes** 4 servings

- 1 **pound ground beef**
- 1 **can (19 ounces) Campbell's® Chunky™ Roadhouse–Beef & Bean Chili**
- ¾ **cup Pace® Picante Sauce**
- ¾ **cup water**
- 8 **corn tortillas (6-inch) *or* 6 flour tortillas (8-inch), cut into 1-inch pieces**
- ⅔ **cup shredded Cheddar cheese**

1. Heat the oven to 400°F.

2. Cook the beef in a 10-inch skillet over medium-high heat until well browned, stirring often to separate the meat. Pour off any fat.

3. Stir the chili, picante sauce, water, tortillas and **half** the cheese in the skillet. Pour the beef mixture into a 2-quart shallow baking dish. Cover the baking dish.

4. Bake for 30 minutes or until the mixture is hot and bubbling. Sprinkle with the remaining cheese.

balsamic chicken with white beans & spinach

prep 10 minutes I **cook** 25 minutes I **makes** 4 servings

- 2 **tablespoons olive oil**
- 1¼ **pounds skinless, boneless chicken breast halves**
- 3 **cloves garlic, minced**
- ⅓ **cup balsamic vinegar**
- 1 **can (10¾ ounces) Campbell's® Condensed Golden Mushroom Soup**
- 1 **can (about 15 ounces) white kidney beans (cannellini), rinsed and drained**
- 1 **bag (about 7 ounces) fresh baby spinach**

1. Heat the oil in a 12-inch skillet over medium-high heat. Add the chicken and cook for 10 minutes or until well browned on both sides. Remove the chicken from the skillet.

2. Reduce the heat to medium. Add the garlic to the skillet and cook and stir for 1 minute. Stir in the vinegar and cook, scraping up the browned bits from the bottom of the pan.

3. Stir the soup and beans in the skillet and heat to a boil. Stir in the spinach. Return the chicken to the skillet. Reduce the heat to medium. Cover and cook until the chicken is cooked through and the spinach is wilted.

beef sirloin steak with baby spinach

prep 20 minutes | **cook** 20 minutes | **makes** 4 servings

- 2 tablespoons olive oil
- 1 boneless beef sirloin steak, ¾-inch thick (about 1 pound), cut into 4 pieces
- 1 large onion, sliced (about 1 cup)
- 1 small red pepper, chopped (about ½ cup)
- 3 cloves garlic, minced
- 1 can (10¾ ounces) Campbell's® Condensed Cream of Mushroom Soup (Regular **or** 98% Fat Free)
- ½ cup water
- 2 tablespoons balsamic vinegar
- 1 tablespoon chopped fresh rosemary leaves **or** 1 teaspoon dried rosemary leaves, crushed
- 1 bag (about 7 ounces) fresh baby spinach

  Hot mashed potatoes

1. Heat **1 tablespoon** oil in a 12-inch skillet over medium-high heat. Add the beef and cook until well browned on both sides. Remove the beef from the skillet. Pour off any fat.

2. Heat the remaining oil in the skillet. Add the onion and pepper and cook for 1 minute, stirring occasionally. Add the garlic and cook until the vegetables are tender-crisp, stirring often.

3. Stir the soup, water, vinegar and rosemary in the skillet and heat to a boil. Return the beef to the skillet. Reduce the heat to medium. Stir in the spinach. Cover and cook the beef for 2 minutes for medium or until desired doneness. Serve the beef and vegetable mixture with the potatoes.

pasta e fagioli

prep 15 minutes | **cook** 30 minutes | **makes** 4 servings

- 1 **tablespoon olive oil**
- 2 **stalks celery, finely chopped (about 1 cup)**
- 2 **medium carrots, finely chopped (about 1 cup)**
- 1 **medium onion, chopped (about ½ cup)**
- 2 **cloves garlic, minced**
- 2 **cups Swanson® Chicken Broth (Regular, Natural Goodness® *or* Certified Organic)**
- 1 **teaspoon Italian seasoning, crushed**
- 1 **can (14.5 ounces) diced tomatoes, undrained**
- ¾ **cup short tube–shaped ditalini pasta, cooked and drained**
- 1 **can (about 15 ounces) white kidney beans (cannellini), undrained**

1. Heat the oil in a 12-inch skillet over medium heat. Cook the celery, carrots, onion and garlic until they're tender.

2. Stir the broth, Italian seasoning and tomatoes in the skillet. Heat to a boil. Reduce the heat to low and cook for 15 minutes or until the vegetables are tender-crisp.

3. Add the pasta and beans and cook for 5 minutes.

4. Place **half** of the broth mixture into a blender or food processor. Cover and blend until smooth. Pour the puréed mixture into the skillet. Cook over medium heat until the mixture is hot.

sausage bites

prep 1 hour I **bake** 15 minutes I **cool** 10 minutes I **makes** 36 appetizers

½ of a 17.3-ounce package Pepperidge Farm® Puff Pastry Sheets (1 sheet), thawed

½ pound bulk pork sausage

1. Heat the oven to 400°F.

2. Unfold the pastry sheet on a lightly floured surface. Roll the pastry sheet into a 12×9-inch rectangle. Cut into **3** (3-inch) strips.

3. Divide the sausage into thirds. Shape **each** into a cylinder the same length as the pastry. Place **1** piece sausage on the long edge of **each** pastry rectangle. Roll up the pastry around the sausage and press the seams and pinch the edges to seal.

4. Cut **each** roll into **12** (1-inch) slices, making **36** in all. Place the slices, cut-side down, onto a baking sheet.

5. Bake for 15 minutes or until the pastries are golden brown and the sausage is cooked through. Remove the pastries from the baking sheet and let cool on wire racks for 10 minutes.

tips You can substitute Italian sausage (casing removed) for the bulk pork sausage.

To make ahead: Place the unbaked slices onto a baking sheet. Cover and freeze until firm. Remove the frozen slices from the baking sheet and store in a gallon-size resealable plastic bag in the freezer for up to 1 month. Bake the frozen slices on a baking sheet at 400°F. for 20 minutes or until the pastry is golden brown and the sausage is cooked through.

beef & broccoli

prep 10 minutes I **cook** 20 minutes I **makes** 4 servings

1 **tablespoon vegetable oil**

1 **pound boneless beef sirloin steak *or* beef top round steak, ¾–inch thick, cut into thin strips**

1 **can (10¾ ounces) Campbell's® Condensed Tomato Soup**

3 **tablespoons soy sauce**

1 **tablespoon vinegar**

1 **teaspoon garlic powder**

¼ **teaspoon crushed red pepper (optional)**

3 **cups fresh *or* thawed frozen broccoli florets**

4 **cups hot cooked rice**

1. Heat the oil in a 10-inch skillet over medium-high heat. Add the beef and stir-fry until well browned.

2. Stir the soup, soy sauce, vinegar, garlic powder and red pepper, if desired, in the skillet and heat to a boil. Stir in the broccoli and cook until it's tender-crisp. Serve the beef mixture over the rice.

tip *To make slicing easier, freeze the beef for 1 hour.*

3-cheese pasta bake

prep 20 minutes | **bake** 20 minutes | **makes** 4 servings

- 1 can (10¾ ounces) Campbell's® Condensed Cream of Mushroom Soup (Regular *or* 98% Fat Free)
- 1 package (8 ounces) shredded two–cheese blend (about 2 cups)
- ⅓ cup grated Parmesan cheese
- 1 cup milk
- ¼ teaspoon ground black pepper
- 3 cups corkscrew-shaped pasta (rotini), cooked and drained

1. Stir the soup, cheeses, milk and black pepper in a 1½-quart casserole. Stir in the pasta.

2. Bake at 400°F. for 20 minutes or until the mixture is hot and bubbling.

 *Substitute* ***2 cups*** *of your favorite shredded cheese for the two-cheese blend.*

broccoli & cheese stuffed shells

prep 25 minutes | **bake** 25 minutes | **makes** 6 servings

1 **container (15 ounces) ricotta cheese**
1 **package (10 ounces) frozen chopped broccoli, thawed and well drained**
1 **cup shredded mozzarella cheese (about 4 ounces)**
⅓ **cup grated Parmesan cheese**
¼ **teaspoon black pepper**
18 **jumbo shell-shaped pasta, cooked and drained**
1 **jar (24 ounces) Prego® Chunky Garden Combination Italian Sauce**

1. Stir the ricotta cheese, broccoli, ½ **cup** of the mozzarella cheese, Parmesan cheese and black pepper in a medium bowl. Spoon **about 2 tablespoons** of the cheese mixture into **each** shell.

2. Spread **1 cup** of the Italian sauce in a 13×9×2-inch shallow baking dish. Place the filled shells on the sauce. Pour the remaining sauce over the shells. Sprinkle with the remaining mozzarella cheese.

3. Bake at 400°F. for 25 minutes or until it's hot and bubbling.

tip *To save time:* Thaw the broccoli in the microwave on HIGH for 4 minutes.

chicken & shrimp jambalaya

prep 25 minutes | **cook** 45 minutes | **stand** 10 minutes | **makes** 6 servings

   1 **tablespoon olive oil**
1¼ **pounds skinless, boneless chicken breast halves, cut into 1-inch pieces**
   1 **large onion, diced (about 1 cup)**
   1 **medium green pepper, diced (about 1 cup)**
   2 **teaspoons Cajun seasoning**
   1 **can (10¾ ounces) Campbell's® Condensed Tomato Soup**
   2 **cups water**
   1 **cup _uncooked_ regular long-grain white rice**
   ½ **pound fresh _or_ thawed frozen medium shrimp, peeled and deveined**
   1 **large tomato, chopped (about 1½ cups)**
      Chopped fresh parsley (optional)

1. Heat the oil in a 12-inch skillet over medium-high heat. Add the chicken and cook until well browned, stirring occasionally.

2. Stir the onion, pepper and Cajun seasoning in the skillet and cook for 2 minutes.

3. Stir the soup, water and rice in the skillet and heat to a boil. Reduce the heat to low. Cover and cook for 20 minutes. Stir in the shrimp and cook, uncovered, for 10 minutes or until the shrimp are cooked through and the rice is tender. Stir in the tomato and parsley, if desired. Let stand for 10 minutes.

tip *For a more classic jambalaya flavor,* stir in **1 cup** chopped smoked ham with the soup.

dilled tuna & egg sandwiches

prep 10 minutes | **makes** 3 servings

1 can (6 ounces) low-sodium chunk white tuna in water, drained

2 hard-cooked egg whites, chopped

⅓ cup nonfat sour cream

2 tablespoons chopped green onions

2 teaspoons Dijon-style mustard

2 teaspoons chopped fresh dill weed (optional)

6 slices Pepperidge Farm® 100% Natural Nine Grain Bread, toasted

Romaine lettuce leaves

1. Stir the tuna, egg whites, sour cream, green onions, mustard and dill weed, if desired, in a medium bowl.

2. Divide the tuna mixture among **3** bread slices. Top with the lettuce and remaining bread slices.

baked potatoes olé

prep 5 minutes | **cook** 15 minutes | **makes** 4 servings

1 pound ground beef

1 tablespoon chili powder

1 cup Pace® Picante Sauce

4 hot baked potatoes, split

Shredded Cheddar cheese

1. Cook the beef and chili powder in a 10-inch skillet over medium-high heat until the beef is well browned, stirring often to separate the meat. Pour off any fat.

2. Stir the picante sauce in the skillet. Reduce the heat to low. Cook until the mixture is hot and bubbling. Serve the beef mixture over the potatoes. Top with the cheese.

tip *To bake the potatoes, pierce the potatoes with a fork. Bake at 400°F. for 1 hour or microwave on HIGH for 12 minutes or until fork-tender.*

easy pasta primavera

prep 20 minutes | **cook** 15 minutes | **makes** 4 servings

- 2 **tablespoons cornstarch**
- 1¾ **cups Swanson® Natural Goodness® Chicken Broth**
- 1 **teaspoon dried oregano leaves, crushed**
- ¼ **teaspoon garlic powder *or* 2 garlic cloves, minced**
- 2 **cups broccoli florets**
- 2 **medium carrots, sliced (about 1 cup)**
- 1 **medium onion, cut into wedges**
- 1 **medium tomato, diced (about 1 cup)**
- ½ **of a 1-pound package thin spaghetti, cooked and drained (about 4 cups)**
- 3 **tablespoons grated Parmesan cheese**

1. Stir the cornstarch and ¾ **cup** broth in a small bowl until the mixture is smooth.

2. Heat the remaining broth, oregano, garlic powder, broccoli, carrots and onion in a 4-quart saucepan over medium heat to a boil. Reduce the heat to low. Cover and cook for 5 minutes or until the vegetables are tender-crisp.

3. Stir the cornstarch mixture in the saucepan. Cook and stir until the mixture boils and thickens. Stir in the tomato. Add the spaghetti and toss to coat. Sprinkle with the cheese.

dripping roast beef sandwiches with melted provolone

prep 5 minutes I **cook** 5 minutes I **bake** 3 minutes I **makes** 4 servings

1 can (10½ ounces) Campbell's® Condensed French Onion Soup

1 tablespoon reduced-sodium Worcestershire sauce

¾ pound thinly sliced deli roast beef

4 Pepperidge Farm® Classic Soft Hoagie Rolls with Sesame Seeds

4 slices deli provolone cheese, cut in half

¼ cup drained hot **or** mild pickled banana pepper rings

1. Heat the oven to 400°F.

2. Heat the soup and Worcestershire in a 2-quart saucepan over medium-high heat to a boil. Add the beef and heat through, stirring occasionally.

3. Divide the beef evenly among the rolls. Top the beef with the cheese slices and place the sandwiches onto a baking sheet.

4. Bake for 3 minutes or until the sandwiches are toasted and the cheese is melted. Spoon the soup mixture onto the sandwiches. Top **each** sandwich with **1 tablespoon** pepper rings.

 *You may substitute ½ **of a 11.25-ounce package** Pepperidge Farm® Texas Toast (4 slices), prepared according to package directions, for the rolls in this recipe. Serve the sandwiches open-faced.*

beefy pasta skillet

prep 10 minutes **|** **cook** 15 minutes **|** **makes** 4 servings

- 1 **pound ground beef**
- 1 **medium onion, chopped (about ½ cup)**
- 1 **can (10¾ ounces) Campbell's® Condensed Tomato Soup (Regular *or* Healthy Request®)**
- ¼ **cup water**
- 1 **tablespoon Worcestershire sauce**
- ½ **cup shredded Cheddar cheese**
- 1½ **cups corkscrew-shaped pasta (rotini), cooked and drained**

1. Cook the beef and onion in a 10-inch skillet over medium-high heat until the beef is well browned, stirring often to separate the meat. Pour off any fat.

2. Stir the soup, water, Worcestershire, cheese and pasta in the skillet and cook until the mixture is hot and bubbling.

> **tip** *You can substitute 1 cup uncooked elbow pasta, cooked and drained, for the corkscrew pasta, if you like.*

quick bean & rice casserole

prep 5 minutes **|** **cook** 25 minutes **|** **makes** 6 servings

- 2½ **cups water**
- ¾ **cup *uncooked* regular long-grain white rice**
- 1 **envelope (about 1 ounce) dry onion soup and recipe mix**
- 1 **can (16 ounces) Campbell's® Pork and Beans**
- ¼ **cup maple-flavored syrup**

1. Heat the water in a 3-quart saucepan over medium-high heat to a boil. Stir in the rice and soup mix. Reduce the heat to low. Cover and cook for 20 minutes or until the rice is tender.

2. Stir the beans and syrup in the saucepan and cook until the mixture is hot and bubbling.

broccoli & noodles supreme

prep 10 minutes   I   **cook** 25 minutes   I   **makes** 5 servings

3 cups **uncooked** medium egg noodles

2 cups fresh **or** frozen broccoli florets

1 can (10¾ ounces) Campbell's® Condensed Cream of Chicken Soup
   (Regular **or** 98% Fat Free)

½ cup sour cream

⅓ cup grated Parmesan cheese

⅛ teaspoon ground black pepper

1. Cook the noodles according to the package directions. Add the broccoli for the last 5 minutes of cooking time. Drain the noodle mixture well in a colander. Return the noodle mixture to the saucepan.

2. Stir the soup, sour cream, cheese and black pepper in the saucepan and cook over medium heat until the mixture is hot and bubbling, stirring often.

one-dish chicken & rice bake

prep 5 minutes | **bake** 45 minutes | **makes** 4 servings

1 **can (10¾ ounces) Campbell's® Condensed Cream of Mushroom Soup (Regular _or_ 98% Fat Free)**

1 **cup water***

¾ **cup _uncooked_ regular long-grain white rice**

¼ **teaspoon paprika**

¼ **teaspoon ground black pepper**

4 **skinless, boneless chicken breast halves (about 1 pound)**

For creamier rice, increase the water to 1⅓ cups.

1. Stir the soup, water, rice, paprika and black pepper in a 2-quart shallow baking dish. Top with the chicken. Season with additional paprika and black pepper. Cover the baking dish.

2. Bake at 375°F. for 45 minutes or until the chicken is cooked through and the rice is tender.

cheddar penne with sausage & peppers

prep 20 minutes | **cook** 20 minutes | **makes** 6 servings

- 1 **tablespoon olive oil**
- 1 **pound sweet Italian pork sausage, cut into ½-inch slices**
- 1 **large green pepper, cut into 2-inch-long strips (about 2 cups)**
- 1 **large onion, sliced (about 1 cup)**
- 3 **cloves garlic, minced**
- 1 **can (10¾ ounces) Campbell's® Condensed Cheddar Cheese Soup**
- ½ **cup milk**
- 2 **cups penne pasta, cooked and drained**

1. Heat the oil in a 10-inch skillet over medium-high heat. Add the sausage and cook until well browned, stirring occasionally. Remove the sausage from the skillet. Pour off any fat.

2. Add the pepper and onion to the skillet and cook until the vegetables are tender, stirring occasionally. Add the garlic and cook and stir for 1 minute. Stir in the soup and milk and heat to a boil. Return the sausage to the skillet. Reduce the heat to low. Cook until the sausage is cooked through, stirring occasionally.

3. Place the pasta into a large bowl. Add the sausage mixture and toss to coat.

tip *You may substitute hot Italian sausage for the sweet Italian sausage in this recipe.*

chili mac

prep 15 minutes I **cook** 30 minutes I **makes** 4 servings

- 1   **pound ground beef**
- 1   **cup Pace® Picante Sauce**
- 1   **tablespoon chili powder**
- 1   **can (14.5 ounces) whole peeled tomatoes, drained and cut up**
- 1   **cup frozen whole kernel corn**
- 1½   **cups elbow macaroni, cooked and drained (about 3 cups)**
- ½   **cup shredded Cheddar cheese**
-     **Sliced avocado *and* sour cream**

1. Cook the beef in a 10-inch skillet over medium-high heat until it's well browned, stirring often to separate the meat. Pour off any fat.

2. Stir the picante sauce, chili powder, tomatoes and corn in the skillet and heat to a boil. Reduce the heat to low. Cook for 10 minutes.

3. Stir in the macaroni. Top with the cheese. Cover and cook until the cheese is melted. Garnish with the avocado and sour cream.

easy chicken & cheese enchiladas

prep 15 minutes | **bake** 40 minutes | **makes** 6 servings

- 1 **can (10¾ ounces) Campbell's® Condensed Cream of Chicken Soup (Regular *or* 98% Fat Free)**
- ½ **cup sour cream**
- 1 **cup Pace® Picante Sauce**
- 2 **teaspoons chili powder**
- 2 **cups chopped cooked chicken**
- ½ **cup shredded Monterey Jack cheese**
- 6 **flour tortillas (6-inch), warmed**
- 1 **small tomato, chopped (about ½ cup)**
- 1 **green onion, sliced (about 2 tablespoons)**

1. Heat the oven to 350°F. Stir the soup, sour cream, picante sauce and chili powder in a medium bowl.

2. Stir **1 cup** soup mixture, chicken and cheese in a large bowl.

3. Divide the chicken mixture among the tortillas. Roll up the tortillas and place seam-side up in a 2-quart shallow baking dish. Pour the remaining soup mixture over the filled tortillas. Cover the baking dish.

4. Bake for 40 minutes or until the enchiladas are hot and bubbling. Top with the tomato and onion.

> **tip** *Stir ½ **cup** canned black beans, rinsed and drained, into the chicken mixture before filling the tortillas.*

italian-style skillet pork chops

prep 5 minutes | **cook** 25 minutes | **makes** 6 servings

- 1 **tablespoon vegetable oil**
- 6 **pork chops, ¾-inch thick**
- 1 **jar (24 ounces) Prego® Fresh Mushroom Italian Sauce**
- ½ **of a 16-ounce package tube-shaped pasta (ziti), cooked and drained (about 6 cups)**

1. Heat the oil in a 12-inch skillet over medium-high heat. Add the chops and cook until they're browned on both sides. Remove the chops. Pour off any fat.

2. Stir the Italian sauce in the skillet. Heat to a boil. Reduce the heat to low. Return the chops to the skillet. Cover and cook for 10 minutes or until cooked through, stirring occasionally. Serve with the pasta.

pan-grilled veggie & cheese sandwiches

prep 5 minutes I **cook** 15 minutes I **makes** 4 servings

Vegetable cooking spray

2 **portobello mushrooms, cut into ½-inch slices**

1 **medium red pepper, cut into strips (about 1½ cups)**

2 **slices onions, ½-inch thick *each***

8 **slices eggplants, ¼-inch thick *each***

Garlic powder (optional)

½ **cup shredded fat-free mozzarella cheese**

2 **tablespoons balsamic vinegar**

8 **slices Pepperidge Farm® 100% Natural 100% Whole Wheat Bread**

1. Spray a nonstick grill pan with the cooking spray and heat over medium heat for 1 minute.

2. Add the mushrooms, pepper and onion to one side of the pan. Add the eggplant to the other side. Sprinkle the garlic powder over all, if desired. Cook until the vegetables are tender. Sprinkle the eggplant with the cheese and cook until the cheese is melted.

3. Place the mushrooms, pepper and onions into a medium bowl. Add the vinegar and toss to coat. Divide the eggplant slices among **4** bread slices. Top with the mushroom mixture and remaining bread slices.

tip *If you don't have a grill pan, this recipe can be made in a 12-inch nonstick skillet.*

italian sausage & peppers with penne

prep 15 minutes I **cook** 35 minutes I **makes** 6 servings

- 2 **tablespoons olive oil**
- 1½ **pounds sweet *or* hot Italian pork sausage, cut into ½-inch slices**
- 2 **medium green *and/or* red peppers, cut into 2 long strips (about 3 cups)**
- 2 **medium onions, thickly sliced (about 1½ cups)**
- 3 **cups Prego® Traditional Italian Sauce *or* Organic Tomato & Basil Italian Sauce**
- 4 **cups tube-shaped pasta (penne *or* ziti), cooked and drained**
   Grated Parmesan cheese

1. Heat **1 tablespoon** of the oil in a 12-inch skillet over medium-high heat. Add the sausage in 2 batches and cook until it's well browned, stirring often. Remove the sausage from the skillet. Pour off any fat.

2. Reduce the heat to medium and add the remaining oil. Stir the peppers and onions in the skillet and cook for 5 minutes.

3. Stir the Italian sauce in the skillet. Heat to a boil. Return the sausage to the skillet and reduce the heat to low. Cover and cook for 20 minutes or until the sausage is cooked through and the vegetables are tender. Serve over the pasta and sprinkle with the cheese.

buffalo burgers

prep 10 minutes | **grill** 10 minutes | **cook** 10 minutes | **makes** 4 servings

- 1 **pound ground beef**
- 1 **can (10¾ ounces) Campbell's® Condensed Tomato Soup (Regular _or_ Healthy Request®)**
- ½ **teaspoon Louisiana-style hot sauce**
- ½ **cup crumbled blue cheese _or_ 4 slices blue cheese**
- 4 **Pepperidge Farm® Classic Sandwich Buns with Sesame Seeds, split**
     Lettuce leaves, red onion slices, tomato slices (optional)

1. Shape the beef into **4** (½-inch-thick) burgers.

2. Lightly oil the grill rack and heat the grill to medium. Grill the burgers for 10 minutes for medium or to desired doneness, turning the burgers over once halfway through the grilling time.

3. Heat the soup and hot sauce in a 1-quart saucepan over medium heat to a boil. Reduce the heat to low. Cover and cook for 5 minutes. Top the burgers with the soup mixture. Sprinkle with the cheese. Serve the burgers on the buns with the lettuce, onion and tomato, if desired.

tip _Any leftover soup mixture can also be a great dipping sauce for French fries._

chicken quesadillas & fiesta rice

prep 5 minutes I **cook** 20 minutes I **bake** 5 minutes I **stand** 5 minutes I **makes** 4 servings

- 1¼ **pounds skinless, boneless chicken breast halves, cut into cubes**
- 1 **can (10¾ ounces) Campbell's® Condensed Cheddar Cheese Soup**
- 1 **cup Pace® Picante Sauce**
- 10 **flour tortillas (8-inch), warmed**
- 1 **can (10½ ounces) Campbell's® Condensed Chicken Broth**
- ½ **cup water**
- 2 **cups *uncooked* instant white rice**

1. Heat the oven to 425°F.

2. Cook the chicken in a 10-inch nonstick skillet over medium-high heat until well browned and cooked through, stirring often. Stir in the soup and ½ **cup** picante sauce. Cook until the mixture is hot and bubbling.

3. Spread **about** ⅓ **cup** chicken mixture onto **half** of **each** tortilla to within ½ inch of the edge. Brush the edges of the tortillas with water. Fold the tortillas over the filling and press to seal. Place the filled tortillas onto **2** baking sheets.

4. Bake for 5 minutes or until the quesadillas are hot. Cut **each** quesadilla in half.

5. Heat the broth, water and remaining picante sauce in a 1-quart saucepan over medium-high heat to a boil. Stir in the rice. Cover the saucepan and remove from the heat. Let stand 5 minutes. Serve the rice with the quesadillas.

broccoli & cheese casserole

prep 10 minutes | **bake** 30 minutes | **makes** 6 servings

- 1 **can (10¾ ounces) Campbell's® Condensed Cream of Mushroom Soup (Regular *or* 98% Fat Free)**
- ½ **cup milk**
- 2 **teaspoons yellow mustard**
- 1 **bag (16 ounces) frozen broccoli florets, thawed**
- 1 **cup shredded Cheddar cheese (4 ounces)**
- ⅓ **cup dry bread crumbs**
- 2 **teaspoons butter, melted**

1. Stir the soup, milk, mustard, broccoli and cheese in a 1½-quart casserole.

2. Stir the bread crumbs and butter in a small bowl. Sprinkle the crumb mixture over the broccoli mixture.

3. Bake at 350°F. for 30 minutes or until the mixture is hot and bubbling.

Rice Is Nice: Add **2 cups** cooked white rice to the broccoli mixture before baking.

Cheese Change-Up: Substitute mozzarella cheese for the Cheddar.

chicken sorrento

prep 20 minutes I **cook** 20 minutes I **makes** 4 servings

- 1 tablespoon vegetable oil
- 1 pound skinless, boneless chicken breast halves
- 1 jar (24 ounces) Prego® Veggie Smart® Chunky & Savory Italian Sauce
- 2 tablespoons balsamic vinegar
- 2 tablespoons chopped fresh basil leaves
- 3 cups penne pasta, cooked and drained (about 4½ cups)
- ¼ cup grated Parmesan cheese

1. Heat the oil in a 10-inch skillet over medium-high heat. Add the chicken and cook for 10 minutes or until well browned on both sides. Remove the chicken from the skillet.

2. Stir the Italian sauce and vinegar in the skillet and cook for 2 minutes, stirring often. Stir in the basil. Return the chicken to the skillet. Reduce the heat to low. Cover and cook for 5 minutes or until the chicken is cooked through.

3. Slice the chicken. Serve the chicken and sauce over the penne. Sprinkle with the cheese.

beef taco bake

- **1 pound ground beef**
- **1 can (10¾ ounces) Campbell's® Condensed Tomato Soup**
- **1 cup Pace® Picante Sauce**
- **½ cup milk**
- **6 flour tortillas (8-inch) *or* corn tortillas (6-inch), cut into 1-inch pieces**
- **1 cup shredded Cheddar cheese (about 4 ounces)**

1. Cook the beef in a 10-inch skillet over medium-high heat until well browned, stirring often. Pour off any fat.

2. Stir the soup, picante sauce, milk, tortillas and **half** the cheese in the skillet. Spoon the beef mixture into a 2-quart shallow baking dish. Cover the baking dish.

3. Bake at 400°F. for 30 minutes or until the beef mixture is hot and bubbling. Sprinkle with the remaining cheese.

chicken & broccoli alfredo

prep 10 minutes | **cook** 20 minutes | **makes** 4 servings

½ **of a 16-ounce package linguine**

1 **cup fresh *or* frozen broccoli florets**

2 **tablespoons butter**

4 **skinless, boneless chicken breast halves (about 1 pound), cut into 1½-inch pieces**

1 **can (10¾ ounces) Campbell's® Condensed Cream of Mushroom Soup**
   (Regular, 98% Fat Free *or* Healthy Request®)

½ **cup milk**

½ **cup grated Parmesan cheese**

¼ **teaspoon ground black pepper**

1. Prepare the linguine according to the package directions in a 3-quart saucepan. Add the broccoli during the last 4 minutes of the cooking time. Drain the linguine mixture well in a colander.

2. Heat the butter in a 10-inch skillet over medium-high heat. Add the chicken and cook until it's well browned, stirring often.

3. Stir the soup, milk, cheese, black pepper and linguine mixture in the skillet and cook until the chicken is cooked through, stirring occasionally. Serve with additional Parmesan cheese.

Grilled Chicken & Broccoli Alfredo: Substitute grilled chicken breasts for the skinless, boneless chicken.

Shrimp & Broccoli Alfredo: Substitute *1 pound* fresh extra large shrimp, shelled and deveined, for the chicken. Cook as directed for the chicken above, until the shrimp are cooked through.

Spanish-Inspired Tip: Reduce the chicken to ½ *pound* and omit the Parmesan cheese. Prepare as directed above. Stir ½ *pound* peeled cooked shrimp, ¼ *pound* chorizo *or* ham, diced and *1 teaspoon* paprika into the soup mixture.

Indian-Inspired Tip: Omit the Parmesan cheese. Substitute *3 cups* cooked basmati rice and ¾ *cup* cooked broccoli florets for the linguine and *uncooked* broccoli. Stir *1 teaspoon* curry powder and ½ *teaspoon* ground cumin into the skillet with the chicken. Sprinkle with toasted slivered almonds, if desired.

Asian-Inspired Tip: Omit the Parmesan cheese. Substitute *1 package* (6 ounces) rice noodles for the linguine. Prepare as directed above. Stir *1 tablespoon* soy sauce, *2* cloves garlic, minced and *2 teaspoons* minced fresh ginger root in the skillet and cook with the chicken.

> **tip** *You can substitute spaghetti **or** fettuccine for the linguine in this recipe.*

family spaghetti pie

prep 25 minutes I **bake** 30 minutes I **stand** 5 minutes I **makes** 6 servings

- 1 **pound ground beef**
- 1 **cup Pace® Picante Sauce**
- 1 **cup Prego® Fresh Mushroom Italian Sauce**
- ⅓ **of a 16-ounce package spaghetti, cooked and drained (about 3 cups)**
- ⅓ **cup grated Parmesan cheese**
- 1 **egg, beaten**
- 1 **tablespoon butter, melted**
- 1 **cup ricotta cheese**
- 4 **ounces shredded mozzarella cheese (about 1 cup)**

1. Cook the beef in a 10-inch skillet over medium-high heat until meat is well browned, stirring often to separate the meat. Pour off any fat. Stir the picante sauce and Italian sauce into the skillet and cook until it's hot and bubbling.

2. Stir the spaghetti, Parmesan cheese, egg and butter in a medium bowl. Spread the mixture on the bottom and up the side of greased 10-inch pie plate. Spread the ricotta cheese in the spaghetti shell. Top with the beef mixture.

3. Bake at 350°F. for 30 minutes or until it's hot and bubbling. Sprinkle with the mozzarella cheese. Let stand for 5 minutes before serving. Cut into **6** wedges.

hot sausage casserole

prep 30 minutes I **bake** 1 hour I **makes** 6 servings

- 1 **pound bulk hot Italian pork sausage**
- 1 **large green pepper, chopped (about 1 cup)**
- 1 **large onion, chopped (about 1 cup)**
- 2 **stalks celery, chopped (about 1 cup)**
- 1 **cup _uncooked_ regular long-grain white rice**
- 2 **cans (10¾ ounces _each_) Campbell's® Condensed Cream of Chicken Soup**
- 1 **can (10¾ ounces) Campbell's® Condensed Cream of Mushroom Soup**
   Vegetable cooking spray

1. Cook the sausage in a 10-inch skillet over medium-high heat until well browned, stirring often to separate the meat. Pour off any fat. Stir the pepper, onion, celery, rice, soups and **1 can** of water in the skillet.

2. Spray a 3-quart casserole with the cooking spray. Spoon the sausage mixture into the casserole. Bake at 400°F. covered for 45 minutes. Remove cover, stir and cook 15 minutes more.

mac & cheese veggie bake

prep 20 minutes **|** **bake** 30 minutes **|** **makes** 6 servings

  2 cans (10¾ ounces **each**) Campbell's® Condensed Cheddar Cheese Soup

1½ cups milk

  2 tablespoons Dijon-style mustard

1½ cups frozen sugar snap peas

  1 medium green **or** red pepper, diced (about 1 cup)

  3 cups elbow macaroni, cooked and drained

  ¼ cup water

  2 tablespoons butter, melted

  4 cups Pepperidge Farm® Corn Bread Stuffing

1. Stir the soup, milk, mustard, snap peas, pepper and macaroni in a 3-quart shallow baking dish.

2. Stir the water and butter in a large bowl. Add the stuffing and mix lightly to coat. Sprinkle the stuffing over the macaroni mixture.

3. Bake at 400°F. for 30 minutes or until it's hot and bubbling.

linguine with savory meat sauce

prep 20 minutes | **cook** 25 minutes | **makes** 6 servings

1 **pound ground beef**

1 **large onion, minced (about 1 cup)**

4 **large carrots, diced (about 2 cups)**

2 **cloves garlic, minced**

1 **can (14.5 ounces) diced tomatoes, undrained**

1 **can (10¾ ounces) Campbell's® Condensed Cream of Mushroom Soup (Regular *or* 98% Fat Free)**

½ **cup water**

3 **tablespoons thinly sliced fresh basil leaves**

1 **package (16 ounces) linguine, cooked and drained**

Grated Parmesan cheese

1. Cook the beef, onion, carrots and garlic in a 12-inch skillet over medium-high heat until the beef is well browned, stirring often to separate the meat. Pour off any fat.

2. Stir the tomatoes with juice, soup and water in the skillet and heat to a boil. Reduce the heat to low. Cook for 15 minutes, stirring occasionally. Stir in the basil.

3. Place the linguine into a large bowl. Add the beef mixture and toss to coat. Serve with the cheese.

tip *You may substitute **2 cups** shredded carrots for the diced carrots in this recipe. Pre-shredded carrots are available in the produce section or salad bar of most grocery stores.*

mexican beans and rice

prep 10 minutes | **cook** 30 minutes | **makes** 5 servings

1¾ **cups Swanson® Chicken Broth**

½ **teaspoon ground cumin**

⅛ **teaspoon ground black pepper**

1 **medium onion, chopped (about ½ cup)**

1 **small green pepper, chopped (about ½ cup)**

¾ **cup *uncooked* regular long-grain white rice**

1 **can (about 15 ounces) kidney beans, rinsed and drained**

1. Heat the broth, cumin, black pepper, onion and green pepper in a 3-quart saucepan over medium heat to a boil. Stir in the rice. Reduce the heat to low. Cover and cook for 20 minutes or until the rice is tender.

2. Stir the beans in the saucepan and cook until the mixture is hot.

souper sloppy joes

prep 5 minutes | **cook** 15 minutes | **makes** 6 servings

- 1 **pound ground beef**
- 1 **can (10¾ ounces) Campbell's® Condensed Tomato Soup**
- ¼ **cup water**
- 1 **tablespoon prepared yellow mustard**
- 6 **Pepperidge Farm® Classic Sandwich Buns with Sesame Seeds**

1. Cook the beef in a 10-inch skillet over medium-high heat until well browned, stirring often to separate the meat. Pour off any fat.

2. Stir the soup, water and mustard in the skillet and cook until the mixture is hot and bubbling. Spoon the beef mixture on the buns.

puff pastry vegetable pizza

thaw 40 minutes | **prep** 20 minutes | **bake** 15 minutes | **makes** 4 servings

- ½ of a 17.3-ounce package Pepperidge Farm® Puff Pastry Sheets (1 sheet), thawed
- 2 teaspoons vegetable oil
- 1 cup broccoli florets
- 1 cup sliced mushrooms (about 3 ounces)
- 1 small green *or* red pepper, chopped (about ½ cup)
- 1 small onion, chopped (about ¼ cup)
- ¾ cup Prego® Traditional Italian Sauce
- 1½ cups shredded mozzarella cheese *or* shredded Swiss cheese (about 6 ounces)

1. Heat the oven to 400°F.

2. Unfold the pastry sheet on a lightly floured surface. Roll the pastry sheet into a 15×10-inch rectangle and place onto a baking sheet. Fold over the edges ½ inch on all sides, pressing firmly to form a rim. Prick the center of the pastry thoroughly with a fork.

3. Bake for 10 minutes or until the pastry is golden brown.

4. Heat the oil in a 10-inch skillet over medium heat. Add the broccoli, mushrooms, pepper and onion and cook until they're tender, stirring occasionally.

5. Spread the Italian sauce on the pastry. Top with the vegetable mixture. Sprinkle with the cheese.

6. Bake for 5 minutes or until the cheese is melted.

tip *This recipe serves 16 as an appetizer.*

*Flavor Variation: Add any of your favorite pizza toppers: pepperoni, sliced pitted olives **or** cooked crumbled sausage.*

mexi-mac

prep 5 minutes | **cook** 20 minutes | **makes** 4 servings

- 1   **pound ground beef**
- 1   **cup Pace® Picante Sauce**
- 1   **tablespoon chili powder**
- 1   **can (14.5 ounces) whole peeled tomatoes, cut up**
- 1   **cup frozen whole kernel corn**
- 3   **cups cooked elbow macaroni**
- ½   **cup shredded Cheddar cheese**
-     **Sliced avocado**
-     **Sour cream**

1. Cook the beef in a 10-inch skillet over medium-high heat until well browned, stirring to separate the meat. Pour off any fat.

2. Stir the picante sauce, chili powder, tomatoes and corn in the skillet. Heat to a boil. Reduce the heat to low. Cook for 10 minutes. Add the macaroni. Sprinkle with the cheese. Cover and heat until the cheese melts. Garnish with avocado and sour cream.

mexican pizza

thaw 40 minutes I **prep** 20 minutes I **bake** 15 minutes I **makes** 4 servings

½ **of a 17.3-ounce package Pepperidge Farm® Puff Pastry Sheets (1 sheet), thawed**

¾ **cup Prego® Traditional Italian Sauce**

¼ **cup Pace® Picante Sauce**

¾ **cup shredded mozzarella cheese**

¾ **cup shredded Cheddar cheese**

¼ **cup sliced pitted ripe olives**

1. Heat the oven to 400°F.

2. Unfold the pastry sheet on a lightly floured surface. Roll the pastry sheet into a 15×10-inch rectangle. Place the pastry onto a baking sheet. Prick the pastry thoroughly with a fork. Bake for 10 minutes or until the pastry is golden brown.

3. Stir the Italian sauce and picante sauce in a small bowl. Spread the sauce mixture on the pastry to within ½ inch of the edge. Top with the cheeses and sprinkle with the olives. Bake for 5 minutes or until the cheese is melted.

sirloin, pepper & onion skillet

prep 20 minutes I **cook** 20 minutes I **makes** 4 servings

2 tablespoons olive oil

1 boneless beef sirloin steak, ¾-inch thick (about 1 pound), cut into 4 pieces

1 large onion, sliced (about 1 cup)

2 medium red **and/or** green peppers, cut into 2-inch-long strips (about 3 cups)

3 cloves garlic, minced

1 tablespoon red wine vinegar **or** balsamic vinegar

1 can (10¾ ounces) Campbell's® Condensed Golden Mushroom Soup

½ cup water

1 cup shredded Cheddar Jack cheese **or** Cheddar cheese (about 4 ounces)

1. Heat **1 tablespoon** oil in a 10-inch skillet over medium-high heat. Add the beef and cook until well browned on both sides. Remove the beef from the skillet. Pour off any fat. Reduce the heat to medium.

2. Heat the remaining oil in the skillet. Add the onion and peppers and cook for 3 minutes, stirring occasionally. Add the garlic and cook until the vegetables are tender-crisp, stirring often.

3. Add the vinegar to the skillet and cook and stir for 1 minute. Stir in the soup and water and heat to a boil. Return the beef to the skillet. Reduce the heat to low. Cover and cook the beef for 2 minutes for medium or until desired doneness. Sprinkle with the cheese.

vegetable chili

prep 15 minutes I **cook** 30 minutes I **makes** 6 servings

- 1 tablespoon olive oil *or* vegetable oil
- 1 large onion, chopped (about 1 cup)
- 1 tablespoon chili powder
- ¼ teaspoon garlic powder *or* 1 clove garlic, minced
- 1½ cups Campbell's® Tomato Juice
- 1 can (10¾ ounces) Campbell's® Condensed Golden Mushroom Soup
- 1 package (about 10 ounces) frozen baby lima beans *or* whole kernel corn
- 3 large carrots, chopped (about 1½ cups)
- 1 can (about 15 ounces) black beans *or* pinto beans, rinsed and drained
- 2 cups regular long-grain white rice, cooked according to package directions (about 6 cups)
  Sour cream (optional)
  Sliced green onions (optional)

1. Heat the oil in a 4-quart saucepan over medium heat. Add the onion, chili powder and garlic powder and cook until the onion is tender.

2. Stir the tomato juice, soup, lima beans and carrots in the saucepan and heat to a boil. Reduce the heat to low. Cover and cook for 20 minutes or until the vegetables are tender.

3. Add the black beans and heat through. Serve over the rice. Top with sour cream and green onion, if desired.

whole wheat chicken salad sandwiches

prep 10 minutes | **makes** 4 servings

- 2 cans (4.5 ounces **each**) Swanson® Premium White Chunk Chicken Breast in Water, drained
- ¼ cup chopped celery
- 1 tablespoon finely chopped onion
- 2 tablespoons nonfat mayonnaise
- 2 tablespoons nonfat plain yogurt
- ⅛ teaspoon ground black pepper
- 8 slices Pepperidge Farm® Whole Grain 100% Whole Wheat Bread
- 8 tomato slices
- 4 lettuce leaves

1. Stir the chicken, celery, onion, mayonnaise, yogurt and pepper in a small bowl.

2. Divide the chicken mixture among **4** bread slices. Top **each** with **2** slices tomato, **1** leaf lettuce and **1** remaining bread slice.

family favorites

Nothing brings families together like good food.

teriyaki burgers

prep 10 minutes | **cook** 15 minutes | **makes** 6 servings

1½ **pounds ground beef**

1 **can (10½ ounces) Campbell's® Condensed Beef Broth**

1 **tablespoon soy sauce**

2 **teaspoons brown sugar**

¼ **teaspoon ground ginger**

6 **Pepperidge Farm® Classic Sandwich Buns with Sesame Seeds, split**

1. Shape the beef into **6** (½-inch thick) burgers.

2. Cook the burgers in a 12-inch skillet over medium-high heat until well browned on both sides. Pour off any fat.

3. Stir the broth, soy sauce, brown sugar and ginger in the skillet and heat to a boil. Reduce the heat to low. Cover and cook for 5 minutes for medium or to desired doneness. Serve the burgers and sauce on the buns.

create family favorite memories in your home

What do you get when you combine family favorite dinners with fun activities? Memories that will last a lifetime for you and your family. Here are a few memory-making ideas you can serve up along with your great dinners.

■ *Eat dinner together at the table as often as possible.* Not only is it a good time for family bonding, but this conversational period actually promotes good digestion.

■ *Every other month, go formal.* Get out the good china, glassware and candles, and have the kids set a formal table. Besides being fun, this is a great way to learn which side of the plate the fork goes on and what all those different glasses are for. It's also a perfect time to teach manners and etiquette. Don't worry about making fancy, unfamiliar food for these affairs—family favorites work just fine.

■ *Plan an indoor picnic on rainy or snowy days.* Throw a blanket on the living room floor and, if you have a fireplace, build a fire for atmosphere. Stuck on menu ideas? A winter barbecue is always fun and, of course, great tasting. BBQ chicken and potato salad taste terrific any time of the year!

■ *Share the cooking with one of the kids.* Nothing boosts a child's self esteem more than a sense of accomplishment and spending time with a grownup in the kitchen.

7-layer meatless tortilla pie

prep 20 minutes I **bake** 40 minutes I **makes** 6 servings

- 2 cans (about 15 ounces **each**) pinto beans, rinsed and drained
- 1 cup Pace® Picante Sauce
- ¼ teaspoon garlic powder **or** 1 clove garlic, minced
- 2 tablespoons chopped fresh cilantro leaves
- 1 can (about 15 ounces) black beans, rinsed and drained
- 1 small tomato, chopped (about ½ cup)
- 7 flour tortillas (8-inch)
- 8 ounces shredded Cheddar cheese (about 2 cups)

1. Mash the pinto beans in a medium bowl with a fork. Stir in ¾ **cup** picante sauce and the garlic powder.

2. Stir the remaining picante sauce, cilantro, black beans and tomato in a medium bowl.

3. Place **1** tortilla onto a baking sheet. Spread ¾ **cup** pinto bean mixture over the tortilla to within ½ inch of the edge. Top with ¼ **cup** cheese. Top with **1** tortilla and ⅔ **cup** black bean mixture. Top with ¼ **cup** cheese. Repeat the layers twice more. Top with the remaining tortilla and spread with the remaining pinto bean mixture. Cover with aluminum foil.

4. Bake at 400°F. for 40 minutes or until the filling is hot. Uncover the pie. Top with the remaining cheese. Cut the pie into 6 wedges. Serve with additional picante sauce and sprinkle with additional cilantro, if desired.

chicken cacciatore & pasta skillet

prep 10 minutes I **cook** 30 minutes I **makes** 4 servings

 1 **tablespoon vegetable oil**

1¼ **pounds skinless, boneless chicken breast halves *or* skinless, boneless chicken thighs**

1¾ **cups Swanson® Chicken Broth *or* Swanson® Chicken Stock**

 1 **teaspoon dried oregano leaves, crushed**

 1 **teaspoon garlic powder**

 1 **can (14.5 ounces) diced tomatoes**

 1 **small green pepper, cut into 2-inch-long strips (about 1 cup)**

 1 **medium onion, cut into wedges**

 ¼ **teaspoon ground black pepper**

 ½ **of a 1-pound package *uncooked* medium shell-shaped pasta (about 2½ cups)**

1. Heat the oil in a 10-inch skillet over medium-high heat. Add the chicken and cook for 10 minutes or until well browned on both sides.

2. Stir the broth, oregano, garlic powder, tomatoes, green pepper, onion and black pepper in the skillet and heat to a boil. Stir in the pasta. Reduce the heat to low. Cover and cook for 15 minutes or until the pasta is tender.

cheesy chicken pizza

prep 15 minutes | **bake** 15 minutes | **makes** 4 servings

- 1   **package (about 13 ounces) refrigerated pizza dough**
- ½   **cup Pace® Picante Sauce**
- ½   **cup Prego® Traditional Italian Sauce *or* Roasted Garlic & Herb Italian Sauce**
- 1   **cup chopped cooked chicken *or* turkey**
- ½   **cup sliced pitted ripe olives**
- 2   **green onions, sliced (about ¼ cup)**
- 4   **ounces shredded mozzarella cheese (about 1 cup)**

1. Heat the oven to 425°F.

2. Unroll the dough onto a greased 12-inch pizza pan. Press the dough into a 12-inch circle. Pinch up the edge to form a rim.

3. Stir the picante sauce and Italian sauce in a small bowl. Spread the picante sauce mixture over the crust to the rim. Top with the chicken, olives, onions and cheese.

4. Bake for 15 minutes or until the cheese is melted and the crust is golden brown.

tip *For a crispier crust, prepare the dough as directed in step 2. Bake the dough for 5 minutes. Remove the dough from the oven and proceed as directed in steps 3 and 4.*

lasagna primavera

prep 40 minutes I **bake** 45 minutes I **stand** 10 minutes I **makes** 8 servings

  4 tablespoons reduced-fat butter

  2 tablespoons all-purpose flour

1½ cups skim milk

 ¼ teaspoon ground nutmeg

 ¼ teaspoon ground black pepper

  2 medium zucchini **or** summer squash, halved lengthwise and thinly sliced (about 3 cups)

  1 package (10 ounces) cremini mushrooms, sliced (about 3¾ cups)

  1 medium red pepper, cut into 2-inch-long strips (about 1½ cups)

 ½ pound asparagus, trimmed and cut into 2-inch-long pieces (about 2 cups)

  3 cups Prego® Heart Smart Ricotta Parmesan Italian Sauce

12 oven-ready lasagna noodles (no boil)

1. Heat **2 tablespoons** butter in a 1-quart saucepan over medium heat. Stir in the flour. Cook and stir for 2 minutes or the mixture turns a golden color. **Gradually** stir in the milk with a whisk. Cook and stir for 5 minutes or until the milk mixture boils and thickens. Stir in the nutmeg and black pepper. Remove the saucepan from the heat.

2. Heat the remaining butter in a 12-inch nonstick skillet over medium heat. Add the zucchini, mushrooms, red pepper and asparagus and cook for 10 minutes or until the vegetables are tender-crisp.

3. Layer ½ **cup** Italian sauce, **4** lasagna noodles, another ¾ **cup** Italian sauce, **one-third** of the milk mixture and **half** of the vegetable mixture in a 13×9×2-inch baking dish. Repeat the layers. Top with the remaining lasagna noodles, sauce and milk mixture.

4. Loosely cover the baking dish with foil and bake for 45 minutes at 375°F. or until the lasagna is hot and bubbling. Let stand for 10 minutes before serving.

crispy italian chicken

prep 15 minutes | **bake** 20 minutes | **makes** 4 servings

Vegetable cooking spray

2 **cups Pepperidge Farm® Four Cheese and Garlic Croutons**

1 **egg**

4 **skinless, boneless chicken breast halves (about 1 pound)**

1 **cup Prego® Traditional Italian Sauce *or* Tomato Basil & Garlic Italian Sauce, heated**

¼ **cup shredded mozzarella cheese**

1. Heat the oven to 375°F. Spray a baking sheet with the cooking spray. Place the croutons into a gallon size resealable plastic bag. Seal the bag and crush the croutons with a rolling pin.

2. Beat the egg in a shallow dish with a fork or whisk. Dip the chicken into the egg. Add the chicken to the bag. Seal the bag and shake to coat. Place the chicken onto the baking sheet. Spray the chicken with the cooking spray.

3. Bake for 20 minutes or until the chicken is cooked through. Spoon the Italian sauce over the chicken and sprinkle with the cheese.

tip *You can substitute your favorite Pepperidge Farm® croutons for the Four Cheese and Garlic.*

asian chicken with peanuts

prep 15 minutes | **cook** 20 minutes | **makes** 4 servings

- 2 **tablespoons cornstarch**
- 1¾ **cups Swanson® Chicken Stock**
- 2 **tablespoons soy sauce**
- ½ **teaspoon ground ginger**
- ½ **teaspoon sesame oil (optional)**
- 2 **tablespoons vegetable oil**
- 1 **pound skinless, boneless chicken breasts, cut into strips**
- 2 **cups broccoli florets**
- 2 **small red peppers, cut into 2-inch-long strips (about 2 cups)**
- 2 **cloves garlic, minced**
- ½ **cup salted peanuts**
  Hot cooked regular long-grain white rice

1. Stir the cornstarch, stock, soy sauce, ginger and sesame oil, if desired, in a medium bowl until the mixture is smooth.

2. Heat **1 tablespoon** of the oil in a 12-inch skillet over medium-high heat. Add the chicken and stir-fry until well browned, stirring often. Remove the chicken from the skillet.

3. Reduce the heat to medium. Heat the remaining vegetable oil in the skillet. Add the broccoli, peppers and garlic and stir-fry until the vegetables are tender-crisp. Stir the cornstarch mixture in the skillet. Cook and stir until the mixture boils and thickens. Return the chicken to the skillet. Stir in the peanuts and cook until the mixture is hot and bubbling. Serve over the rice.

chicken fusilli with spinach & asiago cheese

prep 10 minutes | **cook** 20 minutes | **makes** 6 servings

½ of a 1-pound package ***uncooked*** fusilli pasta (about 2½ cups)

1 bag (about 7 ounces) fresh baby spinach

2 tablespoons olive oil

1¼ pounds skinless, boneless chicken breast halves, cut into 1½-inch pieces

3 cloves garlic, minced

1 package (3 ounces) sun-dried tomato halves (about ¾ cup)

1 can (10¾ ounces) Campbell's® Condensed Cream of Chicken Soup (Regular *or* 98% Fat Free)

½ teaspoon crushed red pepper

1 cup shredded Asiago cheese (about 4 ounces)

1. Prepare the fusilli according to the package directions in a 6-quart saucepot. Add the spinach during the last minute of the cooking time. Drain the fusilli mixture well in a colander, reserving **1 cup** cooking liquid.

2. Heat the oil in a 12-inch skillet over medium-high heat. Add the chicken and cook until well browned, stirring occasionally.

3. Add the garlic to the skillet and cook and stir for 1 minute. Stir in the tomatoes, soup, **½ cup** cooking liquid and red pepper and heat to a boil. Reduce the heat to low. Cook until the chicken is cooked through, stirring occasionally. Stir in the fusilli mixture and cook until the mixture is hot and bubbling. Stir in the remaining cooking liquid as needed until desired consistency. Sprinkle with the cheese.

tip *You may substitute* **1 package** *(about 9 ounces) refrigerated fully-cooked chicken strips for the chicken breast halves. Stir in the chicken with the soup.*

slow-cooked taco shredded beef

prep 10 minutes | **cook** 6 hours | **stand** 10 minutes | **makes** 16 servings

- 1 can (10¾ ounces) Campbell's® Condensed French Onion Soup
- 1 tablespoon chili powder
- ½ teaspoon ground cumin
-    2-pound boneless beef chuck roast
- 2 tablespoons finely chopped fresh cilantro leaves
- 16 taco shells
- 1 cup shredded Cheddar cheese (about 4 ounces)
-    Shredded lettuce
-    Sour cream

1. Stir the soup, chili powder and cumin in a 4-quart slow cooker. Add the beef and turn to coat.

2. Cover and cook on LOW for 6 to 7 hours* or until the beef is fork-tender.

3. Remove the beef from the cooker to a cutting board and let stand for 10 minutes. Using 2 forks, shred the beef. Return the beef to the cooker. Stir the cilantro in the cooker.

4. Spoon **about** ¼ **cup** beef mixture into **each** taco shell. Top **each** with **about** **1 tablespoon** cheese. Top with the lettuce and the sour cream.

Or on HIGH for 4 to 5 hours.

cheese steak pockets

prep 10 minutes | **cook** 15 minutes | **makes** 8 servings

- 1 **tablespoon vegetable oil**
- 1 **medium onion, cut in half and sliced (about ½ cup)**
- ½ **of a 24-ounce package frozen beef *or* frozen chicken sandwich steaks (8 steaks)**
- 1 **can (10¾ ounces) Campbell's® Condensed Cheddar Cheese Soup**
- 1 **jar (about 4½ ounces) sliced mushrooms, drained**
- 4 **pita breads (6-inch) cut in half, forming *8* pockets**

1. Heat the oil in a 10-inch skillet over medium-high heat. Add the onion and cook until tender stirring occasionally. Add the sandwich steaks in batches and cook until well browned on both sides. Pour off any fat.

2. Stir the soup and mushrooms in the skillet and cook until the mixture is hot and bubbling. Divide the sandwich steaks and soup mixture among the pita halves.

2-step inside-out chicken pot pie

prep 10 minutes | **cook** 15 minutes | **makes** 4 servings

- 4 **skinless, boneless chicken breast halves (about 1 pound), cut into 1-inch pieces**
- 1 **can (10¾ ounces) Campbell's® Condensed Cream of Chicken Soup (Regular *or* 98% Fat Free)**
- 1 **bag (16 ounces) frozen vegetable combination (broccoli, cauliflower, carrots)**
- 8 **hot biscuits, split**

1. Cook the chicken in a 10-inch nonstick skillet over medium-high heat until well browned, stirring often.

2. Stir the soup and vegetables in the skillet. Reduce the heat to low. Cover and cook until the chicken is cooked through. Serve the chicken and sauce over the biscuits.

beef enchiladas

prep 15 minutes | **bake** 20 minutes | **makes** 6 servings

- 1 **pound ground beef**
- 1 **jar (16 ounces) Pace® Picante Sauce**
- 2 **cups shredded cheese**
- 12 **corn *or* flour tortillas (10-inch), warmed**

1. Heat the oven to 350°F.

2. Cook the beef in a 10-inch skillet over medium-high heat until well browned. Pour off any fat. Stir in ½ **cup** picante sauce and 1 **cup** cheese.

3. Spread ½ **cup** picante sauce in 13×9×2-inch baking dish.

4. Spoon **about 2 tablespoons** meat mixture down center of **each** tortilla. Roll up and place seam-side down in prepared dish. Top with remaining sauce and cheese.

5. Bake for 20 minutes until the cheese melts.

miracle lasagna

prep 10 minutes | **bake** 1 hour | **stand** 5 minutes | **makes** 6 servings

- 1 **jar (24 ounces) Prego® Traditional Italian Sauce *or* Tomato Basil & Garlic Italian Sauce**
- 6 ***uncooked* lasagna noodles**
- 1 **container (15 ounces) ricotta cheese**
- 8 **ounces shredded mozzarella cheese (about 2 cups)**
- ¼ **cup grated Parmesan cheese**

1. Spread **about 1 cup** of the Italian sauce in a 2-quart shallow baking dish. Top with **3 uncooked** noodles, ricotta cheese, **1 cup** mozzarella cheese, Parmesan cheese and **1 cup** sauce. Top with the remaining **3 uncooked** noodles and the remaining sauce. **Cover** the dish.

2. Bake at 375°F. for 1 hour. Uncover the dish and top with the remaining mozzarella cheese. Let stand for 5 minutes.

chicken & stir-fry vegetable pizza

prep 5 minutes | **cook** 5 minutes | **bake** 10 minutes | **makes** 4 servings

1 **can (10¾ ounces) Campbell's® Condensed Cream of Mushroom Soup (Regular *or* 98% Fat Free)**

1 **prepared pizza crust (12-inch)**

1 **tablespoon vegetable oil**

3 **cups frozen vegetables**

⅛ **teaspoon garlic powder**

1 **package (about 10 ounces) refrigerated cooked chicken strips**

1 **cup shredded Cheddar cheese (about 4 ounces)**

Dried oregano leaves *or* crushed red pepper

1. Spread the soup on the crust to within ¼ inch of the edge. Bake at 450°F. for 5 minutes.

2. Heat the oil in a 10-inch skillet over medium heat. Add the vegetables and garlic powder and cook until the vegetables are tender-crisp, stirring occasionally.

3. Spoon the vegetables on the pizza. Top with the chicken and cheese. Sprinkle with the oregano, if desired.

4. Bake for 5 minutes or until the cheese is melted.

creamy beef stroganoff

prep 15 minutes I **cook** 8 hours I **makes** 9 servings

2 cans (10¾ ounces **each**) Campbell's® Condensed Cream of Mushroom Soup

¼ cup water

2 tablespoons Worcestershire sauce

1 package (8 ounces) sliced white mushrooms

3 medium onions, coarsely chopped (about 1½ cups)

3 cloves garlic, minced

½ teaspoon ground black pepper

2 pounds boneless beef bottom round steaks, sliced diagonally into strips

1 cup sour cream

Hot cooked egg noodles

Chopped fresh parsley (optional)

1. Stir the soup, water, Worcestershire sauce, mushrooms, onions, garlic and black pepper in a 6-quart slow cooker. Add the beef and stir to coat.

2. Cover and cook on LOW for 8 to 9 hours* or until the beef is cooked through.

3. Stir the sour cream into the cooker. Serve with the egg noodles. Top with the parsley, if desired.

*Or on HIGH for 4 to 5 hours.

> **tip** *For more overall flavor and color, brown the beef before adding it to the slow cooker.*

tomato & onion pork chops
with cannellini beans

prep 10 minutes I **cook** 45 minutes I **makes** 6 servings

¼ **cup olive oil**

6 **boneless pork chops, ½-inch thick *each* (about 1½ pounds)**

3 **garlic cloves, minced**

1 **large onion, finely chopped (about 1 cup)**

3 **cups Prego® Chunky Garden Tomato, Onion & Garlic Italian Sauce**

1 **can (about 15 ounces) white kidney beans (cannellini) *or* navy beans, undrained**

1 **package (10 ounces) Pepperidge Farm® Mozzarella Garlic Bread**

2 **tablespoons chopped fresh basil leaves**

1. Heat **3 tablespoons** of the oil in a 6-quart saucepot over medium-high heat. Add the pork and cook until well browned on both sides. Remove the pork from the saucepot.

2. Heat the remaining oil in the saucepot over medium heat. Add the garlic and onion and cook for 3 minutes or until the onion is tender.

3. Preheat the oven to 400°F. for the bread.

4. Return the pork to the saucepot. Stir the Italian sauce in the saucepot and heat to a boil. Reduce the heat to low. Cover and cook for 20 minutes or until the pork is cooked through. Stir in the beans and cook until the mixture is hot and bubbling.

5. Meanwhile, bake the bread according to the package directions.

6. Sprinkle the pork mixture with the basil. Cut the bread into 2-inch diagonal slices. Serve the bread with the pork.

chicken crunch

prep 10 minutes | **bake** 20 minutes | **cook** 5 minutes | **makes** 4 servings

 1 **can (10¾ ounces) Campbell's® Condensed Cream of Chicken Soup (Regular *or* 98% Fat Free)**

 ½ **cup milk**

 4 **skinless, boneless chicken breast halves (about 1 pound)**

 2 **tablespoons all-purpose flour**

1½ **cups Pepperidge Farm® Herb Seasoned Stuffing, finely crushed**

 2 **tablespoons butter, melted**

1. Heat the oven to 400°F. Stir ⅓ **cup** soup and ¼ **cup** milk in a shallow dish. Coat the chicken with the flour. Dip the chicken in the soup mixture. Coat the chicken with the stuffing. Place the chicken onto a baking sheet. Drizzle with the butter.

2. Bake for 20 minutes or until the chicken is cooked through.

3. Heat the remaining soup and milk in a 1-quart saucepan over medium-high heat until the mixture is hot and bubbling. Serve the sauce with the chicken.

chicken fajitas

prep 5 minutes | **marinate** 30 minutes | **grill** 15 minutes | **makes** 6 servings

- ¼ cup Italian salad dressing
- 6 skinless, boneless chicken breast halves (about 1½ pounds)
- 1 can (10¾ ounces) Campbell's® Condensed Cheddar Cheese Soup
- ½ cup Pace® Picante Sauce
- 12 flour tortillas (8–inch), warmed
- 4 green onions, thinly sliced (about ½ cup)
- 1 small avocado, peeled, pitted and sliced (optional)

1. Pour the dressing into a shallow nonmetallic dish or gallon-size resealable plastic bag. Add the chicken and turn to coat. Cover the dish or seal the bag and refrigerate for 30 minutes. Remove the chicken from the marinade. Discard the marinade.

2. Lightly oil the grill rack and heat the grill to medium. Grill the chicken for 15 minutes or until cooked through, turning it over once halfway through grilling.

3. Heat the soup and picante sauce in a 1-quart saucepan over medium-high heat until the mixture is hot and bubbling.

4. Cut the chicken into thin strips. Divide the chicken among the tortillas. Top with the soup mixture, onions and avocado, if desired. Fold the tortillas around the filling.

chicken pasta salad italiano

prep 20 minutes | **chill** 30 minutes | **makes** 4 servings

- 3 cups corkscrew-shaped pasta (rotini), cooked and drained
- 2 cans (4.5 ounces **each**) Swanson® Premium White Chunk Chicken Breast in Water, drained
- 1 small cucumber, cut in half lengthwise and sliced
- 1 medium tomato, chopped (about ½ cup)
- ½ cup frozen peas, thawed
- ¾ cup fat free Italian salad dressing **or** reduced fat creamy Italian salad dressing

Place the pasta, chicken, cucumber, tomato and peas in a large bowl. Add the dressing and toss to coat. Cover and refrigerate for 30 minutes.

 *This simple salad lends itself to variation…it's a great way to use the leftover veggies in your fridge.*

25-minute chicken & noodles

prep 5 minutes | **cook** 20 minutes | **makes** 4 servings

- 1¾ cups Swanson® Chicken Stock
- 1 teaspoon dried basil leaves, crushed
- ¼ teaspoon ground black pepper
- 2 cups frozen vegetable combination (broccoli, cauliflower, carrots)
- 2 cups **uncooked** medium egg noodles
- 2 cups cubed cooked chicken

1. Heat the stock, basil, black pepper and vegetables in a 10-inch skillet over medium heat to a boil. Reduce the heat to low. Cover and cook for 5 minutes or until the vegetables are tender-crisp.

2. Stir the noodles in the skillet. Cover and cook for 5 minutes or until the noodles are tender. Stir in the chicken and cook until the mixture is hot and bubbling.

sun-dried tomato bow tie pasta

prep 10 minutes | **cook** 20 minutes | **makes** 4 servings

1 tablespoon olive oil

1 large onion, finely chopped (about 1 cup)

⅓ cup sun-dried tomatoes, cut into thin strips

2 cloves garlic, minced

1 can (10¾ ounces) Campbell's® Condensed Cream of Chicken Soup
   (Regular **or** 98% Fat Free)

1 cup milk

2 tablespoons thinly sliced fresh basil leaves

1 package (1 pound) bow tie pasta (farfalle) (about 6 cups), cooked and drained

2 tablespoons grated Parmesan cheese

   Freshly ground black pepper

1. Heat the oil in a 10-inch skillet over medium heat. Add the onion and cook until tender.

2. Add the tomatoes and garlic and cook for 1 minute. Stir the soup, milk and basil in the skillet. Cook until the mixture is hot and bubbling, stirring occasionally.

3. Place the pasta into a large serving bowl. Pour the soup mixture over the pasta and toss to coat. Sprinkle with the cheese. Season with the black pepper, if desired.

tip *For a thinner sauce, reserve ¼ **cup** of the pasta cooking water and add it to the skillet with the soup and milk.*

crunchy chicken with ham sauce

prep 15 minutes | **bake** 20 minutes | **makes** 6 servings

- 1 can (10¾ ounces) Campbell's® Condensed Cream of Chicken Soup (Regular *or* 98% Fat Free)
- ¾ cup milk
- 6 skinless, boneless chicken breast halves (about 1½ pounds)
- 3 tablespoons all-purpose flour
- 2 cups Pepperidge Farm® Herb Seasoned Stuffing, crushed
- 2 tablespoons butter, melted
- ½ cup shredded Swiss cheese
- ⅓ cup chopped cooked ham
- 6 cups hot cooked noodles

1. Stir ⅓ **cup** soup and ¼ **cup** milk in a shallow dish. Coat the chicken with the flour. Dip the chicken in the soup mixture. Coat the chicken with the stuffing. Place the chicken on the baking sheet. Drizzle with the butter.

2. Bake at 400°F. for 20 minutes or until the chicken is cooked through.

3. Heat the remaining soup, remaining milk, cheese and ham in a 1-quart saucepan over medium heat until the cheese is melted, stirring often. Serve the chicken and sauce with the noodles.

spaghetti bolognese

prep 15 minutes | **cook** 4 hours | **makes** 8 servings

6 slices bacon, cut into
½-inch pieces

1 large onion, diced
(about 1 cup)

3 cloves garlic, minced

2 pounds ground beef

4 cups Prego® Traditional
Italian Sauce

1 cup milk

1 pound spaghetti, cooked
and drained*

Grated Parmesan cheese

*Reserve some of the cooking water from
the spaghetti. You can use it to adjust the
consistency of the finished sauce, if you
like.*

1. Cook the bacon in a 12-inch skillet over medium-high heat until crisp. Remove the bacon from the skillet. Pour off all but **1 tablespoon** of the drippings.

2. Add the onion and cook in the hot drippings until tender, stirring occasionally. Add the garlic and beef and cook until the beef is well browned, stirring often to separate the meat. Pour off any fat.

3. Stir the bacon, beef mixture, Italian sauce and milk in a 6-quart slow cooker.

4. Cover and cook on HIGH for 4 to 5 hours.** Serve with the spaghetti and cheese.

**Or on LOW for 7 to 8 hours.

hot chicken & potato salad

prep 15 minutes | **bake** 25 minutes | **makes** 8 servings

- **1 can (6 ounces) French fried onions**
- **⅓ cup chopped walnuts**
- **4 cups diced cooked chicken**
- **2 cups frozen peas and carrots, thawed**
- **1 can (10¾ ounces) Campbell's® Condensed Cream of Mushroom Soup (Regular *or* 98% Fat Free)**
- **1½ cups shredded Monterey Jack cheese *or* shredded Swiss cheese (about 6 ounces)**
- **¾ cup plain yogurt**
- **1 large potato, cut into cubes**

1. Stir ½ **can** onions and walnuts in a medium bowl.

2. Stir the remaining onions, chicken, peas and carrots, soup, cheese, yogurt and potato in a large bowl. Pour the chicken mixture into a 2-quart baking dish.

3. Bake at 350°F. for 20 minutes or until the chicken mixture is hot and bubbling. Stir the chicken mixture. Sprinkle with the walnut mixture.

4. Bake for 5 minutes or until the walnut mixture is golden brown.

burgers stroganoff

prep 10 minutes | **cook** 30 minutes | **makes** 6 servings

1½ **pounds ground beef**
1 **can (10¾ ounces) Campbell's® Condensed Cream of Mushroom Soup (Regular *or* 98% Fat Free)**
2 **tablespoons ketchup**
⅓ **cup sour cream**
6 **bagels, split**

1. Shape the beef into **6** (½-inch thick) burgers.

2. Cook the burgers in batches in a 10-inch skillet over medium-high heat until well browned on both sides. Remove the burgers from the skillet. Pour off any fat.

3. Stir the soup and ketchup in the skillet and heat to a boil. Return the burgers to the skillet. Reduce the heat to low. Cover and cook for 10 minutes or until the burgers are cooked though.

4. Stir in the sour cream. Serve the burgers and sauce on the bagels.

easy chicken stroganoff

prep 20 minutes | **cook** 25 minutes | **makes** 4 servings

2 **tablespoons butter**
1 **pound skinless, boneless chicken breast halves, cut into strips**
6 **ounces sliced mushrooms (about 2 cups)**
1 **medium onion, chopped (about ½ cup)**
1 **can (10¾ ounces) Campbell's® Condensed Cream of Chicken Soup (Regular *or* 98% Fat Free)**
½ **cup sour cream *or* plain yogurt**
4 **cups medium egg noodles, cooked and drained**
Chopped fresh parsley (optional)

1. Heat **1 tablespoon** butter in a 10-inch skillet over medium heat. Add the chicken and cook until browned, stirring often. Remove the chicken from the skillet and set aside.

2. Heat the remaining butter in the skillet. Add the mushrooms and onion and cook until they're tender, stirring occasionally.

3. Add the soup and sour cream and heat to a boil. Return the chicken to the skillet and cook until the chicken is cooked through. Serve the chicken mixture over the noodles. Garnish with parsley, if desired.

chicken with savory herbed rice

prep 5 minutes | **cook** 25 minutes | **makes** 4 servings

- **4** skinless, boneless chicken breast halves (about 1 pound)
- **¼** teaspoon garlic powder
- **⅛** teaspoon ground black pepper
- **1¾** cups Swanson® Chicken Stock
- **½** teaspoon dried thyme leaves, crushed
- **1½** cups *uncooked* instant white rice
- **1** cup frozen peas
- **2** tablespoons grated Parmesan cheese

1. Season the chicken with the garlic powder and black pepper.

2. Cook the chicken in a 10-inch nonstick skillet over medium-high heat for 10 minutes or until well browned on both sides. Remove the chicken from the skillet.

3. Heat the stock and thyme in the skillet over medium-high heat to a boil. Stir in the rice. Reduce the heat to low. Cover and cook for 5 minutes. Stir in the peas. Return the chicken to the skillet. Cover and cook for 5 minutes or until the chicken is cooked through and the rice is tender. Stir the cheese into the rice before serving.

crunchy chicken and gravy

prep 10 minutes | **bake** 20 minutes | **cook** 5 minutes | **makes** 4 servings

- 1 **cup Pepperidge Farm® Herb Seasoned Stuffing, crushed**
- 2 **tablespoons grated Parmesan cheese**
- 1 **egg**
- 4 **skinless, boneless chicken breast halves (about 1 pound)**
- 2 **tablespoons butter, melted**
- 1 **jar (12 ounces) Campbell's® Slow Roast Chicken Gravy**

1. Stir the stuffing and cheese on a plate. Beat the egg in a shallow dish with a fork or whisk. Dip the chicken into the egg. Coat the chicken with the stuffing mixture. Place the chicken onto a baking sheet. Drizzle with the butter.

2. Bake at 400°F. for 20 minutes or until the chicken is cooked through.

3. Heat the gravy in a 1-quart saucepan over medium heat until hot and bubbling. Serve the gravy with the chicken.

easy spaghetti & meatballs

prep 10 minutes | **cook** 8 minutes | **makes** 4 servings

- 1 **pound ground beef**
- 2 **tablespoons water**
- ⅓ **cup seasoned dry bread crumbs**
- 1 **egg, beaten**
- 1 **jar (24 ounces) Prego® Traditional Italian Sauce**
- ½ **of a 16-ounce package spaghetti, cooked and drained (about 4 cups)**

1. Mix **thoroughly** ground beef, water, bread crumbs and egg. Shape **firmly** into **12** (2-inch) meatballs. Arrange the meatballs in a 2-quart microwavable baking dish.

2. Microwave on HIGH for 5 minutes or until they're cooked through. Pour off any fat. Stir the Italian sauce in the dish. **Cover**. Microwave for 3 minutes or until hot. Serve over the spaghetti.

sizzling fajitas

prep 10 minutes | **cook** 15 minutes | **makes** 4 servings

  2 **tablespoons vegetable oil**

  1 **pound skinless, boneless chicken breast *or* beef sirloin steak, cut into strips**

  1 **medium green *or* red pepper, cut into 2-inch-long strips (about 1½ cups)**

  1 **medium onion, sliced (about ½ cup)**

1½ **cups Pace® Picante Sauce**

  8 **flour tortillas (8-inch), warmed**

     Guacamole (optional)

1. Heat the oil in a 12-inch skillet over medium-high heat. Add the chicken and cook until well browned, stirring often.

2. Stir the pepper and onion in the skillet and cook until tender-crisp. Stir the picante sauce in the skillet and cook until the mixture is hot and bubbling.

3. Spoon **about** ½ **cup** chicken mixture down the center of **each** tortilla. Top with additional picante sauce. Fold the tortillas around the filling. Serve with the guacamole, if desired.

good-for-you stuffed peppers

prep 20 minutes | **bake** 45 minutes | **stand** 5 minutes | **makes** 6 servings

½ cup *uncooked* quick-cooking brown rice

1 pound extra lean ground beef

3 cups Prego® Heart Smart Traditional Italian Sauce

6 medium green peppers

4 ounces shredded fat-free mozzarella cheese (about 1 cup)

1. Cook the rice without salt or butter according to the package directions.

2. Cook the beef in a 10-inch skillet over medium-high heat until well browned, stirring often to separate the meat. Pour off any fat. Stir **2 cups** of the Italian sauce and the rice in the skillet.

3. Cut **each** pepper in half lengthwise. Discard the seeds and white membranes. Place the pepper shells in a 17×11-inch roasting pan.

4. Spoon the beef mixture into the pepper shells. Pour the remaining sauce over the filled peppers. **Cover** the dish.

5. Bake at 400° F. for 45 minutes or until the peppers are tender. Top with the cheese. Let stand for 5 minutes or until the cheese is melted.

mediterranean chicken casserole

prep 20 minutes | **bake** 30 minutes | **makes** 4 servings

- 1 can (10¾ ounces) Campbell's® Condensed Cream of Celery Soup (Regular **or** 98% Fat Free)
- ½ cup water
- ½ teaspoon dried oregano leaves, crushed
- ¼ teaspoon ground black pepper
- 1 package (10 ounces) frozen chopped spinach, thawed and well drained
- 2 cups cubed cooked chicken
- ⅔ cup orzo pasta, cooked and drained
- ½ cup shredded Italian cheese blend

1. Stir the soup, water, oregano, black pepper, spinach, chicken and pasta in a 2-quart shallow baking dish. **Cover** the baking dish.

2. Bake at 375°F. for 30 minutes or until the chicken mixture is hot and bubbling. Sprinkle with the cheese.

tip You can substitute **3 cans** (4.5 ounces **each**) Swanson® Premium White Chunk Chicken Breast in Water, drained, for the cubed cooked chicken.

garlic chicken, vegetable & rice skillet

prep 5 minutes | **cook** 40 minutes | **makes** 4 servings

Vegetable cooking spray

1¼ pounds skinless, boneless chicken breast halves

2 cloves garlic, minced

1¾ cups Swanson® Chicken Stock

¾ cup *uncooked* regular long-grain white rice

1 bag (16 ounces) frozen vegetable combination (broccoli, cauliflower, carrots)

⅓ cup grated Parmesan cheese

Paprika

1. Spray a 12-inch skillet with the cooking spray and heat over medium-high heat for 1 minute. Add the chicken and garlic and cook for 10 minutes or until the chicken is well browned on both sides. Remove the chicken from the skillet.

2. Stir the stock, rice and vegetables in the skillet and heat to a boil. Reduce the heat to low. Cover and cook for 15 minutes. Stir in the cheese.

3. Return the chicken to the skillet. Sprinkle the chicken with the paprika. Cover and cook for 10 minutes or until the chicken is cooked through and the rice is tender.

easy turkey & biscuits

prep 20 minutes | **bake** 30 minutes | **makes** 5 servings

1   **can (10¾ ounces) Campbell's® Condensed Cream of Celery Soup (Regular *or* 98% Fat Free)**

1   **can (10¾ ounces) Campbell's® Condensed Cream of Potato Soup**

1   **cup milk**

¼   **teaspoon dried thyme leaves, crushed**

¼   **teaspoon ground black pepper**

4   **cups cooked cut-up vegetables (broccoli, cauliflower, carrots)**

2   **cups cubed cooked turkey *or* cooked chicken**

1   **package refrigerated buttermilk biscuits (10 biscuits)**

1. Stir the soups, milk, thyme, black pepper, vegetables and turkey in a 3-quart shallow baking dish.

2. Bake at 400°F. for 15 minutes. Stir the turkey mixture. Cut **each** biscuit into quarters.

3. Evenly top the turkey mixture with the cut biscuits. Bake for 15 minutes or until the turkey mixture is hot and bubbling and the biscuits are golden brown.

tip *To microwave the vegetables, stir the vegetables in a 2-quart shallow microwave-safe baking dish with ¼ cup water. Cover and microwave on HIGH for 10 minutes.*

lasagna roll-ups

prep 30 minutes | **bake** 35 minutes | **stand** 10 minutes | **makes** 4 servings

    1 cup ricotta cheese
    1 can (about 4 ounces) mushroom stems and pieces, drained
    ½ cup refrigerated pesto sauce
    8 lasagna noodles, cooked and drained
    2 cups Prego® Traditional Italian Sauce **or** Tomato, Basil & Garlic Italian Sauce
    ¾ cup Pace® Picante Sauce
    4 ounces shredded mozzarella cheese (about 1 cup)

1. Stir the ricotta, mushrooms and pesto in a medium bowl. Top **each** noodle with ¼ **cup** of the cheese mixture. Spread to the edges. Roll up like a jelly roll. Place the rolls seam-side down in a 2-quart shallow baking dish.

2. Stir the Italian sauce and picante sauce in a small bowl and pour the mixture over the roll-ups.

3. Bake at 400°F. for 30 minutes or until hot and bubbling. Top with the mozzarella cheese. Bake for 5 minutes or until the cheese is melted. Let stand for 10 minutes.

honey-barbecued ribs

prep 10 minutes I **cook** 40 minutes I **grill** 20 minutes I **makes** 4 servings

1 **rack pork spareribs (about 4 pounds)**
1 **can (10½ ounces) Campbell's® Condensed French Onion Soup**
¾ **cup ketchup**
⅓ **cup honey**
½ **teaspoon garlic powder**
½ **teaspoon ground black pepper**

1. Place the ribs into a 6-quart saucepot and add water to cover. Heat over medium-high heat to a boil. Reduce the heat to low. Cover and cook for 30 minutes or until the meat is tender. Drain the ribs well in a colander.

2. Heat the soup, ketchup, honey, garlic powder and black pepper in a 2-quart saucepan over medium-high heat to a boil. Reduce the heat to low. Cook for 5 minutes.

3. Lightly oil the grill rack and heat the grill to medium. Grill the ribs for 20 minutes or until well glazed, turning and brushing often with the soup mixture. Cut the ribs into serving-size pieces.

monterey chicken tortilla casserole

prep 15 minutes | **bake** 40 minutes | **makes** 4 servings

- 1 **cup coarsely crumbled tortilla chips**
- 2 **cups cubed cooked chicken *or* turkey**
- 1 **can (about 15 ounces) cream-style corn**
- ¾ **cup Pace® Picante Sauce**
- ½ **cup sliced pitted ripe olives**
- 2 **ounces shredded Cheddar cheese (about ½ cup)**
  Chopped green *or* red pepper
  Tortilla chips

1. Layer the crumbled chips, chicken, corn and picante sauce in a 1-quart casserole. Top with the olives and cheese.

2. Bake at 350°F. for 40 minutes or until the mixture is hot and bubbling. Top with the pepper. Serve with the chips.

polynesian burgers

prep 10 minutes I **cook** 20 minutes I **makes** 6 servings

1½ pounds ground beef

1 can (8 ounces) pineapple slices in juice, undrained

1 can (10½ ounces) Campbell's® Condensed French Onion Soup

2 teaspoons packed brown sugar

1 tablespoon cider vinegar

1 loaf French bread, cut crosswise into 6 pieces

1. Shape the beef into **6** (½-inch thick) burgers.

2. Cook the burgers in a 12-inch skillet over medium-high heat until well browned on both sides. Pour
   off an... ...h burger with **1** slice pineapple. Reserve the pineapple juice.

   ...served pineapple juice, brown sugar and vinegar in a small bowl. Add the soup
   ...t and heat to a boil. Reduce the heat to low. Cover and cook for 5 minutes or until
   ...ked through.

   ...ces. Serve the burgers and sauce on the bread.

To: Sionnie
From: Chelsea

italian-style sloppy joes

prep 10 minutes | **cook** 10 minutes | **makes** 6 servings

1 **pound ground beef**

1 **medium onion, chopped (about 1 cup)**

1½ **cups Prego® Traditional *or* Roasted Garlic & Herb Italian Sauce**

1 **tablespoon Worcestershire sauce**

6 **Pepperidge Farm® Classic Sandwich Buns with Sesame Seeds, split and toasted**

1. Cook the beef and onion in a 10-inch skillet over medium-high heat until browned, stirring often to separate the meat. Pour off any fat.

2. Stir the Italian sauce and Worcestershire sauce in the skillet and cook until the mixture is hot and bubbling. Evenly divide the beef mixture among the buns.

broccoli fish bake

prep 15 minutes I **bake** 20 minutes I **makes** 4 servings

1 package (about 10 ounces) frozen broccoli spears, cooked and drained

4 fresh *or* thawed frozen firm white fish fillets (cod, haddock *or* halibut) (about 1 pound)

1 can (10¾ ounces) Campbell's® Condensed Cream of Broccoli Soup

⅓ cup milk

¼ cup shredded Cheddar cheese

2 tablespoons dry bread crumbs

1 teaspoon butter, melted

⅛ teaspoon paprika

1. Place the broccoli into a 2-quart shallow baking dish. Top with the fish. Stir the soup and milk in a small bowl. Pour the soup mixture over the fish. Sprinkle with the cheese.

2. Stir the bread crumbs, butter and paprika in a small bowl. Sprinkle the crumb mixture over all.

3. Bake at 450°F. for 20 minutes or until the fish flakes easily when tested with a fork.

tip You can substitute **1 pound** fresh broccoli spears, cooked and drained, for the frozen.

mushroom bacon burgers

1½ **pounds ground beef**

1 **can (10¾ ounces) Campbell's® Condensed Cream of Mushroom Soup (Regular *or* 98% Fat Free)**

⅓ **cup water**

6 **slices Cheddar cheese**

6 **Pepperidge Farm® Classic Sandwich Buns with Sesame Seeds**

6 **slices bacon, cooked**

6 **red onion slices**

1. Shape the beef into **6** (½-inch thick) burgers.

2. Cook the burgers in a 12-inch skillet over medium-high heat until well browned on both sides. Pour off any fat.

3. Stir the soup and water in the skillet and heat to a boil. Reduce the heat to low. Cover and cook for 5 minutes or until desired doneness.

4. Top the burgers with the cheese and cook until the cheese is melted. Serve the burgers and sauce on the buns. Top with the bacon and onion.

spaghetti squash alfredo

- 1 medium spaghetti squash (about 3 pounds)
- 1 can (10¾ ounces) Campbell's® Condensed Cream of Celery Soup (Regular **or** 98% Fat Free)
- ¾ cup water
- ¼ cup milk
- 1 cup shredded lowfat Swiss cheese (about 4 ounces)
- 2 tablespoons grated Parmesan cheese
   Chopped fresh parsley **or** chives

1. Pierce the squash with a fork.

2. Bake at 350°F. for 50 minutes or until the squash is fork-tender. Cut the squash in half and scoop out and discard the seeds. Scrape the flesh with a fork to separate the spaghetti-like strands.

3. Heat the soup, water and milk in a 3-quart saucepan over medium heat to a boil. Stir in the Swiss cheese. Add the squash and toss to coat. Sprinkle with the Parmesan cheese and parsley.

spicy verde chicken & bean chili

prep 10 minutes | **cook** 40 minutes | **makes** 6 servings

- 2 **tablespoons butter**
- 1 **large onion, chopped (about 1 cup)**
- ¼ **teaspoon garlic powder *or* 1 clove garlic, minced**
- 1 **tablespoon all-purpose flour**
- 2 **cups Swanson® Chicken Stock**
- 2 **cups shredded cooked chicken**
- 1 **can (about 15 ounces) small white beans, undrained**
- 1 **can (4 ounces) chopped green chiles, drained**
- 1 **teaspoon ground cumin**
- 1 **teaspoon jalapeño hot pepper sauce**
- 6 **flour tortillas (8-inch), warmed**
  Shredded Monterey Jack cheese
  Chopped fresh cilantro leaves (optional)

1. Heat the butter in a 12-inch skillet over medium heat. Add the onion and garlic powder. Cook and stir until the onion is tender.

2. Stir the flour into the skillet. Cook and stir for 2 minutes. Gradually stir in the stock. Cook and stir until the mixture boils and thickens.

3. Stir in the chicken, beans, chiles, cumin and hot sauce. Heat to a boil. Reduce the heat to low. Cook for 20 minutes, stirring occasionally.

4. Line **each** of **6** serving bowls with the tortillas. Divide the chili among the bowls. Serve topped with cheese and cilantro, if desired.

weekday pot roast & vegetables

prep 15 minutes **I** **cook** 10 hours **I** **makes** 8 servings

- 1 boneless beef bottom round roast **or** chuck pot roast (2 to 2½ pounds)
- 1 teaspoon garlic powder
- 1 tablespoon vegetable oil
- 1 pound potatoes, cut into wedges
- 3 cups fresh **or** frozen whole baby carrots
- 1 medium onion, thickly sliced (about ¾ cup)
- 2 teaspoons dried basil leaves, crushed
- 2 cans (10¼ ounces **each**) Campbell's® Beef Gravy

1. Season the beef with the garlic powder. Heat the oil in a 10-inch skillet over medium-high heat. Add the beef and cook until well browned on all sides.

2. Place the potatoes, carrots and onion in a 3 ½-quart slow cooker. Sprinkle with the basil. Add the beef to the cooker. Pour the gravy over the beef and vegetables.

3. Cover and cook on LOW for 10 to 11 hours* or until the beef is fork-tender.

*Or on HIGH for 5 to 6 hours.

mexican chicken & rice

prep 10 minutes I **cook** 30 minutes I **makes** 5 servings

1 ¾ cups Swanson® Chicken Stock

½ teaspoon ground cumin

⅛ teaspoon ground black pepper

1 medium onion, chopped (about ½ cup)

1 small green pepper, chopped (about ½ cup)

¾ cup *uncooked* regular long-grain white rice

1 can (about 15 ounces) kidney beans, rinsed and drained

2 cans (4.5 ounces *each*) Swanson® Premium White Chunk Chicken Breast in Water, drained

1. Heat the stock, cumin, black pepper, onion and green pepper in a 3-quart saucepan over medium heat to a boil.

2. Stir the rice in the saucepan. Reduce the heat to low. Cover and cook for 20 minutes or until the rice is tender.

3. Stir in the beans and chicken and cook until the mixture is heated through.

spiced pot roast

prep 5 minutes | **marinate** 12 hours | **bake** 3 hours | **stand** 10 minutes | **makes** 8 servings

- 3 **tablespoons packed brown sugar**
- 2 **teaspoons ground cloves**
- 2 **teaspoons ground allspice**
- 2 **teaspoons ground cinnamon**
- 1 **teaspoon cracked black pepper**
- 1 **boneless beef bottom round roast *or* beef chuck pot roast (about 4 pounds)**
- 2 **cups Swanson® Beef Stock**
- 1 **bottle (12 ounces) dark beer *or* stout**
  Hot boiled potatoes
  Chopped fresh parsley (optional)

1. Stir the brown sugar, cloves, allspice, cinnamon and black pepper in a large bowl. Add the beef and turn to coat. Cover the bowl and refrigerate for 12 hours or overnight.

2. Place the beef in a 6-quart oven-safe saucepot. Pour the stock and beer over the beef. **Cover** the saucepot.

3. Bake at 350°F. for 3 hours or until the beef is fork-tender. Remove the beef from the saucepot and let stand for 10 minutes. Thinly slice the beef. Serve with the stock mixture and the potatoes. Sprinkle with the parsley, if desired.

simple creamy chicken risotto

prep 10 minutes | **cook** 35 minutes | **makes** 4 servings

 1 **tablespoon vegetable oil**
 4 **skinless, boneless chicken breast halves (about 1 pound), cut into 1-inch pieces**
 1 **can (10¾ ounces) Campbell's® Condensed Cream of Mushroom with Roasted Garlic Soup**
 1 **can (10½ ounces) Campbell's® Condensed Chicken Broth**
 ¾ **cup water**
 1 **small carrot, shredded (about ¼ cup)**
 2 **green onions, sliced (about ¼ cup)**
 1 **tablespoon grated Parmesan cheese**
 1 **cup *uncooked* regular long-grain white rice**

1. Heat the oil in a 10-inch skillet over medium-high heat. Add the chicken and cook until well browned, stirring often.

2. Stir the soup, broth, water, carrot, green onions and cheese in the skillet and heat to a boil. Stir in the rice. Reduce the heat to low. Cover and cook for 25 minutes or until the chicken is cooked through and the rice is tender.

pork chops & french onion rice

prep 10 minutes I **cook** 30 minutes I **makes** 6 servings

1 tablespoon vegetable oil

6 bone-in pork chops (about 2 pounds)

1 can (10½ ounces) Campbell's® Condensed French Onion Soup

½ cup water

   Ground black pepper

1 stalk celery, chopped (about ½ cup)

¼ teaspoon dried thyme leaves, crushed

½ cup *uncooked* regular long-grain white rice

1. Heat the oil in a 10-inch skillet over medium-high heat. Add the pork and cook until well browned on both sides. Pour off any fat.

2. Stir the soup, water, black pepper, celery, thyme and rice in the skillet and heat to a boil. Reduce the heat to low. Cover and cook for 30 minutes or until the pork is cooked through and the rice is tender, stirring the rice occasionally.

now & later baked ziti

prep 15 minutes | **bake** 30 minutes | **makes** 12 servings

- 2 **pounds ground beef**
- 1 **large onion, chopped (about 1 cup)**
- 7½ **cups Prego® Fresh Mushroom Italian Sauce**
- 9 **cups tube-shaped pasta (ziti), cooked and drained**
- 12 **ounces shredded mozzarella cheese (about 3 cups)**
- ½ **cup grated Parmesan cheese**

1. Cook the beef and onion in an 8-quart saucepot over medium-high heat until the beef is well browned, stirring often to separate the meat. Pour off any fat.

2. Stir the Italian sauce, ziti and **2 cups** mozzarella cheese in the saucepot. Spoon the beef mixture into **2** (12½×8½×2-inch) disposable foil pans. Top with the remaining mozzarella and Parmesan cheeses.

3. Bake at 350°F. for 30 minutes or until the beef mixture is hot and the cheese is melted.

tip *To make ahead and freeze, prepare the ziti as directed above but do not bake. Cover the pans with foil and freeze. Bake the frozen ziti, uncovered, at 350°F. for 1 hour or until it's hot. Or, thaw the ziti in the refrigerator for 24 hours, then bake, uncovered, at 350°F. for 45 minutes or until it's hot.*

picante chicken & rice bake

prep 10 minutes I **cook** 45 minutes I **makes** 4 servings

- 1 **jar (16 ounces) Pace® Picante Sauce**
- ½ **cup water**
- 1 **cup whole kernel corn**
- ¾ **cup *uncooked* regular long-grain white rice**
- 4 **skinless, boneless chicken breast halves (about 1 pound)**
   Paprika
- ½ **cup shredded Cheddar cheese**

1. Stir the picante sauce, water, corn and rice in a 2-quart shallow baking dish. Top with the chicken. Sprinkle the chicken with the paprika. **Cover** the baking dish.

2. Bake at 375°F. for 45 minutes or until the chicken is cooked through and the rice is tender. Sprinkle with the cheese.

tip *If you don't have Cheddar cheese on hand, you can substitute an equal amount of shredded Monterey Jack **or** a Mexican cheese blend.*

pan-sautéed chicken with vegetables & herbs

prep 20 minutes I **cook** 20 minutes I **bake** 35 minutes I **makes** 4 servings

⅛ **teaspoon ground black pepper**

⅛ **teaspoon paprika**

2 **tablespoons all-purpose flour**

4 **bone-in chicken breast halves (about 2 pounds)**

2 **tablespoons olive oil**

2 **small red onions, cut into quarters**

1 **pound new potatoes, cut into quarters**

8 **ounces fresh whole baby carrots (about 16), green tops trimmed to 1 inch long**

1½ **cups Swanson® Chicken Stock**

3 **tablespoons lemon juice**

1 **tablespoon chopped fresh oregano leaves**

   Chopped fresh thyme leaves (optional)

1. Heat the oven to 350°F. Stir the black pepper, paprika and flour on a plate. Coat the chicken with the flour mixture.

2. Heat the oil in a 12-inch oven-safe skillet over medium-high heat. Add the chicken and cook until well browned on all sides. Remove the chicken from the skillet.

3. Add the onions and potatoes to the skillet and cook for 5 minutes. Add the carrots, stock, lemon juice and oregano and heat to a boil. Return the chicken to the skillet. **Cover** the skillet.

4. Bake for 20 minutes. Uncover the skillet and bake for 15 minutes or until the chicken is cooked through and the vegetables are tender. Sprinkle with the thyme, if desired.

penne bolognese-style

prep 20 minutes **I** **cook** 30 minutes **I** **makes** 4 servings

- 1 **pound lean ground beef**
- 1 **large onion, minced (about 1 cup)**
- 3 **large carrots, shredded (about 2 cups)**
- 1 **jar (24 ounces) Prego® Veggie Smart® Smooth & Simple Italian Sauce**
- ½ **cup water**
- 3 **tablespoons fresh basil leaves, cut into very thin strips**
- 3 **cups penne pasta, cooked and drained (about 4½ cups)**
- 2 **tablespoons grated Parmesan cheese**

1. Cook the beef, onion and carrots in a 12-inch skillet over medium-high heat until the beef is well browned, stirring often to separate the meat. Pour off any fat.

2. Stir the Italian sauce and water in the skillet and heat to a boil. Reduce the heat to low. Cook for 15 minutes or until the vegetables are tender, stirring occasionally. Stir in additional water, if needed, until desired consistency.

3. Place the basil and penne into a large bowl. Add the beef mixture and toss to coat. Sprinkle with the cheese.

comfort classics

Recipes that bring back good memories

and make you feel good.

quick chicken a la king

prep 20 minutes | **cook** 10 minutes | **makes** 4 servings

> 1 **tablespoon butter**
> ¼ **cup chopped green pepper *or* red pepper**
> 1 **can (10¾ ounces) Campbell's® Condensed Cream of Mushroom Soup (Regular *or* 98% Fat Free)**
> ½ **cup milk**
> 1½ **cups cubed cooked chicken *or* ham**
> 4 **cups hot cooked regular long-grain white rice**

1. Heat the butter in a 3-quart saucepan over medium heat. Add the pepper and cook until tender, stirring often.

2. Stir the soup, milk and chicken in the skillet and cook until the mixture is hot and bubbling. Serve the chicken mixture with the rice.

tips for quick comfort

Everyone has their own idea of comfort food. Often with roots in our childhoods, these foods bring back memories of simpler times and make us feel good. The next time you need a little comfort but don't have a lot of time to get there, these tips and ideas will help you feel better in no time!

■ *Use pre-cooked meat for a shortcut to comfort. Swanson*® Premium Chunk Chicken Breast or rotisserie chicken from the store are real time-savers when making classics like chicken noodle soup or pot pie. And instead of making a pot pie crust from scratch, use a *Pepperidge Farm*® Puff Pastry sheet—speedy and delicious!

■ *Top baked potatoes or freshly baked biscuits with quick-cooking chili, purchased guacamole or pimiento cheese from your grocery store's deli section.* Or pour hot *Campbell's*® Chunky™ soups over mashed potatoes, biscuits, or cooked rice for an inexpensive, hearty spin on comfort food.

■ *Refrigerated biscuits make wonderful dumplings and cook in just minutes.* Simply roll the dough into small balls, drop them into a simmering soup or stew, then cover the pot and cook until the dumplings are firm.

■ *Craving beef stew? Speed up prep time by using frozen or prepared vegetables (such as cooked cubed potatoes) from the produce aisle.* Or make an even quicker beef stew by adding cubed leftover roast beef or pork to *Campbell's*® Chunky™ Vegetable soup.

■ *Remember, smaller items cook faster, so make miniature versions of things like meatloaf.* Mini meatloaves cook in about half the time of a full-size recipe!

classic tuna noodle casserole

prep 10 minutes I **bake** 25 minutes I **makes** 4 servings

- 1 can (10¾ ounces) Campbell's® Condensed Cream of Celery Soup (Regular *or* 98% Fat Free)
- ½ cup milk
- 1 cup cooked peas
- 2 tablespoons chopped pimientos
- 2 cans (about 6 ounces *each*) tuna, drained and flaked
- 2 cups hot cooked medium egg noodles
- 2 tablespoons dry bread crumbs
- 1 tablespoon butter, melted

1. Heat the oven to 400°F. Stir the soup, milk, peas, pimientos, tuna and noodles in a 1½-quart baking dish. Stir the bread crumbs and butter in a small bowl.

2. Bake for 20 minutes or until the tuna mixture is hot and bubbling. Stir the tuna mixture. Sprinkle with the bread crumb mixture.

3. Bake for 5 minutes or until the bread crumbs are golden brown.

tip Substitute Campbell's® Condensed Cream of Mushroom Soup for the Cream of Celery. To melt the butter, remove the wrapper and place the butter in a microwavable cup. Cover and microwave on HIGH for 30 seconds.

garlic potato soup

prep 15 minutes | **cook** 25 minutes | **makes** 4 servings

3½ cups Swanson® Chicken Broth (Regular, Natural Goodness® *or* Certified Organic)

4 cloves garlic, minced

4 medium red potatoes, cut into cubes (about 4 cups)

2 medium carrots, diced (about 1 cup)

1 medium onion, chopped (about ½ cup)

1 stalk celery, chopped (about ½ cup)

2 slices bacon, cooked and crumbled

1 cup milk

1 cup instant mashed potato flakes *or* buds

1 tablespoon chopped fresh parsley

1. Heat the broth, garlic, potatoes, carrots, onion, celery and bacon in a 4-quart saucepan over medium-high heat to a boil. Reduce the heat to low. Cover and cook for 15 minutes or until the vegetables are tender.

2. Reduce the heat to medium. Stir the milk, potato flakes and parsley in the saucepan. Cook until the mixture is hot and bubbling, stirring occasionally.

slow cooker veggie beef stew

prep 15 minutes I **cook** 10 hours I **makes** 6 servings

- 2 tablespoons oil
- 1½ pounds beef for stew, cut into 1-inch pieces
- 1 bag (about 24 ounces) frozen vegetables for stew
- 1 beef bouillon cube
- 1½ cups V8® 100% Vegetable Juice
- 1 tablespoon all-purpose flour
- ½ teaspoon dried basil leaves, crushed
- ½ teaspoon dried oregano, crushed
- ½ teaspoon dried thyme leaves, crushed
- ½ teaspoon dried rosemary, crushed
- ½ teaspoon garlic salt

1. Heat the oil in a 12-inch skillet over medium-high heat. Add the beef and cook until well browned, stirring often. Pour off any fat.

2. Place the beef, vegetables and bouillon cube in a 3½-quart slow cooker. Stir the vegetable juice, flour, basil, oregano, thyme, rosemary and garlic salt in a medium bowl and pour it into the slow cooker.

3. Cover and cook on LOW for 10 to 12 hours* or until the beef is fork-tender.

Or on HIGH for 5 to 6 hours.

broth simmered rice

prep 5 minutes I **cook** 25 minutes I **makes** 4 servings

- 1¾ cups Swanson® Chicken Broth (Regular, Natural Goodness® **or** Certified Organic)
- ¾ cup **uncooked** regular long-grain white rice

1. Heat the broth in a 2-quart saucepan over medium-high heat to a boil.

2. Stir in the rice. Reduce the heat to low. Cover and cook for 20 minutes or until the rice is tender.

Florentine Simmered Rice: Add **1 teaspoon** dried Italian seasoning to broth. Add **1 cup** chopped spinach with rice. Stir in ½ **cup** grated Parmesan cheese before serving. Serve with additional cheese.

> **tip** This recipe will work with any variety of Swanson® Broth.

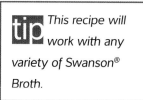

bacon potato chowder

prep 15 minutes I **cook** 3 hours I **makes** 8 servings

- 4 slices bacon, cooked and crumbled
- 1 large onion, chopped (about 1 cup)
- 4 cans (10¾ ounces *each*) Campbell's® Condensed Cream of Potato Soup
- 4 soup cans milk
- ¼ teaspoon ground black pepper
- 2 large russet potatoes, cut into ½-inch pieces (about 3 cups)
- ½ cup chopped fresh chives
- 2 cups shredded Cheddar cheese (about 8 ounces)

1. Stir the bacon, onion, soup, milk, black pepper, potatoes and ¼ **cup** chives in a 6-quart slow cooker.

2. Cover and cook on HIGH for 3 to 4 hours or until the potatoes are tender.

3. Add the cheese and stir until the cheese is melted. Serve with the remaining chives.

green bean casserole

prep 10 minutes **|** **bake** 30 minutes **|** **makes** 5 servings

1 **can (10¾ ounces) Campbell's® Condensed Cream of Mushroom Soup (Regular _or_ 98% Fat Free)**

½ **cup milk**

1 **teaspoon soy sauce**

Dash ground black pepper

2 **packages (10 ounces _each_) frozen cut green beans, cooked and drained**

1 **can (2.8 ounces) French fried onions (1⅓ cups)**

1. Stir the soup, milk, soy sauce, black pepper, green beans and ⅔ **cup** onions in a 1½-quart casserole.

2. Bake at 350°F. for 25 minutes or until hot. Stir the green bean mixture.

3. Sprinkle the remaining onions over the green bean mixture. Bake for 5 minutes more or until onions are golden brown.

tip _You can also make this classic side dish with fresh **or** canned green beans. You will need either 1½ **pounds** fresh green beans, cut into 1-inch pieces, cooked and drained **or** 2 **cans** (about 16 ounces **each**) cut green beans, drained for the frozen green beans._

tomato soup spice cake

prep 20 minutes | **bake** 40 minutes | **cool** 20 minutes | **makes** 12 servings

2 **cups all-purpose flour**

1⅓ **cups sugar**

4 **teaspoons baking powder**

1½ **teaspoons ground allspice**

1 **teaspoon baking soda**

1 **teaspoon ground cinnamon**

½ **teaspoon ground cloves**

1 **can (10¾ ounces) Campbell's® Condensed Tomato Soup**

½ **cup vegetable shortening**

2 **eggs**

¼ **cup water**

Cream Cheese Frosting

1. Heat the oven to 350°F. Grease **2** (8- or 9-inch) cake pans.

2. Stir the flour, sugar, baking powder, allspice, baking soda, cinnamon and cloves in a large bowl. Add the soup, shortening, eggs and water. Beat with an electric mixer on low speed just until blended. Increase the speed to high and beat for 4 minutes. Pour the batter into the pan.

3. Bake for 40 minutes or until a toothpick inserted in the centers comes out clean. Let the cakes cool in the pans on wire racks for 20 minutes. Frost with the Cream Cheese Frosting.

Cream Cheese Frosting: Beat **1 package** (8 ounces) cream cheese, softened, **2 tablespoons** milk and **1 teaspoon** vanilla extract in a medium bowl with an electric mixer on medium speed until the mixture is creamy. Slowly beat in **1 package** (16 ounces) confectioners' sugar until the frosting is desired consistency.

 The cake can also be prepared in a 13×9-inch baking pan.

2-bean chili

prep 10 minutes | **cook** 15 minutes | **makes** 6 servings

1   **pound ground beef**
1   **large green pepper, chopped (about 1 cup)**
1   **large onion, chopped (about 1 cup)**
2   **tablespoons chili powder**
¼   **teaspoon ground black pepper**
3   **cups Campbell's® Tomato Juice**
1   **can (about 15 ounces) kidney beans, rinsed and drained**
1   **can (about 15 ounces) great Northern beans, rinsed and drained**
    Sour cream
    Sliced green onions
    Shredded Cheddar cheese
    Chopped tomato

1. Cook the beef, green pepper, onion, chili powder and black pepper in a 10-inch skillet until the beef is well browned, stirring often to separate the meat. Pour off any fat.

2. Stir the tomato juice and beans in the skillet and cook until the mixture is hot and bubbling. Top the beef mixture with the sour cream, green onions, cheese and tomato before serving.

creamy carrot gingered soup

prep 10 minutes | **cook** 40 minutes | **makes** 6 servings

1   **tablespoon olive oil**

8   **medium carrots, coarsely chopped (about 4 cups)**

1   **large sweet onion, coarsely chopped (about 1½ cups)**

1   **large potato, coarsely chopped (about 1 cup)**

6   **cups Swanson® Vegetable Broth (Regular *or* Certified Organic)**

3   **tablespoons minced fresh ginger**

½   **teaspoon ground black pepper**

1   **tablespoon fresh chopped parsley (optional)**

1. Heat the oil in a 4-quart saucepan over medium-high heat. Add the carrots, onion and potato. Cook for 5 minutes or until the vegetables are tender-crisp.

2. Stir in the broth, ginger and black pepper. Heat to a boil. Reduce the heat to low. Cover and cook for 20 minutes or until the vegetables are tender.

3. Place ⅓ of the carrot mixture into an electric blender or food processor container. Cover and blend until smooth. Pour the mixture into a medium bowl. Repeat the blending process twice more with the remaining carrot mixture. Return all of the puréed mixture to the saucepan. Cook over medium heat until the mixture is hot. Garnish with parsley, if desired.

roasted garlic mashed potatoes

prep 10 minutes | **cook** 1 hour 15 minutes | **makes** 6 servings

- 1 **whole bulb garlic**
- 2⅔ **cups Swanson® Chicken Broth (Regular, Natural Goodness® or Certified Organic)**
- 5 **large potatoes, cut into 1-inch pieces (about 7½ cups)**
- 2 **tablespoons chopped chives or green onion tops (optional)**

1. Cut off the top of the garlic bulb. Drizzle with **about 2 tablespoons** of the broth. Wrap the bulb in aluminum foil and bake at 350°F. for 1 hour or until softened.

2. Place the broth and potatoes in a 3-quart saucepan and heat to a boil over medium-high heat. Reduce the heat to medium. Cover and cook for 10 minutes or until the potatoes are tender. Drain, reserving the broth.

3. Mash the potatoes with 1¼ **cups** of the broth, **2 or 3 cloves** of roasted garlic* and chives, if desired. Add additional broth, if needed, until desired consistency is reached.

*Leftover roasted garlic is perfect for garlic toast, meat gravy, soups, etc.

hearty old fashioned vegetable soup

prep 20 minutes | **cook** 5 minutes | **makes** 2 servings

- 1 **can (10½ ounces) Campbell's® Condensed Old Fashioned Vegetable Soup**
- 1 **soup can water**
- 1 **can (about 8 ounces) stewed tomatoes**
- ¾ **cup corkscrew-shaped pasta (rotini), cooked and drained**
  Grated Parmesan cheese

Heat the soup, water, tomatoes and pasta in a 1-quart saucepan over medium-high heat until the mixture is hot and bubbling. Serve with the cheese.

meatloaf casserole

prep 10 minutes | **bake** 20 minutes | **makes** 4 servings

- 1 **pound ground beef**
- 1 **clove garlic, minced**
- 1 **can (10¾ ounces) Campbell's® Condensed Vegetable Soup**
- 1 **can (10¾ ounces) Campbell's® Condensed Golden Mushroom Soup**
- 1 **tablespoon Worcestershire sauce**
- 2 **cups water**
- 3 **tablespoons butter**
- ¾ **cup milk**
- 2 **cups instant mashed potato flakes *or* buds**

1. Cook beef and garlic in 10-inch skillet over medium-high heat until well browned, stirring to separate the meat. Pour off any fat.

2. Stir beef, vegetable soup, ½ **can** mushroom soup and Worcestershire in 12×8-inch shallow baking dish.

3. Heat remaining mushroom soup, water and butter in 2-quart saucepan over high heat to a boil. Remove from heat. Stir in milk. Slowly stir in potatoes. Spoon potatoes around outer edge of casserole.

4. Bake at 400°F. for 20 minutes or until hot.

classic lasagna

prep 30 minutes | **bake** 30 minutes | **stand** 10 minutes | **makes** 12 servings

- 3 **cups ricotta cheese**
- 12 **ounces shredded mozzarella cheese (about 3 cups)**
- ¾ **cup grated Parmesan cheese**
- 2 **eggs**
- 1 **pound ground beef**
- 1 **jar (45 ounces) Prego® Three Cheese Italian Sauce**
- 12 **lasagna noodles, cooked and drained**

1. Stir the ricotta cheese, mozzarella cheese, ½ **cup** Parmesan cheese and eggs in a medium bowl and set it aside.

2. In a 3-quart saucepan over medium-high heat, cook the beef until well browned, stirring often to separate the meat. Pour off any fat. Stir the Italian sauce in the saucepan.

3. Spoon **1 cup** meat mixture in **each** of two 2-quart shallow baking dishes. Top **each** with **2** lasagna noodles and **about 1¼ cups** cheese mixture. Repeat the layers. Top with the remaining **2** lasagna noodles, remaining meat mixture and the Parmesan cheese.

4. Bake at 400°F. for 30 minutes or until hot and bubbling. Let stand for 10 minutes.

tip To freeze, prepare lasagna but do not bake. Cover tightly with foil and freeze. Bake frozen lasagna, uncovered, at 350°F. for 1 hour 15 minutes or until hot. Or, refrigerate 24 hours to thaw. Bake thawed lasagna, uncovered, at 350°F. for 50 minutes or until hot. Let stand for 10 minutes.

ranchero enchilada casserole

prep 10 minutes | **bake** 25 minutes | **makes** 4 servings

- 1 can (10¾ ounces) Campbell's® Condensed Cream of Chicken Soup (Regular *or* 98% Fat Free)
- ½ cup water
- 1 teaspoon chili powder
- ½ teaspoon garlic powder
- 1 can (about 4 ounces) chopped green chiles
- ¼ cup rinsed, drained canned black beans
- 3 tablespoons tomato paste
- 2 tablespoons chopped red peppers
- 2 cups cubed cooked chicken
- 4 flour tortillas (8-inch) *or* 6 corn tortillas (6-inch), cut into strips
- ½ cup shredded Cheddar cheese

1. Stir the soup, water, chili powder, garlic powder, chiles, beans, tomato paste, red pepper, chicken and tortillas in a large bowl.

2. Spoon the chicken mixture into a 2-quart shallow baking dish. Top with the cheese. Cover the baking dish.

3. Bake at 350°F. for 25 minutes or until the mixture is hot and bubbling.

chicken tortilla soup

prep 15 minutes | **bake** 15 minutes | **cook** 10 minutes | **makes** 4 servings

- 4 **corn tortillas (6-inch), cut into strips**
- 3½ **cups Swanson® Chicken Broth (Regular, Natural Goodness® _or_ Certified Organic)**
- ½ **cup Pace® Picante Sauce**
- 1 **teaspoon garlic powder**
- 1 **can (14.5 ounces) whole peeled tomatoes, cut up**
- 2 **medium carrots, shredded (about 1 cup)**
- 1½ **cups chopped cooked chicken**

1. Heat the oven to 400°F. Place the tortilla strips on a baking sheet.

2. Bake for 15 minutes or until golden.

3. Heat the broth, picante sauce, garlic powder, tomatoes and carrots in a 2-quart saucepan. Heat over medium-high heat to a boil. Reduce the heat to low. Cook for 5 minutes.

4. Stir the chicken in the saucepan and cook until the mixture is hot and bubbling. Top with the tortilla strips before serving.

tip _For 1½ **cups** chopped cooked chicken, heat **4 cups** water in a 2-quart saucepan over medium heat to a boil. Add ¾ **pound** skinless, boneless chicken breast halves **or** thighs, cut into cubes, and cook for 5 minutes or until the chicken is cooked through. Drain the chicken well in a colander._

tomato soup & grilled cheese sandwich

prep 5 minutes I **cook** 5 minutes I **makes** 4 servings

- 2 **cans (10¾ ounces *each*) Campbell's® Condensed Tomato Soup**
- 2 **cans water**
- 8 **teaspoons butter, softened**
- 8 **slices Pepperidge Farm® White Sandwich Bread**
- 8 **slices process American cheese**

1. Heat the soup and water in a 1-quart saucepan over medium heat until the mixture is hot and bubbling, stirring occasionally.

2. Spread the butter on the bread slices.

3. Place **4** bread slices, butter-side down, into a 12-inch skillet. Top with the cheese slices and remaining bread slices, butter-side up. Cook over medium heat until the sandwiches are lightly browned on both sides and the cheese is melted.

country chicken casserole

prep 10 minutes I **bake** 25 minutes I **makes** 5 servings

- 1 **can (10¾ ounces) Campbell's® Condensed Cream of Celery Soup (Regular *or* 98% Fat Free)**
- 1 **can (10¾ ounces) Campbell's® Condensed Cream of Potato Soup**
- 1 **cup milk**
- ¼ **teaspoon dried thyme leaves, crushed**
- ⅛ **teaspoon ground black pepper**
- 4 **cups cooked cut-up vegetables***
- 2 **cups cubed cooked chicken *or* turkey**
- 4 **cups prepared Pepperidge Farm® Herb Seasoned Stuffing**

Use a combination of cut green beans and sliced carrots.

1. Stir the soups, milk, thyme, black pepper, vegetables and chicken in a 3-quart shallow baking dish. Top with the stuffing.

2. Bake at 400°F. for 25 minutes or until the stuffing is golden brown.

lightened up beef & vegetable stir-fry

prep 25 minutes I **cook** 25 minutes I **makes** 4 servings

 Vegetable cooking spray
1 pound boneless beef sirloin steak, ¾-inch thick (about 1 pound), sliced into very thin strips
2 cups broccoli florets
6 ounces sliced mushrooms (about 2 cups)
2 medium onions, cut into wedges
½ teaspoon garlic powder *or* 2 cloves garlic, minced
1 can (10¾ ounces) Campbell's® Healthy Request® Condensed Cream of Mushroom Soup
½ cup water
1 tablespoon low-sodium soy sauce
1 cup regular long-grain white rice, cooked according to package directions without salt (about 3 cups)

1. Spray a 12-inch skillet with the cooking spray and heat over medium-high heat for 1 minute. Add the beef and cook until well browned, stirring often. Remove the beef from the skillet and set aside.

2. Remove the skillet from the heat and spray with the cooking spray. Add the broccoli, mushrooms, onion and garlic powder and cook until the vegetables are tender-crisp, stirring often.

3. Stir the soup, water and soy sauce in the skillet and heat to a boil. Return the beef to the skillet and cook until cooked through. Serve the beef mixture over the rice.

 To make slicing easier, freeze beef for 1 hour.

simply delicious meatloaf & gravy

prep 15 minutes | **bake** 1 hour | **stand** 10 minutes | **makes** 6 servings

1½ **pounds ground beef**
½ **cup Italian-seasoned dry bread crumbs**
1 **egg, beaten**
1 **can (10¾ ounces) Campbell's® Condensed Golden Mushroom Soup**
¼ **cup water**

1. Heat the oven to 350°F. Thoroughly mix the beef, bread crumbs and egg in a large bowl. Place the beef mixture into a shallow 3-quart baking pan and shape firmly into an 8×4-inch loaf.

2. Bake for 30 minutes. Spread ½ **can** soup over the meatloaf.

3. Bake for 30 minutes more or until the meatloaf is cooked through. Let the meatloaf stand for 10 minutes before slicing.

4. Heat **2 tablespoons** pan drippings, remaining soup and water in a 1-quart saucepan over medium heat until the mixture is hot and bubbling. Serve the gravy with the meatloaf.

chocolate velvet torte

thaw 40 minutes I **prep** 15 minutes I **bake** 20 minutes I **cool** 10 minutes I **chill** 2 hours
makes 8 servings

½ **of a 17.3-ounce package Pepperidge Farm® Puff Pastry Sheets (1 sheet), thawed**

16 **ounces semi-sweet chocolate, chopped**

1 **cup heavy cream**

1 **egg yolk**

2 **cups fresh raspberries *or* strawberries**

1. Heat the oven to 425°F.

2. Unfold the pastry sheet on a lightly floured surface. Roll the pastry sheet into a 12-inch square. Cut off the corners to make a circle. Press the pastry into the bottom and up the sides of a 9-inch springform pan. Prick the pastry with a fork.

3. Bake for 20 minutes or until the pastry is golden brown. Let the pastry cool in the pan on a wire rack for 10 minutes.

4. Heat and stir the chocolate and cream in a 1-quart heavy saucepan over low heat until the mixture is melted and smooth. Remove the saucepan from the heat. Stir some chocolate mixture into the egg yolk. Return the egg mixture to the remaining chocolate mixture. Cook and stir for 1 minute. Pour the chocolate mixture into the pastry crust. Cover and refrigerate for 2 hours or until firm. Top the torte with the raspberries.

tip *Stirring a bit of the warm chocolate mixture into the egg before adding it to the rest of the chocolate is an important step called "tempering." Tempering keeps the egg from scrambling and the filling smooth.*

meatloaf with roasted garlic potatoes

prep 20 minutes | **bake** 1 hour | **makes** 6 servings

- 1 cup Pace® Picante Sauce
- 1½ pounds ground beef
- 1 cup fresh bread crumbs
- 1 egg, beaten
- 2 tablespoons chopped fresh parsley **or** 2 teaspoons dried parsley flakes
- 1 tablespoon Worcestershire sauce
- 4 cloves garlic, minced **or** ½ teaspoon garlic powder
- 2 tablespoons vegetable oil
- 4 medium potatoes (about 1¼ pounds), **each** cut into **8** wedges
  Paprika

1. Thoroughly mix ½ **cup** picante sauce, beef, bread crumbs, egg, parsley, Worcestershire and ½ the garlic in a large bowl. Firmly shape into 8×4-inch loaf in a baking pan.

2. Mix the oil and remaining garlic. Toss the potatoes with the oil mixture until they're evenly coated. Sprinkle with the paprika. Arrange the potatoes around the meatloaf.

3. Bake at 350°F. for 1 hour or until meatloaf is cooked through. Pour the remaining picante sauce over the meatloaf before serving.

chili & rice

prep 10 minutes | **cook** 25 minutes | **makes** 4 servings

- ¾ **pound ground beef (85% lean)**
- 1 **medium onion, chopped (about ½ cup)**
- 1 **tablespoon chili powder**
- 1 **can (10¾ ounces) Campbell's® Healthy Request® Condensed Tomato Soup**
- ¼ **cup water**
- 1 **teaspoon vinegar**
- 1 **can (about 15 ounces) kidney beans, rinsed and drained**
- 4 **cups hot cooked regular long-grain white rice, cooked without salt**

1. Cook the beef, onion and chili powder in a 10-inch skillet over medium-high heat until the beef is well browned, stirring often. Pour off any fat.

2. Stir the soup, water, vinegar and beans in the skillet and heat to a boil. Reduce the heat to low. Cook for 10 minutes or until the mixture is hot and bubbling. Serve the beef mixture over the rice.

> **tip** *This dish is delicious served topped with shredded reduced-fat Cheddar cheese.*

simple salisbury steak

prep 15 minutes **I** **cook** 20 minutes **I** **makes** 4 servings

- 1 **pound ground beef**
- ⅓ **cup dry bread crumbs**
- 1 **small onion, finely chopped (about ¼ cup)**
- 1 **egg, beaten**
- 2 **tablespoons water**
- 1 **tablespoon vegetable oil**
- 1 **can (10¼ ounces) Campbell's® Beef Gravy**

1. Thoroughly mix the beef, bread crumbs, onion, egg and water in a medium bowl and shape firmly into **4** oval patties, ½ inch thick.

2. Heat the oil in a 10-inch skillet over medium-high heat. Add the patties and cook for 10 minutes or until well browned on both sides. Pour off any fat.

3. Add the gravy and heat to a boil. Reduce the heat to low. Cover and cook for 10 minutes or until the patties are cooked through.

chicken corn chowder

prep 10 minutes | **cook** 5 minutes | **makes** 4 servings

1 **can (10¾ ounces) Campbell's® Condensed Cream of Celery Soup (Regular *or* 98% Fat Free)**

1 **soup can milk**

½ **cup Pace® Picante Sauce**

1 **can (about 8 ounces) whole kernel corn, drained**

1 **cup cubed cooked chicken *or* turkey**

4 **slices bacon, cooked and crumbled**

Shredded Cheddar cheese

Sliced green onion

1. Heat the soup, milk, picante sauce, corn, chicken and bacon in a 3-quart saucepan over medium heat until the mixture is hot and bubbling, stirring occasionally.

2. Sprinkle with the cheese and onion. Drizzle **each** serving with additional picante sauce.

tip *Substitute Campbell's® Condensed Cream of Chicken Soup for the Cream of Celery.*

roasted tomato & barley soup

prep 10 minutes | **roast** 25 minutes | **cook** 40 minutes | **makes** 8 servings

- **1** can (about 28 ounces) diced tomatoes, undrained
- **2** large onions, diced (about 2 cups)
- **2** cloves garlic, minced
- **2** tablespoons olive oil
- **4** cups Swanson® Chicken Broth (Regular, Natural Goodness® *or* Certified Organic)
- **2** stalks celery, diced (about 1 cup)
- **½** cup *uncooked* pearl barley
- **2** tablespoons chopped fresh parsley

1. Heat the oven to 425°F. Drain the tomatoes, reserving the juice. Place the tomatoes, onions and garlic into a 17×11-inch roasting pan. Pour the oil over the vegetables and toss to coat. Roast for 25 minutes.

2. Place the roasted vegetables into a 3-quart saucepan. Stir in the reserved tomato juice, broth, celery and barley and heat to a boil. Reduce the heat to low. Cover and cook for 35 minutes or until the barley is tender. Stir in the parsley.

skillet cheesy chicken & rice

prep 5 minutes I **cook** 35 minutes I **makes** 4 servings

- 1 **tablespoon vegetable oil**
- 1¼ **pounds skinless, boneless chicken breast halves**
- 1 **can (10¾ ounces) Campbell's® Condensed Cream of Chicken Soup (Regular *or* 98% Fat Free)**
- 1½ **cups water**
- ½ **teaspoon onion powder**
- ¼ **teaspoon ground black pepper**
- 1 **cup *uncooked* regular long-grain white rice**
- 2 **cups frozen mixed vegetables**
- ½ **cup shredded Cheddar cheese**

1. Heat the oil in a 12-inch skillet over medium-high heat. Add the chicken and cook for 10 minutes or until well browned on both sides. Remove the chicken from the skillet.

2. Stir the soup, water, onion powder, black pepper and rice in the skillet and heat to a boil. Reduce the heat to low. Cover and cook for 15 minutes, stirring once halfway through the cooking time.

3. Stir in the vegetables. Return the chicken to the skillet. Sprinkle with the cheese. Cover and cook for 5 minutes or until the chicken is cooked through and the rice is tender.

slow cooker hearty beef stew

prep 20 minutes I **cook** 10 hours 15 minutes I **makes** 6 servings

1½ pounds beef for stew, cut into 1-inch pieces

Ground black pepper

¼ cup all-purpose flour

1 tablespoon vegetable oil

1 pound medium potatoes, cut into cubes (about 3 cups)

4 medium carrots, sliced (about 2 cups)

2 medium onions, cut into wedges

4 cloves garlic, minced

3¼ cups Swanson® Beef Stock

1 tablespoon Worcestershire sauce

1 teaspoon dried thyme leaves, crushed

1 bay leaf

1 cup thawed frozen peas

1. Season the beef with the black pepper. Coat the beef with **2 tablespoons** of the flour. Heat the oil in a 10-inch skillet over medium-high heat. Add the beef in 2 batches and cook until well browned, stirring often.

2. Place the potatoes, carrots, onions and garlic into a 5-quart slow cooker. Top with the beef. Add **3 cups** of the stock, Worcestershire, thyme and bay leaf.

3. Cover and cook on LOW for 10 to 11 hours* or until the beef is fork-tender. Remove and discard the bay leaf.

4. Stir the remaining flour and stock in a small bowl until the mixture is smooth. Stir the flour mixture and peas in the cooker. Increase the heat to HIGH. Cover and cook for 15 minutes or until the mixture boils and thickens.

Or on HIGH for 5 to 6 hours.

sensational chicken noodle soup

prep 5 minutes | **cook** 25 minutes | **makes** 4 servings

- 4 cups Swanson® Chicken Broth (Regular, Natural Goodness® **or** Certified Organic)
  Generous dash ground black pepper
- 1 medium carrot, sliced (about ½ cup)
- 1 stalk celery, sliced (about ½ cup)
- ½ cup **uncooked** extra-wide egg noodles
- 1 cup shredded cooked chicken **or** turkey

1. Heat the broth, black pepper, carrot and celery in a 2-quart saucepan over medium-high heat to a boil.

2. Stir the noodles and chicken into the saucepan. Reduce the heat to medium. Cook for 10 minutes or until the noodles are tender.

Asian Soup: Add **2** green onions cut into ½-inch pieces, **1 clove** garlic, minced, **1 teaspoon** ground ginger and **2 teaspoons** soy sauce. Substitute **uncooked** curly Asian noodles for egg noodles.

Mexican Soup: Add ½ cup Pace® Chunky Salsa, **1 clove** garlic, minced, **1 cup** rinsed and drained black beans and ½ **teaspoon** chili powder. Substitute **2** corn tortillas (4 or 6-inch) cut into thin strips for the noodles, adding them just before serving.

Italian Tortellini Soup: Add **1 can** (about 14.5 ounces) diced tomatoes, drained, **1 clove** garlic, minced, **1 teaspoon** dried Italian seasoning, crushed, and **1 cup** spinach leaves. Substitute ½ **cup** frozen cheese tortellini for egg noodles. Serve with grated Parmesan cheese.

slow-cooked pulled pork sandwiches

prep 15 minutes I **cook** 8 hours I **stand** 10 minutes I **makes** 12 servings

  1   **tablespoon vegetable oil**
  1   **boneless pork shoulder roast (3½ to 4 pounds), netted _or_ tied**
  1   **can (10½ ounces) Campbell's® Condensed French Onion Soup**
  1   **cup ketchup**
  ¼   **cup cider vinegar**
  3   **tablespoons packed brown sugar**
 12   **Pepperidge Farm® Sandwich Buns, split**

1. Heat the oil in a 10-inch skillet over medium-high heat. Add the pork and cook until well browned on all sides.

2. Stir the soup, ketchup, vinegar and brown sugar in a 5-quart slow cooker. Add the pork and turn to coat.

3. Cover and cook on LOW for 8 to 9 hours* or until the pork is fork-tender.

4. Remove the pork from the cooker to a cutting board and let stand for 10 minutes. Using 2 forks, shred the pork. Return the pork to the cooker.

5. Spoon the pork and sauce mixture on the buns.

Or on HIGH for 4 to 5 hours.

easy mushroom soup

prep 15 minutes | **cook** 25 minutes | **makes** 4 servings

1¾ cups Swanson® 50% Less Sodium Beef Broth

1¾ cups Swanson® Natural Goodness® Chicken Broth

⅛ teaspoon ground black pepper

⅛ teaspoon dried rosemary leaves, crushed

2 cups sliced fresh mushrooms (about 8 ounces)

¼ cup thinly sliced carrot

¼ cup finely chopped onion

¼ cup sliced celery

¼ cup fresh *or* frozen peas

1 tablespoon sliced green onion

1. Heat the beef broth, chicken broth, black pepper, rosemary, mushrooms, carrots, onion, celery and peas in a 4-quart saucepan over medium heat to a boil. Reduce the heat to low. Cover and cook for 15 minutes.

2. Add the green onion. Cook for 5 minutes or until the vegetables are tender.

spicy barbecued chicken

prep 10 minutes | **bake** 1 hour | **makes** 4 servings

4 bone-in chicken breast halves (about 2 pounds), skin removed

1 can (10¾ ounces) Campbell's® Healthy Request® Condensed Tomato Soup

2 tablespoons packed brown sugar

3 tablespoons vinegar

1 tablespoon Worcestershire sauce

¼ teaspoon garlic powder

2 teaspoons Louisiana-style hot sauce (optional)

4 cups hot cooked rice, cooked without salt

1. Place the chicken in a 2-quart shallow baking dish and bake at 375°F. for 30 minutes.

2. Stir the soup, brown sugar, vinegar, Worcestershire, garlic powder and hot sauce, if desired, in a small bowl. Spoon the soup mixture over the chicken and bake for 30 minutes or until the chicken is cooked through. Remove the chicken from the dish and stir the sauce. Serve the chicken and sauce with the rice.

best of the season

Embrace the change of the seasons

with delicious inspiration.

orange beef steak

prep 10 minutes | **broil** 25 minutes | **makes** 6 servings

1 jar (12 ounces) Campbell's® Slow Roast Beef Gravy
1 tablespoon grated orange zest
2 tablespoons orange juice
½ teaspoon garlic powder **or** 2 cloves garlic, minced
1 boneless beef top round steak, 1½-inch thick (about 1½ pounds)

1. Stir the gravy, orange zest, orange juice and garlic powder in a 1-quart saucepan.

2. Heat the broiler. Place the beef on a rack in a broiler pan. Broil 4 inches from the heat for 25 minutes for medium or to desired doneness, turning the beef over halfway through cooking and brushing often with the gravy mixture. Thinly slice the beef.

3. Heat the remaining gravy mixture over medium-high heat to a boil. Serve the gravy mixture with the beef.

seasonal favorites

Focus on the season and the availability of foods whenever you can. Not only will you get the freshest ingredients available, but you'll save money too—fruits and vegetables in season are often abundant and cheaper as a result.

■ *Check out local farmers' markets,* both outdoors and indoors, in your community to see what's hot right now.

■ *Buy produce in season* for the best price, flavor and nutrition.

■ *Experiment with different recipes,* swap out ingredients to suit your taste buds, and enjoy the beauty and taste every season has to offer.

herb roasted turkey

prep 15 minutes I **roast** 4 hours I **stand** 10 minutes I **makes** 12 servings

1 ¾ cups Swanson® Chicken Stock

  3 tablespoons lemon juice

  1 teaspoon dried basil leaves, crushed

  1 teaspoon dried thyme leaves, crushed

 ⅛ teaspoon ground black pepper

     12- to 14-pound turkey

  2 cans (14½ ounces *each*) Campbell's® Turkey Gravy

1. Stir the stock, lemon juice, basil, thyme and black pepper in a small bowl.

2. Roast the turkey according to the package directions, basting occasionally with the stock mixture during cooking. Let the turkey stand for 10 minutes before slicing. Discard any remaining stock mixture.

3. Heat the gravy in a 1-quart saucepan over medium heat until hot and bubbling. Serve with the turkey.

tip The turkey may be roasted in an oven bag, following the package directions, pouring the stock mixture over the turkey before closing the bag.

ratatouille tart

thaw 40 minutes | **prep** 50 minutes | **bake** 1 hour 15 minutes | **makes** 8 servings

- ½ of a 17.3-ounce package Pepperidge Farm® Puff Pastry Sheets (1 sheet), thawed
- ¼ cup olive oil
- 1 medium eggplant, peeled and cut into ½-inch cubes (about 5½ cups)
- 1 medium onion, chopped (about ½ cup)
- 3 cloves garlic, minced
- 3 medium zucchini, peeled and diced (about 2 cups)
- 1 medium green pepper, diced (about 1 cup)
- 1 teaspoon dried oregano leaves, crushed
- ½ teaspoon ground black pepper
- 1 can (8 ounces) tomato sauce
- 1 tablespoon tomato paste
- 1 tablespoon red wine vinegar
- All-purpose flour
- 5 small Italian plum tomatoes, sliced
- 2 small zucchini, sliced (about 2 cups)
- 1 tablespoon dry bread crumbs

1. Heat the oven to 350°F.

2. Heat the oil in a 12-inch skillet over medium heat. Add the eggplant, onion and garlic and cook for 5 minutes, stirring occasionally. Add the zucchini and green pepper. Cook until the vegetables are tender. Season with the oregano and black pepper.

3. Stir the tomato sauce, tomato paste and vinegar in the skillet. Cook for 5 minutes.

4. Sprinkle the flour on the work surface. Unfold the pastry sheet on the work surface. Roll the pastry sheet into a 12-inch square. Cut off the corners to make a circle. Press the pastry into the bottom and up the sides of a 10-inch tart pan with a removable bottom. Trim off the excess pastry. Prick the pastry thoroughly with a fork. Place a piece of aluminum foil onto the pastry. Add pie weights or dried beans.

5. Bake for 15 minutes or until the pastry is golden brown. Remove the foil and weights. Let the pastry cool in the pan on a wire rack for 10 minutes.

6. Spoon the eggplant mixture into the crust. Arrange the tomatoes and zucchini in concentric circles to completely cover the eggplant mixture. Sprinkle with the bread crumbs.

7. Bake for 1 hour or until the zucchini and tomatoes are browned.

Ratatouille-Stuffed Portobello Mushrooms: Omit the puff pastry. Prepare the eggplant filling as directed above. Cook **5** to **6** portobello mushrooms top-side down in **1 tablespoon** olive oil in a 12-inch skillet over medium-high heat for 10 minutes or until golden brown. Turn over and cook about 5 minutes more or until tender. Divide the eggplant mixture among the mushrooms. Sprinkle with ¼ **cup** chopped fresh parsley.

roasted orange cranberry sauce

prep 5 minutes | **roast** 25 minutes | **chill** 2 hours | **makes** 10 servings

- 1 **package (12 ounces) fresh *or* frozen cranberries**
- 1 **cup coarsely chopped orange**
- 1 **cup packed brown sugar**
- 1 **teaspoon ground cinnamon**
- 1¾ **cups Swanson® Chicken Broth (Regular, Natural Goodness® *or* Certified Organic)**

1. Stir cranberries, orange, brown sugar and cinnamon in a 17×15-inch roasting pan. Pour the broth over the fruit mixture.

2. Roast at 450°F. for 25 minutes or until the mixture thickens. Pour into a medium bowl. Cover and refrigerate for at least 2 hours.

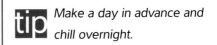
Make a day in advance and chill overnight.

meatloaf with a twist

prep 10 minutes | **bake** 1 hour | **cook** 5 minutes | **makes** 6 servings

- 1 **can (10¼ ounces) Campbell's® Mushroom Gravy**
- 1½ **pounds ground beef**
- ½ **cup dry bread crumbs**
- 1 **egg, beaten**
- ½ **cup Pace® Picante Sauce**

1. Thoroughly mix ¼ **cup** gravy, beef, bread crumbs, egg and ¼ **cup** picante sauce in a large bowl. Shape the beef mixture **firmly** into an 8×4-inch loaf in a baking pan.

2. Bake at 350°F. for 1 hour or until the meatloaf is cooked through.

3. Heat **2 tablespoons** drippings, the remaining gravy and the remaining picante sauce in a 1-quart saucepan over medium heat until hot and bubbling. Serve the gravy mixture with the meatloaf.

sweet potato pie

prep 15 minutes | **bake** 1 hour | **cool** 3 hours | **makes** 8 servings

- 3 large sweet potatoes, peeled and cut into cubes (about 3 cups)
- ¼ cup heavy cream
- 1 can (10¾ ounces) Campbell's® Condensed Tomato Soup
- 1 cup packed brown sugar
- 3 eggs
- 1 teaspoon vanilla extract
- ½ teaspoon ground cinnamon
- ½ teaspoon ground nutmeg
- 1 (9-inch) frozen pie crust

1. Heat the oven to 350°F.

2. Place potatoes into a 3-quart saucepan and add water to cover. Heat over medium-high heat to a boil. Reduce the heat to low. Cover and cook for 10 minutes or until the potatoes are tender. Drain the potatoes well in a colander.

3. Place the potatoes and heavy cream into a large bowl. Beat with an electric mixer on medium speed until the mixture is fluffy. Beat in the soup, brown sugar, eggs, vanilla extract, cinnamon and nutmeg. Pour the potato mixture into the pie crust and place onto a baking sheet.

4. Bake for 1 hour or until set. Cool the pie in the pan on a wire rack about 3 hours.

 Substitute 1¾ cups drained and mashed canned sweet potatoes for the fresh mashed sweet potatoes.

roasted turkey breast with herbed au jus

prep 10 minutes | **cook** 1 hour 45 minutes | **stand** 10 minutes | **makes** 6 servings

1 **tablespoon all-purpose flour**
1 **plastic oven bag, turkey size**
1 **cup Swanson® Chicken Stock**
½ **teaspoon *each* ground dried sage leaves, dried rosemary *and* thyme leaves, crushed**
   6- to 8-pound bone-in turkey breast
½ **teaspoon paprika (optional)**
1 **can (10½ ounces) Campbell's® Turkey Gravy**

1. Add the flour to the oven bag. Close and shake the bag to distribute the flour. Place the bag in a 13×9×2-inch baking pan. Add the stock, sage, rosemary and thyme to the bag. Squeeze the bag to blend in the flour.

2. Rinse the turkey with cold water and pat dry with a paper towel. Sprinkle the turkey evenly with the paprika, if desired. Add the turkey to the bag. Close the bag with the nylon tie. Cut **6** (½-inch) slits in the top of the bag. Insert a meat thermometer through a slit in the bag into the thickest part of the meat, making sure the thermometer is not touching the bone.

3. Roast the turkey at 350°F. for 1¾ to 2 hours*. Begin checking for doneness after 1½ hours of roasting time. Let the turkey stand for 10 minutes before slicing.

4. Remove the turkey from the bag. Pour the turkey liquid from bag into large cup. Skim off the fat.

5. Heat the turkey liquid and gravy in a 2-quart saucepan over medium heat until hot. Serve with the turkey.

*The internal temperature of the turkey should reach 170°F.

tomato walnut pesto penne

prep 15 minutes I **cook** 5 minutes I **makes** 8 servings

¼ cup walnuts, toasted

2 cloves garlic

½ cup loosely-packed fresh basil leaves

4 cups loosely-packed fresh baby spinach

3 cups Prego® Heart Smart Ricotta Parmesan Italian Sauce

1 package (16 ounces) penne pasta, cooked and drained (about 9 cups)

2 tablespoons grated Parmesan cheese (optional)

1. Place the walnuts and garlic into a food processor or blender. Cover and process until the mixture is finely chopped. Add the basil and spinach and process until the mixture forms a smooth paste.

2. Heat the Italian sauce and the walnut mixture in a 2-quart saucepan over medium heat for 5 minutes or until the mixture is hot and bubbling.

3. Toss the sauce mixture with the pasta. Sprinkle with the cheese.

tip *If you're using a blender, reserve ¼ cup pasta water and add it to the walnut mixture to help the blending.*

graveyard cupcakes

prep 20 minutes | **makes** 24 servings

24 Pepperidge Farm® Milano® Cookies **and/or** Brussels® Distinctive Cookies **and/or** Old Fashioned Homestyle Sugar Cookies

4 tubes (4.25 ounces **each**) decorating icing (black, white, orange **and** green) **or** 4 tubes (.68 ounces **each**) decorating gel (black, white, orange **and** green)

Orange-colored sugar crystals

24 store-purchased frosted cupcakes

1. Decorate the Milano® cookies using the black and white icing to resemble tombstones and ghosts.

2. Decorate the Brussels® or Sugar cookies using the orange and green icing and sugar crystals to resemble pumpkins and spider webs.

3. Press the decorated cookies into the tops of the cupcakes.

ratatouille soup

prep 15 minutes | **cook** 35 minutes | **makes** 5 servings

1 pound ground beef

1 jar (24 ounces) Prego® Traditional Italian Sauce **or** Tomato, Basil & Garlic Italian Sauce

1 can (10½ ounces) Campbell's® Condensed Beef Broth

2 cups water

1 small eggplant, cut into cubes (about 3½ cups)

1 medium zucchini, cut into cubes (about 1½ cups)

1 large green pepper, chopped (about 1 cup)

½ cup **uncooked** elbow macaroni

1. Cook the beef in a 4-quart saucepot over medium-high heat until well browned, stirring often to separate the meat. Pour off any fat.

2. Stir the Italian sauce, broth, water, eggplant, zucchini and pepper in the saucepot and heat to a boil over medium-high heat. Reduce the heat to low. Cover and cook for 15 minutes.

3. Stir the macaroni in the saucepot. Increase the heat to medium and cook for 10 minutes or until the macaroni is tender, stirring occasionally.

cranberry apple bread pudding

prep 10 minutes I **stand** 20 minutes I **bake** 40 minutes I **makes** 6 servings

Vegetable cooking spray

4 cups Pepperidge Farm® Cubed Herb Seasoned Stuffing **or** Herb Seasoned Stuffing

¾ cup dried cranberries

4 eggs

2½ cups milk

½ cup sugar

½ cup chunky sweetened applesauce

1 teaspoon vanilla extract

Brandied Butter Sauce

1. Heat the oven to 350°F. Spray a 2-quart shallow baking dish with the cooking spray. Place the stuffing into the dish. Sprinkle the cranberries over the stuffing.

2. Beat the eggs, milk, sugar, applesauce and vanilla extract in a medium bowl with a fork or whisk. Pour the milk mixture over the stuffing mixture. Stir and press the stuffing mixture into the milk mixture to coat. Let stand for 20 minutes.

3. Bake for 40 minutes or until a knife inserted in the center comes out clean. Serve warm with the *Brandied Butter Sauce.*

Brandied Butter Sauce: Heat ½ **cup** (1 stick) butter in a 1-quart saucepan over medium heat until the butter is melted. Add ½ **cup** packed light brown sugar. Cook and stir until the sugar dissolves and the mixture is hot and bubbling. Remove the saucepan from the heat. Whisk in **2 tablespoons** brandy. Makes 1 cup.

tip *Both the bread pudding and the Brandied Butter Sauce can be prepared in advance. Prepare the pudding as directed but do not bake. Prepare the sauce as directed above. Cover the pudding and the sauce and refrigerate for up to 24 hours. Bake the pudding as directed above. Microwave the sauce in a microwavable bowl on MEDIUM for 1 minute or until hot.*

spicy turkey, corn and zucchini skillet

prep 15 minutes I **cook** 20 minutes I **makes** 4 servings

- 2 **teaspoons olive oil**
- 2 **cloves garlic, chopped**
- 1 **onion, finely chopped (about 1 cup)**
- 2 **medium zucchini, finely chopped (about 3 cups)**
- 1 **pound lean ground turkey**
- 2 **medium tomatoes, chopped (about 2 cups)**
- 1 **carton (18.3 ounces) Campbell's® V8® Southwestern Corn Soup**
- 2 **cups baked tortilla chips (fat free)**
- 2 **ounces fat free shredded Cheddar cheese (about ½ cup)**
  Chopped fresh cilantro leaves

1. Heat the oil in a 10-inch nonstick skillet over medium-high heat. Add the garlic, onion and zucchini and cook for 5 minutes. Add the turkey and cook until well browned, stirring often to separate the meat. Stir the tomatoes in the skillet and cook for 2 minutes.

2. Stir the soup in the skillet and heat to a boil. Reduce the heat to low. Cook for 5 minutes or until the turkey mixture is hot and bubbling. Top with the tortilla chips and cheese. Garnish with the cilantro.

game-winning drumsticks

prep 10 minutes I **marinate** 4 hours I **bake** 1 hour I **makes** 6 servings

- 15 chicken drumsticks (about 4 pounds)
- 1¾ cups Swanson® Chicken Stock
- ½ cup Dijon–style mustard
- ⅓ cup Italian–seasoned dry bread crumbs

1. Place the chicken in a single layer into a 15×10-inch disposable foil pan.

2. Stir the stock and mustard in a small bowl. Pour the stock mixture over the chicken and turn to coat. Sprinkle the bread crumbs over the chicken. Cover the pan and refrigerate for 4 hours.

3. Bake at 375°F. for 1 hour or until the chicken is cooked through. Serve hot or at room temperature.

tip *Keep disposable foil pans on hand for convenience to tote casseroles to friends' parties **or** covered-dish suppers. As a safety reminder, be sure to support the bottom of the filled pan when handling them in and out of the oven.*

baked apple cranberry stuffing

prep 20 minutes | **bake** 35 minutes | **makes** 11 servings

Non-stick aluminum foil
3 **tablespoons butter**
4 **stalks celery, sliced (about 2 cups)**
1 **large onion, chopped (about 1 cup)**
2¼ **cups Swanson® Chicken Broth (Regular, Natural Goodness® *or* Certified Organic)**
1 **medium Granny Smith apple, chopped**
1 **cup dried cranberries**
1 **package (12 ounces) Pepperidge Farm® Herb Seasoned Cubed Stuffing**

1. Heat the oven to 350°F. Line a 3-quart shallow baking pan with the foil, dull-side down.

2. Heat the butter in a 3-quart saucepan over medium heat. Add the celery and onion and cook until tender, stirring occasionally. Stir in the broth, apple and cranberries. Remove the saucepan from the heat. Add the stuffing and mix lightly. Spoon the stuffing mixture into the baking pan.

3. Bake for 35 minutes or until the stuffing mixture is hot.

citrus chicken and rice

prep 5 minutes I **cook** 35 minutes I **makes** 4 servings

- 4 skinless, boneless chicken breast halves (about 1 pound)
- 1¾ cups Swanson® Chicken Stock
- ¾ cup orange juice
- 1 medium onion, chopped (about ½ cup)
- 1 cup *uncooked* regular long-grain white rice
- 3 tablespoons chopped fresh parsley

1. Cook the chicken in a 10-inch nonstick skillet over medium-high heat for 10 minutes or until well browned on both sides. Remove the chicken from the skillet.

2. Stir the stock, orange juice, onion and rice in the skillet and heat to a boil. Reduce the heat to low. Cover and cook for 10 minutes.

3. Return the chicken to the skillet. Cover and cook for 10 minutes or until the chicken is cooked through and the rice is tender. Stir in the parsley.

tip *For a special touch, cook orange slices in a nonstick skillet over medium-high heat until lightly browned. Serve over the chicken.*

slow cooker fall harvest pork stew

prep 20 minutes I **cook** 7 hours I **makes** 8 servings

- 2 pounds boneless pork shoulder, cut into 2-inch pieces
- 1 can (10¾ ounces) Campbell's® Condensed French Onion Soup
- ½ cup apple cider *or* apple juice
- 3 large Granny Smith apples, cut into thick slices (about 3 cups)
- 3 cups butternut squash peeled, seeded and cut into 2-inch pieces
- 2 medium parsnips, peeled and cut into 1-inch pieces (about 2 cups)
- ½ teaspoon dried thyme leaves, crushed

1. Stir the pork, soup, cider, apples, squash, parsnips and thyme in a 6-quart slow cooker.

2. Cover and cook on LOW for 7 to 8 hours* or until the pork is fork-tender.

Or on HIGH for 4 to 5 hours.

tip *For thicker gravy, stir ¼ cup all-purpose flour and ½ cup water in a small bowl until the mixture is smooth. Stir the flour mixture in the cooker. Cover and cook on HIGH for 10 minutes or until the mixture boils and thickens.*

herb-simmered beef stew

prep 15 minutes | **cook** 1 hour 30 minutes | **makes** 6 servings

2 pounds beef for stew, cut into
    1-inch cubes

    Ground black pepper

2 tablespoons all-purpose flour

2 tablespoons olive oil

3 cups thickly-sliced mushrooms
    (about 8 ounces)

3 cloves garlic, minced

½ teaspoon dried marjoram leaves,
    crushed **or** 1½ teaspoons fresh
    marjoram leaves

½ teaspoon dried thyme leaves,
    crushed **or** 1½ teaspoons fresh
    thyme leaves

½ teaspoon dried rosemary leaves,
    crushed **or** 1½ teaspoons fresh
    rosemary leaves

1 bay leaf

1¾ cups Swanson® Beef Stock

3 cups fresh **or** frozen whole baby
    carrots

12 whole small red potatoes

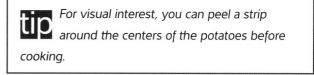

tip *For visual interest, you can peel a strip around the centers of the potatoes before cooking.*

1. Season the beef with the black pepper. Coat the beef with the flour.

2. Heat the oil in a 6-quart saucepot over medium-high heat. Add the beef in 2 batches and cook until well browned, stirring often. Pour off any fat.

3. Add the mushrooms, garlic, herbs and bay leaf to the saucepot and cook until the mushrooms are tender. Stir in the stock and heat to a boil. Reduce the heat to low. Cover and cook for 45 minutes.

4. Increase the heat to medium-high. Stir in the carrots and potatoes and heat to a boil. Reduce the heat to low. Cover and cook for 30 minutes or until the beef is fork-tender. Remove and discard the bay leaf.

twice-baked squash medley

prep 30 minutes | **bake** 1 hour 30 minutes | **makes** 8 servings

- 3 spaghetti squash (about 1½ pounds **each**)
- ½ teaspoon ground black pepper
- 2 cups chopped pecans
- 1 cup raisins
- ¼ cup packed brown sugar
- 1 tablespoon pumpkin pie spice
- 8 acorn squash (about 1 pound **each**)
- 24 Pepperidge Farm® Golden Butter Distinctive Crackers, crushed (about 1 cup)
- 4 tablespoons butter (½ stick), melted

1. Heat the oven to 350°F.

2. Cut **each** spaghetti squash in half lengthwise. Scoop out and discard the seeds. Sprinkle the inside cavity of each squash with black pepper and place them cut-side down in a 17×11-inch roasting pan.

3. Bake for 45 minutes or until the squash is fork-tender.

4. Scrape the squash with a fork to separate the spaghetti-like strands and place the strands in a large bowl. Stir in the pecans, raisins, brown sugar and pumpkin pie spice.

5. Cut off the "tops" of the acorn squash, about 1 inch from the stem end and reserve. Scoop out the seeds and discard. Cut a small portion off the bottom of each squash to make a flat base. Place the squash shells in the roasting pan.

6. Spoon the spaghetti squash mixture evenly into the cavities of each acorn squash. Stir the cracker crumbs and butter in a small bowl with a fork. Sprinkle the crumbs evenly over the squash mixture.

7. Bake for 45 minutes or until the mixture is heated through. Place the reserved squash "tops" on a baking sheet and bake for the last 5 minutes of baking time. Top each squash with an acorn "top."

baked eyeballs casserole

prep 15 minutes I **bake** 25 minutes I **stand** 10 minutes I **makes** 8 servings

    Vegetable cooking spray

1 **jar (24 ounces) Prego® Italian Sausage & Garlic Italian Sauce**

1 **container (15 ounces) part-skim ricotta cheese**

¾ **cup grated Parmesan cheese**

7 **cups bow tie–shaped pasta, cooked and drained**

1 **container (8 ounces) small fresh mozzarella cheese balls (about 1 inch)**

2 **tablespoons sliced pitted ripe olives**

1. Spray a 13×9×2-inch shallow baking dish with the cooking spray.

2. Mix 1½ **cups** of the Italian sauce, ricotta cheese, ½ **cup** Parmesan cheese and pasta in the prepared dish. Spread the remaining sauce over the pasta mixture. Sprinkle with the remaining Parmesan cheese and cover the dish with foil.

3. Bake at 400°F. for 25 minutes or until hot and bubbling. Arrange the cheese balls randomly over the pasta mixture. Place a sliced olive on **each** cheese ball. Let stand for 10 minutes before serving.

tip *If fresh mozzarella cheese balls are not available, substitute **1 package** (8 ounces) fresh mozzarella cheese. Cut crosswise into thirds. Cut **each** third into **6** wedges, for triangle-shaped eyes.*

holiday potato pancakes

prep 25 minutes | **cook** 30 minutes | **makes** 36 pancakes

- 8 medium all-purpose potatoes (about 3 pounds), peeled and grated (about 7 cups)
- 2 cans (10¾ ounces **each**) Campbell's® Condensed Broccoli Cheese Soup (Regular **or** 98% Fat Free)
- 3 eggs, beaten
- 2 tablespoons all-purpose flour
- ¼ teaspoon freshly ground black pepper
- ½ cup vegetable oil
  Sour cream
  Chopped chives

1. Wrap the grated potatoes in a clean dish or paper towel. Twist the towel and squeeze to wring out as much of the liquid as possible.

2. Mix the soup, eggs, flour, black pepper and potatoes in a 3-quart bowl.

3. Heat ¼ **cup** oil in a deep nonstick 12-inch skillet over medium-high heat. Drop a scant ¼ **cup** potato mixture into the pan, making **4** pancakes at a time. Press on **each** pancake to flatten to 3 or 4 inches. Cook 4 minutes, turning once or until pancakes are dark golden brown. Remove the pancakes and keep warm. Repeat with the remaining potato mixture, adding more of the remaining oil as needed. Serve with the sour cream and chives.

golden chicken & autumn vegetables

prep 10 minutes **I** **cook** 30 minutes **I** **makes** 4 servings

- 1 **tablespoon vegetable oil**
- 4 **skinless, boneless chicken breast halves (about 1 pound)**
- 1 **cup Swanson® Chicken Stock**
- 2 **tablespoons minced garlic**
- ½ **teaspoon dried rosemary leaves, crushed**
- ½ **teaspoon dried thyme leaves, crushed**
- ¼ **teaspoon ground black pepper**
- 2 **large sweet potatoes, cut into ½-inch pieces**
- 2 **cups fresh _or_ frozen whole green beans**

1. Heat the oil in a 12-inch skillet over medium-high heat. Add the chicken and cook for 10 minutes or until well browned on both sides. Remove the chicken from the skillet.

2. Stir the stock, garlic, rosemary, thyme, black pepper, potatoes and green beans in the skillet and heat to a boil. Cook for 5 minutes.

3. Reduce the heat to low. Return the chicken to the skillet. Cover and cook for 10 minutes or until the chicken is cooked through and the potatoes are tender. Season as desired.

Herbed Chicken Dijon with Wine: Add ¼ **_cup_** white wine, **_1 teaspoon_** lemon juice and **_2 tablespoons_** Dijon-style mustard with the stock in step 2. Substitute Yukon Gold potatoes for the sweet potatoes.

tip _You can substitute **4 bone-in** chicken breast halves (about 2 pounds), skin removed, for the skinless, boneless chicken. Increase the cooking time to 20 minutes or until the chicken is cooked through._

slow cooker jambalaya

prep 15 minutes | **cook** 7 hours 10 minutes | **makes** 8 servings

- 3 cups Swanson® Chicken Broth **or** Swanson® Chicken Stock
- 1 tablespoon Creole seasoning
- 1 large green pepper, diced (about 1½ cups)
- 1 large onion, diced (about 1 cup)
- 2 cloves garlic, minced
- ½ teaspoon ground black pepper
- 2 large stalks celery, diced (about 1 cup)
- 1 can (about 14½ ounces) diced tomatoes
- 1 pound kielbasa, diced (about 3 cups)
- ¾ pound skinless, boneless chicken thighs, cut into cubes
- 1 cup **uncooked** regular long-grain white rice
- ½ pound fresh medium shrimp, peeled and deveined

1. Stir the broth, Creole seasoning, green pepper, onion, garlic, black pepper, celery, tomatoes, kielbasa, chicken and rice in a 6-quart slow cooker.

2. Cover and cook on LOW for 7 to 8 hours* or until the chicken is cooked through.

3. Add the shrimp to the cooker. Cover and cook for 10 minutes or until the shrimp are cooked through.

Or on HIGH for 4 to 5 hours.

red wine braised short ribs with smashed fall vegetables

prep 35 minutes | **cook** 1 hour 50 minutes | **makes** 6 servings

- 5 pounds beef short ribs, cut into serving-sized pieces
- ⅓ cup all-purpose flour
- 1 tablespoon olive oil
- 2 large onions, sliced (about 2 cups)
- 3 large carrots, cut into 2-inch pieces (about 1½ cups)
- 2 stalks celery, cut into 2-inch pieces (about 1½ cups)
- 4 cloves garlic, chopped
- 1 tablespoon chopped fresh rosemary leaves
- 4 cups Swanson® Beef Stock
- 1 cup dry red wine
- 2 cups Swanson® Vegetable Broth (Regular **or** Certified Organic) **or** Swanson® Chicken Stock
- 1 small butternut squash (about 1½ pounds), peeled and cut into 1-inch pieces (about 4 cups)
- 1 medium sweet potato, diced (about 2 cups)
- ½ pound turnip, cut into quarters (about 1½ cups)
- ½ pound parsnip, thickly sliced (about 1 cup)
- 1 Spanish onion, cut into quarters
- 3 cloves garlic, minced

1. Coat the ribs with the flour.

2. Heat the oil in an 8-quart saucepot over medium-high heat. Add the ribs in 2 batches and cook until well browned on all sides. Remove the ribs from the saucepot.

3. Add the onions to the saucepot and cook for 5 minutes. Stir in the carrots, celery, chopped garlic and rosemary and cook for 3 minutes. Stir in the beef stock and wine. Return the ribs to the saucepot and heat to a boil. Reduce the heat to low. Cover and cook for 1 hour or until the ribs are fork-tender.

4. Heat the vegetable broth, squash, sweet potato, turnips, parsnips, onion and minced garlic in a 4-quart saucepan over high heat to a boil. Reduce the heat to low. Cover and cook for 20 minutes or until the vegetables are tender. Drain the vegetables well in a colander, reserving the cooking liquid.

5. Mash the vegetables with ½ **cup** cooking liquid. Add additional cooking liquid, if needed, until the vegetables are the desired consistency. Serve the vegetables with the ribs.

summer bruschetta

prep 15 minutes | **makes** 4 servings

- 1 tablespoon balsamic vinegar
- 1 tablespoon olive oil
- ¼ cup fresh basil leaves, cut into thin strips
- 1 tablespoon minced garlic
- 8 plum tomatoes, seeded and chopped
- 8 slices Pepperidge Farm® 100% Natural 100% Whole Wheat Bread, toasted *or* grilled and cut diagonally into quarters
- ¼ cup shredded Parmesan cheese

1. Beat the vinegar, oil, basil and garlic in a small bowl with a fork or whisk. Stir in the tomatoes.

2. Divide the tomato mixture among the bread quarters. Top with the cheese.

holiday turkey with cranberry pecan stuffing

prep 30 minutes   I   **roast** 3 hours 30 minutes   I   **stand** 10 minutes   I   **makes** 12 servings

¼ cup (½ stick) butter

2 stalks celery, chopped (about 1 cup)

1 large onion, chopped (about 1 cup)

1¾ cups Swanson® Chicken Broth (Regular, Natural Goodness® *or* Certified Organic)

½ cup dried cranberries

½ cup chopped pecans

1 package (14 ounces) Pepperidge Farm® Herb Seasoned Stuffing

1 turkey (12 to 14 pounds)

Vegetable oil

1. Heat the butter in a 3-quart saucepan over medium heat. Add the celery and onion and cook until tender, stirring occasionally. Stir in the broth. Remove the saucepan from the heat. Stir in the cranberries and pecans. Add the stuffing and mix lightly.

2. Remove the package of giblets and neck from the turkey cavity. Rinse the turkey with cold water and pat dry. Spoon the stuffing mixture lightly into the neck and body cavities. Fold the loose skin over the stuffing mixture. Tie the ends of the drumsticks together.

3. Place the turkey, breast side up, on a rack in a large roasting pan. Brush the turkey with the oil. Insert a meat thermometer into the thickest part of the meat, not touching the bone.

4. Roast at 325°F. for 3½ hours or until the thermometer reads 180°F., basting occasionally with the pan drippings. Begin checking for doneness after 3 hours of roasting time. Let the turkey stand for 10 minutes before slicing.

Cooking for a Crowd: This recipe can be doubled. Double all ingredients and use a 20-pound turkey. Prepare the stuffing mixture in a 6-quart saucepot. Proceed as directed above and roast for 5 hours, checking for doneness after 4½ hours of roasting time.

tips *Bake any remaining stuffing mixture in a covered casserole with the turkey for the last 30 minutes of roasting time or until the stuffing mixture is hot. Use an instant-read thermometer to check that the center of the stuffing mixture both in the turkey and in the casserole reaches 165°F.*

You may use walnuts instead of the pecans in this recipe.

vegetable beef stew

prep 20 minutes I **cook** 2 hours 15 minutes I **makes** 4 servings

- 2 tablespoons all-purpose flour
- ⅛ teaspoon ground black pepper
- 1 pound beef for stew, cut into 1-inch cubes
- 1 tablespoon vegetable oil
- 1¾ cups Swanson® Vegetable Broth (Regular *or* Certified Organic)
- ½ teaspoon dried thyme leaves, crushed
- 1 bay leaf
- 3 medium carrots, cut into 1-inch pieces (about 1½ cups)
- 2 medium potatoes, cut into cubes (about 2 cups)
- 2 stalks celery, cut into 1-inch pieces (about 1½ cups)

1. Stir the flour and pepper on a plate. Coat the beef with the flour mixture.

2. Heat the oil in a 4-quart saucepot over medium-high heat. Add the beef and cook until well browned, stirring often. Set the beef aside. Pour off any fat.

3. Stir the broth, thyme and bay leaf in the saucepot and heat to a boil. Return the beef to the saucepot. Reduce the heat to low. Cover and cook for 1 hour.

4. Stir the carrots, potatoes and celery in the saucepot. Cover and cook for 1 hour or until the beef is fork-tender, stirring occasionally. Discard the bay leaf.

toasted corn & sage harvest risotto

prep 15 minutes | **cook** 35 minutes | **makes** 6 servings

- 1 tablespoon olive oil
- 1 cup fresh *or* drained canned whole kernel corn
- 1 large orange *or* red pepper, chopped (about 1 cup)
- 1 medium onion, chopped (about ½ cup)
- 1¾ cups *uncooked* regular long-grain white rice
- 4 cups Swanson® Chicken Broth (Regular, Natural Goodness® *or* Certified Organic)
- 1 teaspoon ground sage
- 1 can (10¾ ounces) Campbell's® Condensed Cream of Celery Soup (Regular *or* 98% Fat Free)
- ¼ cup grated Parmesan cheese

1. Heat the oil in a 4-quart saucepan over medium heat. Add the corn, pepper and onion and cook for 5 minutes or until the vegetables are lightly browned.

2. Add the rice to the saucepan and cook and stir for 30 seconds. Stir in the broth and sage and heat to a boil. Reduce the heat to low. Cover and cook for 20 minutes or until the rice is tender.

3. Stir in the soup. Cook for 2 minutes or until the rice mixture is hot. Sprinkle with the cheese.

tip *If you want a meatless side dish, substitute Swanson® Vegetable Broth (Regular or Certified Organic) for the Chicken Broth.*

moist & savory stuffing

prep 10 minutes | **cook** 10 minutes | **bake** 30 minutes | **makes** 10 servings

2½ cups Swanson® Chicken Broth (Regular, Natural Goodness® *or* Certified Organic)
    Generous dash ground black pepper

2 stalks celery, coarsely chopped (about 1 cup)

1 large onion, coarsely chopped (about 1 cup)

1 package (16 ounces) Pepperidge Farm® Herb Seasoned Stuffing

1. Heat the broth, pepper, celery and onion in a 3-quart saucepan over medium-high heat to a boil. Reduce the heat to low. Cover and cook for 5 minutes or until the vegetables are tender, stirring often. Remove the saucepan from the heat. Add the stuffing and mix lightly.

2. Spoon the stuffing mixture into a greased 3-quart shallow baking dish. Cover the baking dish.

3. Bake at 350°F. for 30 minutes or until the stuffing is hot.

Cranberry & Pecan Stuffing: Stir ½ *cup each* dried cranberries *and* chopped pecans into the stuffing mixture.

Sausage & Mushroom Stuffing: Add *1 cup* sliced mushrooms to the vegetables during cooking. Stir ½ *pound* pork sausage, cooked and crumbled, into the stuffing mixture before baking.

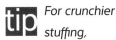 *For crunchier stuffing, bake the casserole uncovered.*

sweet potato dip

prep 10 minutes | **cook** 20 minutes | **makes** 18 servings

- 2 medium sweet potatoes (about 1¼ pounds)
- 2 tablespoons pure maple syrup
- 1 tablespoon butter, melted
- 1 tablespoon lemon juice
- ½ teaspoon ground ginger
- ⅛ teaspoon ground nutmeg
- Dash ground black pepper
- 4 tablespoons chopped pecans, toasted
- 2 packages (6 ounces *each*) Pepperidge Farm® Baked Naturals® Cracker Chips (any variety)

1. Place the potatoes into a 3-quart saucepan and add water to cover. Heat over medium-high heat to a boil. Reduce the heat to medium and cook for 15 minutes or until the potatoes are tender. Drain the potatoes well in a colander. Peel the potatoes. Return the potatoes to the saucepan. Mash the potatoes.

2. Stir the potatoes, syrup, butter, lemon juice, ginger, nutmeg, black pepper and **3 tablespoons** pecans in a medium bowl. Sprinkle with the remaining pecans. Serve with the cracker chips for dipping.

For a savory twist, omit the ginger and nutmeg. Stir in ½ *teaspoon each* ground cumin and garlic powder and *2* green onions, sliced (about ¼ *cup*).

tip For a sweet, tart twist, stir in ¼ *cup* chopped dried cranberries.

thick & hearty two-bean chili

prep 5 minutes | **cook** 35 minutes | **makes** 4 servings

- 1 **pound ground beef**
- 2 **cups Pace® Picante Sauce**
- 1 **can (about 16 ounces) fat free refried beans**
- 1 **can (about 14.5 ounces) whole peeled tomatoes, cut up**
- 1 **tablespoon chili powder**
- ¼ **teaspoon garlic powder _or_ 2 cloves garlic, minced**
- 1 **can (about 15 ounces) kidney beans, rinsed and drained**
  Shredded Cheddar cheese

1. Cook the beef in a 4-quart saucepan over medium-high heat until well browned, stirring often to separate the meat. Pour off any fat.

2. Stir the picante sauce, refried beans, tomatoes, chili powder and garlic powder in the saucepan and heat to a boil. Reduce the heat to low. Cover and cook for 20 minutes. Stir in the kidney beans and cook until the mixture is hot and bubbling. Sprinkle with the cheese.

roasted sweet potato soup

prep 30 minutes I **cook** 20 minutes I **makes** 8 servings

5 medium sweet potatoes (about 2 pounds)

2 tablespoons butter

1 medium onion, chopped (about 1 cup)

2 stalks celery, chopped (about 1 cup)

6 cups Swanson® Chicken Broth (Regular, Natural Goodness® **or** Certified Organic)

1 medium potato, peeled and cut into cubes (about 1 cup)

⅓ cup maple syrup

⅛ teaspoon ground white pepper

2 tablespoons light cream (optional)

1. Pierce the sweet potatoes with a fork. Microwave on HIGH for 8 to 13 minutes or bake at 400°F. for 1 hour or until fork-tender. Cut in half lengthwise. Scoop out sweet potato pulp and set aside.

2. Heat the butter in a 6-quart saucepot over medium heat. Add the onion and celery to the saucepot and cook until tender. Add the broth and potato. Heat to a boil. Reduce the heat to low. Cook for 15 minutes or until the potato is tender. Add the maple syrup, white pepper and reserved sweet potato.

3. Place ⅓ of the broth mixture into an electric blender or food processor container. Cover and blend until smooth. Pour the mixture into a large bowl. Repeat the blending process twice more with the remaining broth mixture. Return all of the puréed mixture to the saucepot. Add the cream, if desired. Cook over medium heat until the mixture is hot. Season to taste.

tip *Substitute 3¾ cups mashed, drained, canned sweet potatoes for the fresh sweet potatoes.*

savory herb-crusted turkey pot pie

thaw 40 minutes | **prep** 15 minutes | **cook** 10 minutes | **bake** 25 minutes
cool 20 minutes | **makes** 6 servings

- 1 **egg**
- 1 **tablespoon water**
- 6 **cups diced cooked turkey *or* chicken**
- 5 **cups frozen mixed vegetables *or* your favorite frozen vegetable blend**
- 2 **tablespoons butter**
- ½ **cup all-purpose flour**
- 2 **cups Swanson® Chicken Broth *or* Swanson® Chicken Stock**
- ¼ **teaspoon ground black pepper**
- ½ **of a 17.3-ounce package Pepperidge Farm® Puff Pastry Sheets (1 sheet), thawed according to package directions**
- 2 **tablespoons coarsely chopped fresh herbs (parsley, thyme *and/or* oregano)**

1. Heat the oven to 400°F. Beat the egg and water in a small bowl with a fork.

2. Stir the turkey and vegetables in a 3-quart (13×9-inch) shallow baking dish.

3. Heat the butter in a 2-quart saucepan over medium heat. Add the flour and cook and stir for 3 minutes. Gradually stir the broth into the saucepan. Cook and stir for 5 minutes or until the mixture boils and thickens. Stir in the black pepper. Pour the broth mixture over the turkey mixture.

4. Unfold the pastry sheet on a lightly floured surface. Roll the pastry sheet into a 13×9-inch rectangle. Place the pastry over the filling. Press the pastry to the rim to seal. Brush the pastry with the egg mixture and sprinkle with the herbs. Cut several slits in the pastry.

5. Bake for 25 minutes or until the pastry is golden brown and the filling is hot and bubbling. Let cool on a wire rack for 20 minutes.

---

tips *For a more striking presentation, you can flute the edges of the pastry as you press it to the rim.*

*We like to keep a 32-ounce package of frozen mixed vegetables on hand. Use **5 cups** for this recipe, then save the remainder to easily stir vegetables into soups, stews **or** casseroles.*

---

root vegetable gratin

prep 20 minutes I **cook** 5 minutes I **bake** 1 hour 5 minutes I **stand** 10 minutes I **makes** 6 servings

- 3 tablespoons unsalted butter, softened
- 1 small butternut squash (about 1½ pounds), peeled and thinly sliced (about 4 cups)
- 1 pound red potato, peeled and thinly sliced (about 3 cups)
- 1 bulb celery root (celeriac), about 1 pound, peeled, cut in half and thinly sliced (about 1 cup)
- 1 bunch leeks, washed well, white part only, thinly sliced (about 1 cup)
- 1¾ cups Swanson® Vegetable Broth (Regular *or* Certified Organic)
- ½ cup heavy cream
- 1 teaspoon minced fresh thyme leaves
- ½ teaspoon ground nutmeg
- ⅓ cup grated Parmesan cheese

1. Heat the oven to 400°F. Spread the butter in a 13×9×2-inch baking dish. Add the squash, potatoes, celery root and leeks to the prepared dish.

2. Heat the broth, cream, thyme and nutmeg in a 2-quart saucepan over medium heat to a boil. Season to taste.

3. Pour the broth mixture over the vegetables and toss to coat.

4. Bake for 25 minutes. Reduce the temperature to 350°F. and bake for 40 minutes more, or until golden brown and the vegetables are tender. (If the vegetables are browning too fast in the first 25 minutes, cover the dish loosely with foil.)

5. Sprinkle with the cheese. Let stand for 10 minutes.

tip *Use a Japanese mandoline to slice the potatoes to a ⅛-inch thickness.*

kids' top picks

Help your kids explore and discover

the great taste of food.

cheesy broccoli

prep 5 minutes I **cook** 5 minutes I **makes** 4 servings

1 can (10¾ ounces) Campbell's® Condensed
    Cheddar Cheese Soup

¼ cup milk

4 cups frozen broccoli florets

1. Stir the soup and milk in a 2-quart microwavable casserole. Stir in the broccoli.

2. Cover and microwave on HIGH for 5 minutes or until the broccoli is tender-crisp, stirring once during cooking.

kid-friendly ideas

Getting some kids to eat anything can be challenging at best. But don't get frustrated—try some of these ideas to see if they "bite."

- *Stacked foods always taste better!* You can do it or the kids can stack some of their foods into towers. Same goes for skewers—for big drama, thread meats, vegetables, or fruits onto bamboo skewers, then stand them in a mound of mashed potatoes! (For kids under age 6, take out the skewers after presenting the food.)

- *Use naturally bright-colored ingredients in recipes,* such as blueberries or raspberries for smoothies, blue cornmeal, green spinach, blue potatoes...that's right, blue potatoes! Many grocery stores and farmers' markets carry them, and they make a lasting impression!

- *Use fun shaped foods,* such as bowtie or wagon-wheel pasta, crackers, and unique fruits like starfruit.

- *Go mini with tiny tacos, sliders, and sandwiches.* Kids like things scaled down to their size.

- *Every once in a while,* serve breakfast for dinner to shake up the routine.

- *Let kids pick out their own plates and cups to eat from.* And have a "special" plate for days of particular importance or achievements, like birthdays or straight-A report cards.

- *Make "walking tacos."* Take a lunch-size bag of tortilla or corn chips, crush slightly, then open the bag and fill with taco-seasoned meat, grated cheese, shredded lettuce, and sour cream; top with *Pace*® Chunky salsa or Picante sauce and eat it straight from the bag with a fork! It's a great party idea for 7- or 8-year-old kids—plus, it's super-easy to clean up!

- *Use a slice of whole wheat bread and a slice of white bread to make a sandwich.* Slice the sandwich into nine squares, then flip over every other square to make a checkerboard.

tuna melts

prep 10 minutes | **broil** 3 minutes | **makes** 2 servings

- 1 **can (about 6 ounces) tuna, drained and flaked**
- ¼ **cup chopped celery**
- 2 **tablespoons mayonnaise**
- 4 **slices Pepperidge Farm® Farmhouse™ Soft Hearty White Bread, toasted**
- 4 **slices Cheddar cheese *or* process American cheese (about 4 ounces)**

1. Stir the tuna, celery and mayonnaise in a medium bowl.

2. Place the toast on a rack in a broiler pan. Divide the tuna mixture evenly among the toast and spread to the edges. Top the tuna mixture with the cheese.

3. Heat the broiler. Broil 4 inches from heat for 3 minutes or until the cheese is melted.

tip **Microwave directions:** *In Step 2, place the toast on a microwave-safe plate. Divide the tuna mixture evenly among the toast. Top with the cheese. Microwave on HIGH for 1½ minutes or until the cheese is melted.*

picnic chicken salad sandwiches

prep 15 minutes | **cook** 2 hours | **makes** 6 servings

- 1 can (10¾ ounces) Campbell's® Condensed Cream of Celery Soup (Regular *or* 98% Fat Free)
- 2 tablespoons mayonnaise
- ¼ teaspoon ground black pepper
- 2 cups chopped cooked chicken
- 2 stalks celery, sliced (about 1 cup)
- 1 small onion, finely chopped (about ¼ cup)
- 6 Pepperidge Farm® Classic Sandwich Buns with Sesame Seeds, split
  Lettuce leaves
  Tomato slices

1. Stir the soup, mayonnaise and black pepper in a large bowl. Add the chicken, celery and onion and toss to coat. Cover and refrigerate for 2 hours.

2. Place the lettuce and tomato on the buns. Divide the chicken mixture among the buns.

goldfish® pizzas

prep 15 minutes I **bake** 10 minutes I **makes** 4 servings

  2 **pieces Pepperidge Farm® Goldfish® 100% Whole Wheat Sandwich Bread, split**
  ¼ **cup Prego® Traditional Italian Sauce**
  ½ **cup shredded part-skim mozzarella cheese**
    Pitted ripe olives (optional)

1. Heat the oven to 350°F. Place the bread pieces, split-side up, onto a baking sheet.

2. Spread **1 tablespoon** Italian sauce on **each** bread piece. Top **each** with **2 tablespoons** cheese.

3. Bake for 10 minutes or until the cheese is melted. Decorate the faces of the Goldfish® with the olive slices (or pieces) if desired.

 *For a more crispy crust, split and toast the bread pieces before topping with the sauce and cheese.*

baked macaroni and cheese

prep 20 minutes I **bake** 20 minutes I **makes** 4 servings

- 1 **can (10¾ ounces) Campbell's® Condensed Cheddar Cheese Soup**
- ½ **soup can milk**
- ⅛ **teaspoon ground black pepper**
- 2 **cups corkscrew-shaped pasta (rotini) *or* shell-shaped pasta, cooked and drained**
- 1 **tablespoon dry bread crumbs**
- 2 **teaspoons butter, melted**

1. Stir the soup, milk, black pepper and pasta in a 1-quart baking dish.

2. Stir the bread crumbs and butter in a small bowl. Sprinkle the bread crumb mixture over the pasta mixture.

3. Bake at 400°F. for 20 minutes or until the pasta mixture is hot and bubbling.

terrific tacos

prep 15 minutes **I** **cook** 15 minutes **I** **makes** 24 tacos

- 2 **pounds ground beef**
- 1 **jar (16 ounces) Pace® Picante Sauce**
- 24 **taco shells**
  Shredded Cheddar cheese
  Shredded lettuce
  Chopped tomato
  Sour cream

1. In a 12-inch skillet over medium-high heat, cook ground beef until browned, stirring to separate the meat. Pour off any fat. Add picante sauce. Heat to a boil. Simmer 5 minutes.

2. Spoon taco mixture into taco shells. Top with cheese, lettuce, tomatoes and sour cream.

power breakfast sandwiches

prep 5 minutes **I** **makes** 2 servings

- ¼ **cup peanut butter**
- 4 **slices Pepperidge Farm® Stone Ground 100% Whole Wheat bread**
- ¼ **cup raisins**
- 1 **medium banana, sliced**

Spread the peanut butter on **4** bread slices. Divide the raisins and banana between **2** bread slices. Top with the remaining bread slices, peanut butter-side down. Cut the sandwiches in half.

tip *You can substitute 1 large apple, cored and sliced, for the raisins and banana.*

skillet chicken & rice

prep 5 minutes | **cook** 35 minutes | **makes** 4 servings

1	**pound skinless, boneless chicken breasts, cut into cubes**
1¾	**cups Swanson® Chicken Stock**
½	**teaspoon dried basil leaves, crushed**
½	**teaspoon garlic powder**
¾	**cup *uncooked* regular long-grain white rice**
1	**package (16 ounces) frozen vegetable combination (broccoli, cauliflower, carrots)**

1. Cook the chicken in a 10-inch nonstick skillet over medium-high heat until well browned, stirring often. Remove the chicken from the skillet.

2. Stir in the stock, basil and garlic powder and heat to a boil. Stir in the rice. Reduce the heat to low. Cover and cook for 5 minutes.

3. Stir in the vegetables. Return the chicken to the skillet. Cover and cook for 15 minutes or until the chicken is cooked through and the rice is tender.

awesome grilled cheese sandwiches

prep 10 minutes | **cook** 5 minutes | **makes** 3 servings

- 1 **package (11.25 ounces) Pepperidge Farm® Garlic Texas Toast**
- 6 **slices fontina cheese *or* mozzarella cheese**
- 6 **thin slices deli smoked turkey**
- 3 **thin slices prosciutto**
- 1 **jar (12 ounces) sliced roasted red pepper, drained**

1. Heat a panini or sandwich press according to the manufacturer's directions until hot. (Or, use a cast-iron skillet or ridged grill pan.)

2. Top **3** of the bread slices with **half** of the cheese, turkey, prosciutto, peppers and remaining cheese. Top with the remaining bread slices.

3. Put the sandwiches on the press, closing the lid onto the sandwiches. Cook the sandwiches for 5 minutes (if cooking in a skillet or grill pan, press with a spatula occasionally or weigh down with another cast-iron skillet/foil-covered brick), until lightly browned and the bread is crisp and the cheese melts.

tip *For a spicier flavor, add a dash of crushed red pepper flakes on the cheese when assembling the sandwiches.*

broccoli chicken potato parmesan

prep 10 minutes I **cook** 20 minutes I **makes** 4 servings

- 2 **tablespoons vegetable oil**
- 1 **pound small red potatoes, sliced ¼-inch thick**
- 1 **can (10¾ ounces) Campbell's® Condensed Broccoli Cheese Soup (Regular *or* 98% Fat Free)**
- ½ **cup milk**
- ¼ **teaspoon garlic powder**
- 2 **cups fresh *or* frozen broccoli florets**
- 1 **package (about 10 ounces) refrigerated cooked chicken breast strips**
- ¼ **cup grated Parmesan cheese**

1. Heat the oil in a 10-inch skillet over medium heat. Add the potatoes. Cover and cook for 10 minutes, stirring occasionally.

2. Stir the soup, milk, garlic powder, broccoli and chicken in the skillet. Add the cheese and heat to a boil. Reduce the heat to low. Cover and cook for 5 minutes or until the potatoes are fork-tender.

cheesy jack tacos

prep 5 minutes | **cook** 15 minutes | **makes** 4 servings

1 **pound ground beef**

1 **can (10¾ ounces) Campbell's® Condensed Cream of Chicken Soup (Regular *or* 98% Fat Free)**

½ **cup water**

1 **package (about 1 ounce) taco seasoning mix**

8 **taco shells, warmed**

1 **cup shredded Monterey Jack cheese (about 4 ounces)**

Shredded lettuce

1. Cook the beef in a 10-inch skillet over medium-high heat until well browned, stirring often to separate the meat. Pour off any fat.

2. Stir the soup, water and taco seasoning mix in the skillet and cook until the mixture is hot and bubbling.

3. Spoon **about** ⅓ **cup** beef mixture into the taco shells. Top with the cheese and lettuce.

tip *You can substitute 8 flour tortillas (8-inch), warmed, for the taco shells. Spoon the beef mixture down the center of the tortillas. Top with the cheese and lettuce. Fold the tortillas around the filling.*

pick-your-own-topping pizza night

thaw 40 minutes I **prep** 25 minutes I **bake** 25 minutes I **makes** 8 servings

Sauces (choose one per pizza):
Cheese & Toppings (choose one cheese and two to three toppings per pizza):

- 1 package (17.3 ounces) Pepperidge Farm® Puff Pastry Sheets, thawed
- ½ cup Prego® Traditional Italian Sauce **or** Marinara Italian Sauce
- ¼ cup prepared pesto sauce
- ½ cup prepared Alfredo sauce
- 1 cup shredded mozzarella cheese (about 4 ounces)
- 1 cup shredded fontina cheese (about 4 ounces)
- 1 cup shredded Italian cheese blend **or** 4-cheese pizza cheese blend (about 4 ounces)
- 1 cup cooked mushrooms
- 1 cup caramelized onions
- ¼ cup chopped prosciutto
- ¼ cup sliced pepperoni
- 2 tablespoons chopped fresh basil leaves
- ¼ cup sliced pitted green olives **or** pitted ripe olives

1. Heat the oven to 400°F.

2. Unfold **1** pastry sheet on a lightly floured surface. Roll the pastry sheet into a 12-inch square. Place the pastry onto a baking sheet. Prick the pastry thoroughly with a fork. Repeat with the remaining pastry sheet.

3. Bake for 15 minutes.

4. Spread the Sauce on **each** pastry to within ½ inch of the edge. Sprinkle with the *Cheese & Toppings*.

5. Bake for 10 minutes or until the pastries are golden brown and the cheese is melted.

> **tip** *Each pizza can also be cut into 24 small rectangles to be served as an appetizer.*

honey mustard chicken bites

prep 15 minutes I **bake** 15 minutes I **cook** 5 minutes I **makes** about 40 appetizers

1½ **pounds skinless, boneless chicken breast halves, cut into 1-inch pieces**
1 **jar (12 ounces) refrigerated honey mustard salad dressing**
2 **cups Pepperidge Farm® Herb Seasoned Stuffing, crushed**
2 **tablespoons orange juice**

1. Dip the chicken into ¾ **cup** of the dressing. Coat with the stuffing.

2. Put the chicken on a baking sheet. Bake at 400°F. for 15 minutes or until the chicken is cooked through.

3. Stir the remaining dressing and orange juice in a 1-quart saucepan over medium heat. Cook and stir until hot. Serve with the chicken for dipping.

tip *To microwave dip, mix remaining dressing and orange juice in microwavable bowl. Microwave on HIGH 1 minute or until hot.*

chicken picante pizzas

prep 15 minutes | **bake** 10 minutes | **makes** 6 servings

- 6 **flour tortillas (8-inch)**
  Vegetable cooking spray
- 1 **jar (16 ounces) Pace® Picante Sauce**
- 1½ **cups cubed cooked chicken**
- 1½ **cups shredded Monterey Jack cheese (about 6 ounces)**
- 3 **green onions, sliced (about 6 tablespoons)**

1. Heat the oven to 450°F. Place the tortillas onto **2** baking sheets. Spray the tortillas with the cooking spray. Bake for 5 minutes or until the tortillas are golden.

2. Spread **about** ¼ **cup** picante sauce onto **each** tortilla to within ½ inch of the edge. Top with the chicken, cheese and onions.

3. Bake for 5 minutes or until the cheese is melted.

italian dipping sauce

prep 5 minutes | **cook** 5 minutes | **makes** 8 servings

1   **cup Prego® Traditional Italian Sauce *or* Tomato, Basil & Garlic Italian Sauce**
2   **tablespoons grated Parmesan cheese**
    Assorted fresh vegetables for dipping

Heat the sauce and cheese in a 1-quart saucepan over medium heat until the mixture is hot and bubbling. Serve with the vegetables.

tip *This sauce is also delicious served with chicken nuggets, mozzarella sticks or fish sticks for dipping.*

hamburger pie

prep 15 minutes | **bake** 15 minutes | **makes** 6 servings

1½ **pounds ground beef**

1 **can (10¾ ounces) Campbell's® Condensed Cream of Mushroom Soup (Regular *or* 98% Fat Free)**

2 **packages (8 ounces *each*) refrigerated crescent rolls**

1 **cup of your favorite shredded cheese**

1. Cook the beef in a 10-inch skillet over medium-high heat until well browned, stirring often to separate the meat. Pour off any fat. Stir the soup in the skillet.

2. Unroll **1 package** crescent roll dough and press on the bottom and up the sides of a 9-inch pie plate. Press the seams to seal. Layer **half** the beef mixture and **half** the cheese in the pie plate. Repeat the layers. Unroll the remaining dough. Place the dough over the filling and press the edges to seal, if desired.

3. Bake at 350°F. for 15 minutes or until the crust is golden brown.

mini tacos

prep 20 minutes **|** **bake** 5 minutes **|** **makes** 24 servings

- 24 **wonton wrappers**
- 1 **pound lean ground beef**
- 1 **package (about 1 ounce) taco seasoning mix**
- 2 **tablespoons Pace® Picante Sauce**
- ½ **cup Pace® Chunky Salsa**
- 4 **ounces shredded Mexican cheese blend (about 1 cup)**
  Sour cream (optional)
  Sliced pitted ripe olives (optional)

1. Heat the oven to 425°F. Press the wonton wrappers into **24** (1½-inch) mini muffin-pan cups.

2. Cook the beef in a 10-inch skillet over medium-high heat until well browned, stirring often to separate the meat. Pour off any fat. Stir in the taco seasoning mix and picante sauce.

3. Spoon the beef mixture into the wonton cups. Top with the salsa and cheese.

4. Bake for 5 minutes or until the wontons are golden brown and the cheese is melted.

5. Garnish with sour cream and olives, if desired. Serve immediately with additional salsa.

super simple nacho pasta

prep 15 minutes I **cook** 5 minutes I **makes** 4 servings

- 1 can (10¾ ounces) Campbell's® Condensed Fiesta Nacho Cheese Soup
- ½ cup milk
- 4 cups corkscrew-shaped pasta (rotini), cooked and drained

Stir the soup, milk and pasta in a 3-quart saucepan. Heat through over medium heat.

chocolate and coconut cream fondue

prep 5 minutes I **cook** 10 minutes I **makes** 24 servings

1 **can (15 ounces) cream of coconut**
1 **package (12 ounces) semi-sweet chocolate pieces (about 2 cups)**
1 **teaspoon rum extract *or* 2 tablespoons rum**
   Assorted Dippers

1. Heat the cream of coconut, chocolate and rum, if desired, in a 2-quart heavy saucepan over low heat until the mixture is melted and smooth, stirring occasionally.

2. Pour the chocolate mixture into a fondue pot or slow cooker. Serve warm with *Assorted Dippers*.

Assorted Dippers: Assorted Pepperidge Farm® Cookies, whole strawberries, banana chunks, dried pineapple pieces *and* fresh pineapple chunks

tip *Any remaining fondue can be used as an ice cream or dessert topping. Cover and refrigerate in an airtight container. Heat in a 2-quart saucepan over medium heat until the mixture is warm.*

cookies 'n' yogurt

prep 5 minutes | **makes** 1 serving

1 **container (6- to 8-ounce) fruit-flavored yogurt**

Pepperidge Farm® Nantucket™ Dark Chocolate Chunk Cookies (1 cookie), any variety, crumbled

Fresh blueberries, cut-up strawberries *or* raspberries

1. Spoon **half** the yogurt into a glass. Top with **half** the crumbled cookie and **half** the berries.

2. Top with the remaining yogurt and berries. Sprinkle with the remaining crumbled cookie.

festive taco nachos

prep 5 minutes I **cook** 20 minutes I **bake** 5 minutes I **makes** 8 servings

- 2 **pounds ground beef**
- 1 **jar (16 ounces) Pace® Picante Sauce**
- 8 **ounces tortilla chips**
- 4 **cups shredded Mexican blend *or* shredded Cheddar Jack cheese (about 16 ounces)**
  - **Chopped tomato**
  - **Sliced pitted ripe olives**
  - **Sliced green onions**

1. Heat the oven to 350°F.

2. Cook the beef in a 12-inch skillet over medium-high heat until well browned, stirring often to separate the meat.

3. Stir the picante sauce in the skillet and heat to a boil. Reduce the heat to low. Cook for 5 minutes or until the beef is cooked through.

4. Arrange the tortilla chips on **2** (12-inch) aluminum pizza pans. Top with the beef mixture and cheese. Bake for 5 minutes or until the cheese is melted. Top with the tomato, olives and onions.

garden vegetable pizza

thaw 2 hours | **prep** 20 minutes | **bake** 25 minutes | **makes** 8 servings

- 2 **tablespoons olive oil**
- 1 **medium onion, sliced (about ½ cup)**
- 1 **clove garlic, minced**
- 1 **small eggplant, cubed (about 1½ cups)**
- ½ **cup red pepper, cut into 1-inch pieces**
- ½ **cup sliced zucchini**
- 1 **jar (24 ounces) Prego® Chunky Garden Mushroom Supreme Italian Sauce with Baby Portobello**
- 2 **loaves (1 pound *each*) frozen white bread dough, thawed**
- 6 **ounces shredded mozzarella cheese (about 1½ cups)**

1. Heat the oven to 375°F. Heat the oil in a 12-inch skillet over medium heat. Stir the onion, garlic, eggplant, pepper and zucchini in the skillet and cook until tender-crisp. Stir the Italian sauce in the skillet.

2. Place the bread dough on a greased 15×10-inch baking pan. Pat the dough to cover the bottom of the pan, forming a single large crust. Pinch up the edges to form a rim. Top the dough with the vegetable mixture and spread it to within 1 inch of the edges. Sprinkle with the cheese.

3. Bake for 25 minutes or until the crust is golden brown.

 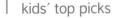

goldfish® checkerboard sandwich

prep 5 minutes I **makes** 1 serving

- 1 **slice Pepperidge Farm® White Sandwich Bread**
- 2 **tablespoons crunchy *or* smooth peanut butter**
- 1 **slice Pepperidge Farm® Whole Grain 100% Whole Wheat Bread**
- 2 **tablespoons grape jelly *or* your favorite jam**
- 4 **Pepperidge Farm® Goldfish® Cheddar Crackers**

1. Spread the white bread with the peanut butter. Spread the whole wheat bread with the jelly and place the **2** slices together with the filling inside.

2. Cut the sandwich into quarters. Turn over **2** quarters and place them back together on plate to resemble a checkerboard. Top **each** quarter with **1** Goldfish® Cracker.

hearty lasagna soup

prep 10 minutes I **cook** 25 minutes I **makes** 4 servings

- 1 **pound ground beef**
- 1 **small onion, chopped (about ¼ cup)**
- 1 **teaspoon minced garlic**
- ¼ **teaspoon dried parsley flakes**
- 3½ **cups Swanson® Beef Broth (Regular, 50% Less Sodium _or_ Certified Organic)**
- 1 **can (14.5 ounces) diced tomatoes**
- ¼ **teaspoon Italian seasoning, crushed**
- 1½ **cups _uncooked_ mafalda _or_ corkscrew–shaped pasta (rotini)**
- ¼ **cup grated Parmesan cheese**

1. Cook the beef, onion, garlic and parsley in a 3-quart saucepan over medium-high heat for 10 minutes, or until well browned, stirring often to separate the meat. Pour off any fat.

2. Stir the broth, tomatoes and Italian seasoning in the saucepan and heat to a boil.

3. Stir the pasta in the saucepan. Reduce the heat to medium and cook for 10 minutes or until the pasta is tender. Stir in the cheese. Serve with additional cheese, if desired.

hidden veggie sloppy joes

prep 10 minutes | **cook** 10 minutes | **makes** 5 servings

- 1 **pound ground beef**
- 1 **medium onion, chopped (about ½ cup)**
- ¾ **cup V8® 100% Vegetable Juice (Regular *or* Low Sodium)**
- ¼ **cup ketchup**
- 1 **tablespoon Worcestershire sauce**
- 5 **Pepperidge Farm® Classic Sandwich Buns with Sesame Seeds**

1. Cook the beef and onion in a 10-inch skillet over medium-high heat until the beef is well browned, stirring often to separate the meat. Pour off any fat.

2. Stir the juice, ketchup and Worcestershire in the skillet and heat until the mixture is hot and bubbling. Serve on the buns.

creative & different ideas

Add excitement to everyday meals with a simple twist to jazz up the ordinary.

stir in flavor

Add some excitement to everyday dinners with a simple twist to a recipe or different plate presentation. They can really jazz up the ordinary.

If mashed potatoes or rice are on the menu, try mixing in a little something to take them to new heights:

Mashed potatoes

- Blue cheese topped with diced fresh tomatoes
- Cooked chopped spinach and crumbled goat cheese
- Roasted garlic (or boil cloves of garlic with the potatoes and mash)
- Diced sautéed bacon and shredded Cheddar cheese
- Minced chipotle chiles in adobo sauce
- Chopped chipotle chiles and shredded Cheddar
- Horseradish and sour cream topped with chives
- Boursin cheese

Rice

- Minced fresh herbs (parsley, chives, cilantro, tarragon)
- Feta cheese and minced lemon zest
- Toasted almonds or pecans
- Roasted or grilled sliced mushrooms
- Sliced green onions
- Cooked peas
- Saffron or ground turmeric (add to the cooking water)
- Coconut milk (use ½ coconut milk and ½ water for cooking the rice)

Vinaigrettes: Prepare a standard vinaigrette (¼ cup vinegar, ¼ cup olive oil, 1 tablespoon Dijon mustard, 1 tablespoon honey), then make it your own by whisking in:

- Blue cheese
- Fresh basil and minced lemon zest
- Herbs, herbs, herbs
- Molasses or maple syrup (use in place of the honey)
- Crushed raspberries
- Orange or apple juice concentrate
- Heavy cream for a slightly creamy dressing

Sour cream, mayonnaise, or yogurt: Stir in the following to jazz up toppings for baked potatoes, chili, or spreads for sandwiches:

- Minced lemon, orange, or lime zest
- Mashed avocado
- Wasabi paste or powder
- Minced chipotle chiles in adobo sauce
- Minced fresh herbs (dill, basil, chives, parsley, cilantro)
- Puréed roasted red pepper
- Horseradish
- Honey

spinach-cheese swirls

thaw 40 minutes **I** **prep** 20 minutes **I** **bake** 15 minutes **I** **cool** 10 minutes **I** **makes** 20 pieces

½ **of a 17.3-ounce package Pepperidge Farm® Puff Pastry Sheets (1 sheet), thawed**

1 **egg**

1 **tablespoon water**

½ **cup shredded Muenster cheese *or* Monterey Jack cheese**

¼ **cup grated Parmesan cheese**

1 **green onion, chopped (about 2 tablespoons)**

⅛ **teaspoon garlic powder**

1 **package (about 10 ounces) frozen chopped spinach, thawed and well drained**

1. Heat the oven to 400°F. Beat the egg and water in a small bowl with a fork or whisk.

2. Stir the Muenster cheese, Parmesan cheese, onion and garlic powder in a medium bowl.

3. Unfold the pastry sheet on a lightly floured surface. Brush the pastry sheet with the egg mixture. Top with the cheese mixture and spinach. Starting with a short side, roll up like a jelly roll. Cut into **20** (½-inch) slices. Place the slices, cut-side down, onto baking sheets. Brush the slices with the egg mixture.

4. Bake for 15 minutes or until the pastries are golden brown. Remove the pastries from the baking sheets and let cool on wire racks for 10 minutes.

tip *Make sure to remove as much liquid as you can from the spinach before adding it to the pastry. If it's too wet, it may make the pastry soggy.*

panhandle pepperoni chicken

prep 10 minutes | **cook** 20 minutes | **makes** 4 servings

- 1 **tablespoon olive oil *or* vegetable oil**
- 4 **skinless, boneless chicken breasts halves (about 1 pound)**
- 1 **cup Pace® Picante Sauce**
- 1 **teaspoon Italian seasoning, crushed**
- 1 **medium green pepper, cut into 1-inch pieces (about 1 cup)**
- ⅓ **cup chopped pepperoni**
   Shredded mozzarella cheese for garnish
- 4 **cups hot cooked rice**

1. Heat the oil in a 10-inch skillet over medium-high heat. Add the chicken and cook for 10 minutes or until well browned on both sides. Remove the chicken and set aside. Pour off any fat.

2. Stir the picante sauce, Italian seasoning, green pepper and pepperoni into the skillet. Heat to a boil. Return chicken to the pan. Reduce heat to low. Cover and cook for 5 minutes or until the chicken is cooked through. Garnish with the cheese. Serve with the rice.

fajita beef potato topper

prep 10 minutes **I** **cook** 15 minutes **I** **makes** 4 servings

- 2 tablespoons vegetable oil
- ½ pound boneless beef sirloin steak *or* beef top round steak, ¾-inch thick, cut into very thin strips
- 1 medium onion, cut into 8 wedges
- ½ cup green pepper, cut into 2-inch strips
- ½ teaspoon dried oregano leaves, crushed
- 1 can (10¾ ounces) Campbell's® Condensed Cream of Mushroom Soup (Regular *or* 98% Fat Free)
- ¼ cup water
- 2 teaspoons lime juice
- ¼ teaspoon ground cumin
- 4 hot baked potatoes, split*
  Pace® Chunky Salsa

To bake potatoes: Using a fork, pierce each potato. Bake at 400°F. for 1 hour or microwave on HIGH for 8 to 10 minutes or until fork-tender.

1. Heat **1 tablespoon** oil in a 10-inch skillet over medium-high heat. Add the beef and cook until well browned, stirring often. Remove the beef and set aside.

2. Heat the remaining oil in the skillet. Add the onion, pepper and oregano and cook until tender.

3. Add the soup, water, lime juice and cumin. Heat to a boil. Return the beef to the skillet and heat until the mixture is hot and bubbling. Spoon the mixture over the potatoes and top with the salsa.

 To make slicing easier, freeze beef for 1 hour.

beef bourguignonne

prep 10 minutes **I** **cook** 30 minutes **I** **makes** 4 servings

- 1 beef sirloin steak **or** top round steak (about 1 pound), cut into 1-inch pieces
- ¼ cup all-purpose flour
- 1 tablespoon olive oil
- 1 medium onion, chopped (about ½ cup)
- 2 cloves garlic, minced
- ⅛ teaspoon dried parsley flakes
- ¼ teaspoon ground black pepper
- 2 cups sliced mushrooms (about 6 ounces)
- 1 teaspoon dried thyme leaves, crushed
- 2 cups fresh **or** frozen whole baby carrots
- 1¾ cups Swanson® Beef Stock
- ½ cup Burgundy **or** other dry red wine
  Hot cooked orzo pasta

1. Coat the beef with the flour.

2. Heat the oil in a 10-inch skillet over medium-high heat. Add the beef and cook until well browned, stirring often. Add the onion, garlic, parsley, black pepper, mushrooms and thyme and cook until the mushrooms are tender.

3. Stir the carrots, stock and wine in the skillet and heat to a boil. Reduce the heat to low. Cover and cook for 20 minutes or until the beef is cooked through. Serve the beef mixture over the orzo.

bacon horseradish burgers

prep 5 minutes I **cook** 20 minutes I **makes** 6 servings

1½ **pounds ground beef**
 1 **can (10¾ ounces) Campbell's® Condensed Bean with Bacon Soup**
 ½ **cup water**
 1 **tablespoon horseradish**
 6 **slices Cheddar cheese (about 6 ounces)**
 6 **Pepperidge Farm® Classic Sandwich Buns with Sesame Seeds, split**

1. Shape the beef into **6** (½-inch-thick) burgers.

2. Cook the burgers in a 12-inch skillet over medium-high heat for 10 minutes or until well browned on both sides. Pour off any fat.

3. Stir the soup, water and horseradish in the skillet and heat to a boil. Reduce the heat to low. Cover and cook for 5 minutes or until the burgers are cooked through. Top the burgers with the cheese and cook until the cheese is melted. Serve the burgers and sauce on the buns.

picante macaroni and cheese

prep 20 minutes I **bake** 30 minutes I **makes** 4 servings

 1 **can (10¾ ounces) Campbell's® Condensed Cream of Mushroom Soup (Regular *or* 98% Fat Free)**
 ½ **cup Pace® Picante Sauce**
 2 **cups shredded Cheddar cheese (about 8 ounces)**
 3 **cups hot cooked elbow macaroni (about 1½ cups dry)**
 ½ **cup crumbled tortilla chips**

1. Stir the soup, picante sauce, 1½ **cups** cheese and macaroni in a 1½-quart casserole.

2. Bake at 400°F. for 25 minutes or until hot and bubbling. Stir the macaroni mixture.

3. Sprinkle with the chips and remaining cheese. Bake for 5 minutes or until the cheese is melted.

stuffed-crust sopressata pizza
with lemony arugula salad

thaw 40 minutes I **prep** 20 minutes I **bake** 20 minutes I **cool** 10 minutes I **makes** 4 servings

1 **egg**

1 **tablespoon water**

1 **package (17.3 ounces) Pepperidge Farm® Puff Pastry Sheets, thawed according to package directions**

4 **ounces whole milk mozzarella cheese**

2 **tablespoons Prego® Traditional Italian Sauce**

4 **thin slices sopressata *or* hard salami, torn into pieces**

1 **tablespoon lemon juice**

2 **tablespoons extra virgin olive oil**

¼ **teaspoon freshly ground black pepper**

8 **cups fresh baby arugula leaves**

1. Heat the oven to 400°F. Beat the egg and water in a small bowl with a fork.

2. Unfold **1** pastry sheet on a lightly floured surface. Using a 9-inch pie plate as a template, cut the pastry sheet into a 9-inch circle. Repeat with the remaining pastry sheet. Reserve the trimmings for another use.

3. Cut **half** the cheese into **about 16** "sticks." Thinly slice the remaining cheese.

4. Brush the edges of the pastry circles with the egg mixture. Place the cheese "sticks" around the edges of the pastry circles. Fold the edges of the pastry over to enclose the cheese and press to seal. Brush the seam and edges of the pastry with the egg mixture. Prick the center of the pastry circles thoroughly with a fork.

5. Spread **1 tablespoon** Italian sauce on **each** pastry circle. Divide the cheese slices and sopressata evenly between the pastry circles.

6. Bake for 20 minutes or until the pastry is golden brown and the cheese is melted. Let the pizzas cool on the baking sheets on wire racks for 10 minutes.

7. Beat the lemon juice, oil and black pepper in a large bowl with a fork or whisk. Add the arugula and toss to coat. Divide the arugula mixture evenly between the pizzas.

zesty turkey burgers

prep 20 minutes | **grill** 11 minutes | **makes** 4 servings

- ⅓ cup regular *or* reduced-calorie mayonnaise
- 3 tablespoons canned cranberry sauce
- 1 tablespoon Dijon-style mustard
- 1¼ pounds ground turkey
- ½ cup Pace® Picante Sauce
- 2 tablespoons chopped fresh cilantro leaves
- 1 teaspoon dried thyme leaves, crushed
- 1 cup shredded Cheddar cheese *or* smoked Cheddar cheese
- 1 large orange, peeled and cut into thin slices
- 4 Pepperidge Farm® Classic Hamburger Buns, split and toasted
  Green leaf lettuce
  Thinly sliced red onion

1. Stir the mayonnaise, cranberry sauce and mustard in a small bowl.

2. Thoroughly mix the turkey, picante sauce, cilantro and thyme in a medium bowl. Shape the turkey mixture into **8** (½-inch thick) burgers. Place ¼ **cup** cheese in the center of **each** of **4** burgers. Top **each** with another burger. Pinch the edges of the burgers to enclose the cheese.

3. Lightly oil the grill rack and heat the grill to medium. Grill the burgers for 10 minutes or until desired doneness, turning them over once halfway through grilling. Grill the orange slices for 1 minute, turning them over once halfway through grilling.

4. Spread the mayonnaise mixture on the top halves of the buns. Place the lettuce leaves on the bottom halves of the buns. Top with the burgers, orange slices and onion.

tip *Also delicious with ground beef, chicken or pork.*

---

savory orange chicken with sage

prep 10 minutes | **cook** 20 minutes | **makes** 4 servings

- **4** skinless, boneless chicken breasts halves (about 1 pound)
- **½** cup all-purpose flour
- **1** tablespoon vegetable oil
- **1** tablespoon butter
- **1¾** cups Swanson® Chicken Stock
- **⅓** cup orange juice
- **¼** cup Chablis *or* other dry white wine
- **1** tablespoon grated orange zest
- **1** tablespoon chopped fresh sage leaves *or* 1 teaspoon ground sage
- **¼** teaspoon ground black pepper
- **2** cups chopped shiitake mushrooms (about 3½ ounces)
- Hot cooked rice

1. Coat the chicken with the flour.

2. Heat the oil and butter in a 12-inch skillet over medium-high heat. Add the chicken and cook for 10 minutes or until well browned on both sides. Remove the chicken from the skillet.

3. Stir the stock, juice, wine, orange zest, sage and black pepper in the skillet and heat to a boil. Stir in the mushrooms. Return the chicken to the skillet. Reduce the heat to low. Cook for 5 minutes or until the chicken is cooked through and liquid is reduced by one-fourth. Serve with the rice.

burgundy beef

prep 10 minutes I **cook** 25 minutes I **makes** 4 servings

 1 **tablespoon butter**
 1 **pound boneless beef sirloin steak, ¾-inch thick, cut into 1-inch pieces**
 1 **can (10½ ounces) Campbell's® Mushroom Gravy**
1½ **cups frozen whole baby carrots**
 ½ **cup frozen whole small white onions**
 ¼ **cup tomato paste**
 ¼ **cup Burgundy wine *or* other dry red wine**
 ⅛ **teaspoon garlic powder**
 ½ **of a 12-ounce package medium egg noodles (about 4 cups), cooked and drained**
    Chopped fresh parsley

1. Heat the butter in a 12-inch skillet over medium-high heat. Add the beef and cook until well browned, stirring often. Pour off any fat.

2. Stir the gravy, carrots, onions, tomato paste, wine and garlic powder in the skillet and heat to a boil. Reduce the heat to low. Cover and cook for 10 minutes or until the beef is cooked through. Serve the beef mixture over the noodles. Sprinkle with the parsley.

tip *For mushroom beef, use* **1 tablespoon** *Worcestershire sauce instead of the wine.*

dee's curry chicken

prep 15 minutes I **cook** 25 minutes I **makes** 6 servings

- 1¼ **pounds skinless, boneless chicken breast halves, cut into 1-inch pieces**
- 1 **tablespoon curry powder**
- 1 **teaspoon cumin**
- 2 **tablespoons vegetable oil**
- 2 **cloves garlic, chopped**
- 1 **large onion, chopped (about 1 cup)**
- 1 **tablespoon soy sauce**
- 1 **can (10¾ ounces) Campbell's® Condensed Cream of Mushroom Soup (Regular *or* 98% Fat Free)**
- 1¾ **cups Swanson® Chicken Broth *or* Swanson® Chicken Stock**
- 1 **medium green pepper, cut into 1-inch pieces (about 1 cup)**
- 1 **can (about 8 ounces) peas and carrots, drained**
- 1 **can (about 4 ounces) sliced mushrooms, drained**
- 1 **medium tomato, cut into wedges**
- 2 **cups regular long-grain white rice, prepared according to package directions (about 6 cups) (optional)**

1. Season the chicken with the curry powder and cumin. Heat **1 tablespoon** oil in a 10-inch skillet over medium-high heat. Add the chicken and cook until well browned, stirring often. Remove the chicken from the skillet.

2. Reduce the heat to medium. Heat the remaining oil in the skillet. Add the garlic and onion and cook until the onion is tender, stirring often.

3. Stir the soy sauce, soup, broth, pepper, peas and carrots, mushrooms and tomato in the skillet. Return the chicken to the skillet. Heat to a boil. Reduce the heat to low. Cover and cook for 5 minutes or until the chicken is cooked through. Serve the chicken mixture over the rice, if desired.

chicken with peas & quinoa

prep 10 minutes I **cook** 30 minutes I **makes** 4 servings

- 1 tablespoon olive oil
- 1 pound skinless, boneless chicken tenders
- 1 teaspoon smoked paprika
- 1 cup *uncooked* quinoa, rinsed
- 1½ cups Swanson® Chicken Broth **or** Swanson® Chicken Stock
- 1 jar (24 ounces) Prego® Veggie Smart® Smooth & Simple Italian Sauce
- 1 package (10 ounces) frozen peas, thawed

1. Heat the oil in a 12-inch skillet over medium-high heat. Add the chicken and cook for 10 minutes or until well browned on both sides. Remove the chicken from the skillet, cover and keep warm.

2. Add the paprika and quinoa to the skillet and stir to coat. Stir in the broth and Italian sauce and heat to a boil. Reduce the heat to medium. Cover and cook for 15 minutes or until the quinoa is tender. Stir in the peas. Return the chicken to the skillet. Cook until the chicken is cooked through.

grilled maui burgers

prep 15 minutes I **grill** 15 minutes I **makes** 4 servings

- 1 can (8 ounces) pineapple slices in juice, drained (4 slices)
- 1 cup Pace® Picante Sauce
- 1 pound lean ground beef
- 4 slices deli Monterey Jack cheese (about 3 ounces)
- 4 Pepperidge Farm® Hamburger Buns, split and toasted
- ½ avocado, peeled, pitted and cut into 4 slices

1. Lightly oil the grill rack and heat the grill to medium. Grill the pineapple for 5 minutes or until tender, turning it over once halfway through the grill time. Remove the pineapple to a cutting board. Dice the pineapple. Stir the pineapple and ⅔ **cup** picante sauce in a medium bowl.

2. Thoroughly mix the beef and the remaining picante sauce in a large bowl. Shape the beef mixture into **4** (½-inch-thick) burgers.

3. Grill the burgers for 10 minutes for medium or until desired doneness, turning the burgers over once halfway through the grill time. Top the burgers with the cheese.

4. Serve the burgers on the buns. Top with the pineapple-picante mixture and the avocado.

wild mushroom ragoût in puff pastry shells

prep 25 minutes | **cook** 25 minutes | **makes** 6 servings

- 1 **package (10 ounces) Pepperidge Farm® Puff Pastry Shells**
- 3 **tablespoons olive oil**
- 6 **cups assorted wild mushrooms (portobello, shiitake, oyster *and/or* cremini), cut into quarters**
- 1 **clove garlic, minced**
- 2 **tablespoons chopped fresh rosemary leaves**
- 2 **tablespoons chopped fresh thyme leaves**
- ¼ **cup white wine**
- ¼ **cup balsamic vinegar**
- 1 **can (10¾ ounces) Campbell's® Condensed Cream of Mushroom Soup (Regular *or* 98% Fat Free)**
- ½ **cup milk *or* heavy cream**
- 1 **tablespoon chopped fresh parsley**

1. Prepare the pastry shells according to the package directions.

2. Heat the oil in a 10-inch skillet over medium-high heat. Add the mushrooms, garlic, rosemary and thyme. Cook until the mushrooms are tender, stirring often.

3. Stir the wine and vinegar in the skillet. Cook until the liquid is reduced by half. Stir in the soup and milk and heat to a boil. Stir in the parsley.

4. Spoon the mushroom mixture into the pastry shells. Serve immediately.

buffalo chicken dip

prep 10 minutes I **bake** 20 minutes I **makes** 32 servings (about 4 cups)

- 1 package (8 ounces) cream cheese, softened
- ½ cup blue cheese salad dressing
- ½ cup any flavor hot pepper sauce
- 2 ounces crumbled blue cheese *or* shredded mozzarella cheese (about ½ cup)
- 2 cans (12.5 ounces *each*) Swanson® Premium White Chunk Chicken Breast in Water, drained
  Assorted fresh vegetables *and* Pepperidge Farm® crackers

1. Heat the oven to 350°F.

2. Stir the cream cheese in a 9-inch deep dish pie plate with a fork or whisk until smooth. Stir in the dressing, hot sauce and blue cheese. Stir in the chicken.

3. Bake for 20 minutes or until the chicken mixture is hot and bubbling. Stir the chicken mixture before serving. Serve with the vegetables and crackers for dipping.

To make in the microwave: Use a microwavable 9-inch-deep dish pie plate. Prepare the dip as directed above in Step 2. Microwave, uncovered, on HIGH for 5 minutes or until the chicken mixture is hot, stirring halfway through the cook time.

To reduce the fat: Use Neufchâtel **or** light cream cheese **and** reduced-fat blue cheese salad dressing.

 *This dip can be kept warm in a small slow cooker **or** fondue pot on the buffet table.*

linguine with easy red clam sauce

prep 20 minutes | **cook** 15 minutes | **makes** 4 servings

- 1   tablespoon olive **or** vegetable oil
- 2   cloves garlic, minced
- 1½ cups Prego® Traditional **or** Marinara Italian Sauce
- ¼   cup Chablis **or** other dry white wine
- 1   tablespoon chopped fresh parsley
- 2   cans (6½ ounces **each**) minced clams, undrained
- ½   package (8 ounces) linguine, cooked and drained (about 4 cups)
     Grated Parmesan cheese (optional)

1. Heat the oil in a 2-quart saucepan over medium heat. Add the garlic and cook until tender, stirring often.

2. Stir the Italian sauce, wine, parsley and clams and juice in the saucepan. Reduce the heat to low. Cover and cook for 10 minutes, stirring occasionally.

3. Serve the clam sauce over the linguine. Top with the cheese, if desired.

 *Angel hair **or** fettuccine can be substituted for the linguine in this recipe.*

onion-crusted meatloaf with roasted potatoes

prep 10 minutes | **cook** 1 hour 3 minutes | **makes** 6 servings

- 1 **can (10¾ ounces) Campbell's® Condensed Tomato Soup**
- 1½ **pounds ground beef**
- 1 **can (2.8 ounces) French fried onions**
- 1 **egg, beaten**
- 1 **tablespoon Worcestershire sauce**
- 6 **small potatoes, cut into quarters**

1. Thoroughly mix ½ **cup** soup, beef, ½ **can** onions, egg and Worcestershire in a large bowl. Place the mixture in a 13×9×2-inch baking pan and firmly shape into an 8×4-inch loaf. Spoon the remaining soup over the meatloaf. Arrange the potatoes around the meatloaf.

2. Bake at 400°F. for 1 hour or until the meatloaf is cooked through. Stir the potatoes. Sprinkle the remaining onions over the meatloaf and bake for 3 minutes or until the onions are golden.

slow cooker mole-style pulled pork

prep 10 minutes **I** **cook** 8 hours **I** **makes** 12 servings

 1 can (10½ ounces) Campbell's® Condensed French Onion Soup
 ¼ cup water
 1 tablespoon chili powder
 1 tablespoon brown sugar
 1 teaspoon ground cumin
 1 teaspoon ground cinnamon
 1 boneless pork shoulder roast (3½ to 4½ pounds)
 2 tablespoons semi-sweet chocolate pieces
12 flour tortillas (8-inch), warmed
 6 plum tomatoes, seeded and chopped
 ¼ cup chopped fresh cilantro leaves

1. Stir the soup, water, chili powder, brown sugar, cumin and cinnamon in a 6-quart slow cooker. Add the pork and turn to coat.

2. Cover and cook on LOW for 8 to 9 hours* or until the pork is fork-tender. Remove the pork to a cutting board. Using 2 forks, shred the pork. Add the chocolate to the cooker and stir until melted. Return the pork to the cooker.

3. Place **about** ½ **cup** pork mixture onto **half** of **each** tortilla. Top with the tomatoes and cilantro. Fold the tortillas over the filling.

Or on HIGH for 5 to 6 hours.

chicken creole with chile cream sauce

prep 10 minutes I **cook** 25 minutes I **makes** 4 servings

  4 **skinless, boneless chicken breast halves (about 1 pound)**

  2 **teaspoons Creole *or* Cajun seasoning**

  1 **tablespoon olive oil**

  1 **can (10¾ ounces) Campbell's® Condensed Cream of Chicken Soup (Regular *or* 98% Fat Free)**

  ½ **cup water**

  1 **can (4.5 ounces) chopped green chiles**

  1 **teaspoon lime juice**

  ¼ **cup sour cream**

    Hot cooked regular long-grain white rice

1. Season the chicken with the Creole seasoning.

2. Heat the oil in a 10-inch skillet over medium-high heat. Add the chicken and cook until well browned on both sides.

3. Stir the soup, water, chiles and lime juice in the skillet and heat to a boil. Reduce the heat to low. Cook for 5 minutes or until the chicken is cooked through.

4. Stir in the sour cream and cook until the mixture is hot and bubbling. Serve the chicken and sauce with the rice.

bandito baked beans

prep 5 minutes I **cook** 15 minutes I **makes** 6 servings

  1 **tablespoon vegetable oil**

  ½ **cup chopped onion**

  1 **cup Pace® Picante Sauce**

  ¼ **cup molasses**

  1 **tablespoon spicy-brown mustard**

  1 **can (about 15 ounces) pork and beans**

  1 **can (about 15 ounces) black beans, rinsed and drained**

1. Heat the oil in a 2-quart saucepan over medium heat. Add the onion and cook until tender.

2. Stir the picante sauce, molasses, mustard, pork and beans and black beans in the saucepan and heat to a boil. Reduce the heat to low. Cook for 5 minutes or until the mixture is hot and bubbling.

spanish chicken & chorizo

prep 15 minutes | **cook** 25 minutes | **makes** 4 servings

8 skinless, boneless chicken thighs (about 1 pound), cut into 2-inch pieces
2 tablespoons paprika
1 tablespoon olive oil
½ pound chorizo sausage, sliced
3 cloves garlic, minced
⅓ cup dry white wine
1 can (10¾ ounces) Campbell's® Condensed Cream of Chicken Soup (Regular *or* 98% Fat Free)
1 teaspoon chopped fresh thyme leaves
Hot cooked rice

1. Season the chicken with the paprika.

2. Heat the oil in a 10-inch skillet over medium-high heat. Add the chicken and cook until well browned, stirring occasionally. Add the sausage and cook until well browned, stirring occasionally.

3. Add the garlic to the skillet and cook and stir for 1 minute. Stir in the wine, soup and thyme and heat to a boil. Reduce the heat to low. Cook until the chicken is cooked through, stirring occasionally. Serve the chicken mixture with the rice.

curried chicken chowder

prep 10 minutes | **cook** 20 minutes | **makes** 6 servings

- 1 can (10¾ ounces) Campbell's® Healthy Request® Condensed Cream of Chicken Soup
- 1 can (10¾ ounces) Campbell's® Healthy Request® Condensed Chicken Rice Soup
- 2 soup cans water
- 1 teaspoon curry powder
- 2 medium potatoes (about 10 ounces), cut into cubes (about 2 cups)
- 1 package (about 9 ounces) frozen mixed vegetables
- ¼ cup diced green *or* red pepper
- 2 cans (4.5 ounces *each*) Swanson® Premium White Chunk Chicken Breast in Water, drained

1. Heat the soups, water, curry powder, potatoes, vegetables and pepper in a 4-quart saucepan over medium-high heat to a boil.

2. Reduce the heat to low. Cover and cook for 10 minutes or until the vegetables are tender. Stir in the chicken. Cook until the mixture is hot and bubbling.

chicken pot pie in a shell

prep 25 minutes | **cook** 20 minutes | **makes** 6 servings

- 1 package (10 ounces) Pepperidge Farm® Puff Pastry Shells
- 1 tablespoon vegetable oil
- 1 medium onion, chopped (about ½ cup)
- 1 can (10¾ ounces) Campbell's® Condensed Cream of Chicken Soup (Regular, 98% Fat Free *or* Healthy Request®)
- ½ cup milk
- 1 package (10 ounces) frozen peas and carrots
- 2 cups cubed cooked chicken *or* turkey

1. Prepare the pastry shells according to the package directions.

2. Heat the oil in a 10-inch skillet over medium-high heat. Add the onion and cook until tender.

3. Stir the soup, milk and peas and carrots in the skillet and heat to a boil. Reduce the heat to low. Cover and cook for 5 minutes or until the vegetables are tender. Add the chicken and cook until the mixture is hot and bubbling. Spoon the chicken mixture into the pastry shells.

savory balsamic herb chicken

prep 10 minutes I **cook** 25 minutes I **makes** 6 servings

1½ pounds skinless, boneless chicken thighs
  2 tablespoons all-purpose flour
  1 tablespoon olive oil
  1 medium onion, chopped (about 1 cup)
  2 cloves garlic, minced
  1 cup Swanson® Chicken Stock
  2 tablespoons balsamic vinegar
  1 teaspoon dried thyme leaves, crushed
    Hot cooked rice

1. Coat the chicken with the flour.

2. Heat the oil in a 10-inch skillet over medium-high heat. Add the chicken in 2 batches and cook until well browned on both sides. Remove the chicken from the skillet.

3. Add the onion and garlic to the skillet and cook until tender. Stir the stock, vinegar and thyme in the skillet and heat to a boil. Return the chicken to the skillet. Reduce the heat to low. Cover and cook for 5 minutes or until the chicken is cooked through. Serve with the rice.

southwestern turkey, corn and chile enchiladas

prep 20 minutes | **bake** 25 minutes | **makes** 8 servings

- 1 carton (18.3 ounces) Campbell's® V8® Southwestern Corn Soup
- ½ cup fat free sour cream
  Vegetable cooking spray
- 1 medium onion, chopped (about ½ cup)
- 2 cups chopped cooked turkey **or** chicken
- 1½ cups chopped plum tomato
- 1 can (4 ounces) chopped green chiles
- 8 flour tortillas (8-inch), warmed
- ½ cup shredded reduced-fat Cheddar cheese **or** Monterey Jack cheese
  Chopped fresh cilantro leaves

1. Stir the soup and sour cream in a small bowl until the mixture is smooth.

2. Spray a 10-inch skillet with the cooking spray and heat over medium-high heat for 1 minute. Add the onion and cook until tender. Stir in the turkey, **1 cup** tomatoes, chiles and **2 tablespoons** soup mixture.

3. Spread ½ **cup** soup mixture on the bottom of a 2-quart shallow baking dish. Spoon **about** ¼ **cup** turkey mixture down the center of **each** tortilla. Roll up the tortillas and place seam-side down in the baking dish. Spoon the remaining soup mixture over the filled tortillas. Top with the cheese.

4. Bake at 350°F. for 25 minutes or until the enchiladas are hot and bubbling. Top with the remaining tomatoes and the cilantro.

tip *You can substitute **3 cans** (4.5 ounces **each**) Swanson® Premium Chunk White Chicken Breast, drained, for the cooked chicken.*

cheesy enchilada stack

prep 20 minutes | **bake** 45 minutes | **makes** 8 servings

1 **pound ground beef**

2 **cups prepared enchilada sauce**

Vegetable cooking spray

6 **flour tortillas (10-inch)**

8 **ounces shredded Cheddar cheese (about 2 cups)**

1 **can (about 16 ounces) refried beans**

2 **cans (4 ounces *each*) chopped green chiles, drained**

Chopped green onions

1. Cook the beef in a 10-inch skillet over medium-high heat until well browned, stirring often to separate the meat. Pour off any fat. Stir ½ **cup** of the enchilada sauce in the skillet. Spray a baking sheet with the cooking spray.

2. Place **1** tortilla onto the baking sheet. Top with ⅓ of the beef mixture and ¼ **cup** cheese. Top with **1** tortilla, ½ of the refried beans, ½ **cup** enchilada sauce, **1 can** chiles and ¼ **cup** cheese. Repeat the layers. Top with **1** tortilla, remaining beef mixture and ¼ **cup** cheese. Top with the remaining tortilla. Cover the stack with aluminum foil.

3. Bake at 400°F. for 40 minutes or until the filling is hot. Uncover the stack. Top with the remaining enchilada sauce, cheese and onions. Bake for 5 minutes or until the cheese is melted. Cut the stack into **8** wedges.

savory stuffed mushrooms

prep 30 minutes | **bake** 10 minutes | **makes** 24 appetizers

- 24 medium mushrooms
- 6 tablespoons butter *or* margarine
- 1 small onion, chopped (about ¼ cup)
- ½ teaspoon garlic powder *or* 2 cloves garlic, minced
- 1 package (3 ounces) cream cheese, softened
- 3 tablespoons grated Parmesan cheese
- 2 tablespoons chopped fresh parsley *or* 2 teaspoons dried parsley flakes
- 1 cup Pepperidge Farm® Herb Seasoned Stuffing

1. Heat the oven to 425°F. Remove the stems from the mushrooms. Chop enough stems to make **1 cup**.

2. Heat **2 tablespoons** butter in a 2-quart saucepan over medium heat until melted. Brush the mushroom caps with the butter and place, top-side down, into a 3-quart shallow baking pan.

3. Heat the remaining butter in the saucepan until melted. Stir in the chopped mushroom stems, onion and garlic powder and cook until the mushrooms are tender. Stir in the cream cheese, Parmesan cheese and parsley. Add the stuffing and mix lightly. Spoon **about 1 tablespoon** stuffing mixture into each mushroom cap.

4. Bake for 10 minutes or until the filling is hot.

 To make ahead: *Prepare as directed above, but do not bake. Cover and refrigerate for up to 24 hours. Bake as directed above.*

chicken in creamy sun-dried tomato sauce

prep 15 minutes I **cook** 7 hours I **makes** 8 servings

- 2 cans (10¾ ounces *each*) Campbell's® Condensed Cream of Chicken with Herbs Soup **or** Campbell's® Condensed Cream of Chicken Soup
- 1 cup Chablis **or** other dry white wine*
- ¼ cup coarsely chopped pitted kalamata **or** oil-cured olives
- 2 tablespoons drained capers
- 2 cloves garlic, minced
- 1 can (14 ounces) artichoke hearts, drained and chopped
- 1 cup drained and coarsely chopped sun-dried tomatoes
- 8 skinless, boneless chicken breast halves (about 2 pounds)
- ½ cup chopped fresh basil leaves (optional)
  Hot cooked rice, egg noodles **or** mashed potatoes

You can substitute Swanson® Chicken Broth for the wine, if desired.

1. Stir the soup, wine, olives, capers, garlic, artichokes and tomatoes in a 3½-quart slow cooker. Add the chicken and turn to coat.

2. Cover and cook on LOW for 7 to 8 hours** or until the chicken is cooked through. Sprinkle with the basil, if desired. Serve with the rice.

**Or on HIGH for 4 to 5 hours.

polenta with mushroom vegetable topping

prep 30 minutes I **cook** 55 minutes I **cool** 10 minutes I **bake** 30 minutes I **makes** 8 servings

2 tablespoons olive oil

1 large onion, chopped (about 1 cup)

2 stalks celery, chopped (about 1 cup)

2 medium carrots, chopped (about ⅔ cup)

½ teaspoon ground black pepper

1 pound mixed wild* *and* white mushrooms, chopped (about 8 cups)

2 medium tomatoes, chopped (about 2 cups)

2 cloves garlic, minced

2 teaspoons dried thyme leaves, crushed

1¾ cups Swanson® Beef Broth (Regular, 50% Less Sodium *or* Certified Organic)

6 cups water

16 ounces *uncooked* instant polenta

½ cup grated Parmesan cheese

Use shiitake, cremini or oyster mushrooms.

tip *To make ahead: This dish can be prepared and completely assembled a day ahead. Cover and refrigerate overnight. Bake at 350°F. for 35 minutes or until the mixture is hot.*

1. Heat the oil in a 12-inch skillet over medium heat. Add the onion, celery, carrots and black pepper and cook until the vegetables are tender.

2. Stir the mushrooms, tomatoes, garlic and thyme in the skillet and cook for 5 minutes. Stir the broth in the skillet and heat to a boil. Reduce the heat to low and cook for 35 minutes or until the mixture is thickened.

3. Heat the oven to 350°F.

4. Heat the water in a 4-quart saucepan over medium-high heat to a boil. Stir in the polenta. Cook and stir for 5 minutes or until the mixture is very thick. Remove the saucepan from the heat. Stir in ¼ **cup** cheese. Spread the polenta in a 3-quart shallow baking dish. Let cool for 10 minutes.

5. Spread the vegetable mixture over the polenta. Sprinkle with the remaining cheese.

6. Bake for 30 minutes or until the vegetable mixture is hot and the cheese is melted.

mediterranean halibut with couscous

prep 15 minutes I **cook** 15 minutes I **makes** 4 servings

- 4 **halibut steaks, about 1-inch thick**
- ¼ **cup all-purpose flour**
- 3 **tablespoons olive oil**
- 2 **shallots, chopped**
- 1 **cup Swanson® Chicken Stock**
- 2 **teaspoons dried oregano leaves, crushed**
- 1 **can (about 14.5 ounces) diced tomatoes, drained**
- ½ **cup kalamata olives, pitted and sliced**
  Hot cooked couscous*

For the couscous: Prepare 1 package (10 ounces) couscous according to the package directions, substituting Swanson® Chicken Broth for the water.

1. Coat the fish with the flour.

2. Heat **2 tablespoons** oil in a 12-inch skillet over medium-high heat. Add the fish and cook for 5 minutes or until well browned on both sides and cooked through. Remove the fish from the skillet and keep warm.

3. Heat the remaining oil in the skillet. Add the shallots and cook for 1 minute. Stir in the stock, oregano, tomatoes and olives and heat to a boil. Cook for 5 minutes or until the sauce is slightly thickened. Season to taste. Serve the sauce with the fish and couscous.

oven-roasted chicken with artichokes, lemon and tomato sauce

prep 15 minutes | **roast** 35 minutes | **makes** 6 servings

- 6 **skinless, boneless chicken breast halves (about 1½ pounds)**
- 1 **package (8 ounces) frozen artichoke hearts, cut into quarters**
- 3 **cups Prego® Heart Smart Roasted Red Pepper & Garlic Italian Sauce**
- 1 **tablespoon lemon juice**
- 1 **teaspoon grated lemon zest**
- 3 **cups hot cooked couscous**

1. Heat the oven to 400°F.

2. Place the chicken and artichoke hearts into a 17×11-inch shallow roasting pan. Stir the Italian sauce, lemon juice and lemon zest in a medium bowl. Pour the sauce mixture over the chicken and artichoke hearts.

3. Roast for 35 minutes or until the chicken is cooked through. Serve the chicken mixture over the couscous.

tip *Try sprinkling the finished dish with some chopped pitted kalamata olives.*

pineapple-picante stir-fried pork & cabbage

prep 20 minutes | **cook** 30 minutes | **makes** 4 servings

- 1 cup Pace® Picante Sauce
- 1 tablespoon rice vinegar
- 2 tablespoons minced peeled fresh ginger root
- 1 can (8 ounces) pineapple chunks in juice, drained, reserving juice
- 1 tablespoon cornstarch
- 2 tablespoons vegetable oil
- 1 boneless pork tenderloin (about 1 pound), cut into thin strips
- 1 medium head green cabbage (about 2 pounds), cut in quarters and very thinly sliced (about 8 cups)
- ¼ cup water

1. Stir the picante sauce, vinegar, ginger root, pineapple juice and cornstarch in a medium bowl.

2. Heat **1 tablespoon** oil in a 12-inch skillet over medium-high heat. Add the pork and stir-fry until well browned. Remove the pork from the skillet.

3. Heat the remaining oil in the skillet. Add the cabbage and stir-fry until tender-crisp. Add the water and cook for 5 minutes, stirring occasionally. Remove the cabbage from the skillet and keep warm.

4. Add the picante sauce mixture to the skillet. Cook and stir over medium heat until the mixture boils and thickens. Stir in the pineapple chunks. Return the pork to the skillet and cook until the mixture is hot and bubbling. Serve the pork mixture over the cabbage.

chicken with wild mushroom cream sauce

prep 15 minutes I **cook** 25 minutes I **makes** 4 servings

- 4 skinless, boneless chicken breast halves (about 1 pound)
  Ground black pepper
- 2 tablespoons all–purpose flour
- 2 tablespoons butter
- 4 ounces sliced mixed wild mushrooms (cremini, shiitake, oyster) (about 2 cups)
- 4 green onions, sliced (about ½ cup)
- 1 cup Swanson® Chicken Stock
- ½ cup chopped roasted red pepper
- ½ cup sour cream
- 2 tablespoons chopped fresh parsley

1. Season the chicken with the black pepper and coat with the flour.

2. Heat the butter in a 10-inch skillet over medium-high heat. Add the chicken and cook for 10 minutes or until well browned on both sides. Add the mushrooms and onions and cook until tender.

3. Stir the stock in the skillet and heat to a boil. Reduce the heat to low. Cover and cook for 5 minutes or until the chicken is cooked through. Stir in the pepper and sour cream and heat through. Sprinkle with the parsley.

 *Dried wild mushrooms can be used instead of fresh ones. Soak **1 ounce** dried mushrooms in Swanson® stock and cover for 10 minutes before slicing.*

salmon with cucumber-dill cream napoleons

thaw 40 minutes **I** **prep** 35 minutes **I** **bake** 15 minutes **I** **cool** 10 minutes **I** **makes** 6 servings

    1 cup sour cream
    ½ cup chopped cucumber
    3 tablespoons chopped fresh dill weed **or** 1 tablespoon dried dill weed
    ½ of a 17.3-ounce package Pepperidge Farm® Puff Pastry Sheets (1 sheet), thawed
 1¾ cups Swanson® Chicken Broth (Regular, Natural Goodness® **or** Certified Organic)
    ¼ cup Chablis **or** other dry white wine
    ¼ teaspoon ground black pepper
    6 salmon fillets, 1-inch thick (about 1½ pounds)

1. Heat the oven to 400°F. Stir the sour cream, cucumber and **2 tablespoons** dill weed in a small bowl. Cover and refrigerate until serving time.

2. Unfold the pastry sheet on a lightly floured surface. Cut the pastry sheet into **3** strips along the fold marks. Cut **each** strip into **2** rectangles. Place the pastry rectangles onto a baking sheet.

3. Bake for 15 minutes or until the pastries are golden brown. Let the pastries cool on the baking sheet on a wire rack for 10 minutes. Split **each** pastry into **2** layers, making **12** layers in all.

4. Heat the broth, wine, black pepper and remaining dill weed in a 10-inch skillet over medium heat to a boil. Add the fish to the skillet. Reduce the heat to low. Cover and cook for 10 minutes or until the fish flakes easily when tested with a fork.

5. Spread **1 tablespoon** sour cream mixture on **each** of **6** bottom pastry layers. Top **each** with **1 fillet** fish, **1 tablespoon** sour cream mixture and a top pastry layer. Discard the broth mixture. Serve the Napoleons with the remaining sour cream mixture.

florentine turkey meatloaf

prep 15 minutes | **bake** 1 hour | **stand** 10 minutes | **makes** 6 servings

1¼ **pounds ground turkey**

1 **cup Prego® Traditional Italian Sauce**

½ **cup Italian-seasoned dry bread crumbs**

½ **cup onion, finely chopped**

2 **eggs *or* 1 egg and 2 egg whites**

2 **tablespoons Parmesan cheese**

½ **teaspoon fennel seed**

1 **package (10 ounces) frozen chopped spinach, thawed and drained**

¾ **cup low-fat shredded mozzarella cheese**

1. Heat the oven to 350°F. Spray an 8- or 9-inch loaf pan with vegetable cooking spray; set aside.

2. Mix the ground turkey, ¼ **cup** Italian sauce, bread crumbs, onion, eggs, Parmesan cheese and fennel in a medium bowl.

3. Press **half** of the turkey mixture into prepared pan. Press a 1-inch indentation down center of the mixture, leaving 1-inch thickness on all sides.

4. Toss the spinach and mozzarella cheese together; spoon into the indentation, mounding in the center. Press the remaining turkey mixture evenly over the top, sealing the edges.

5. Bake for 45 to 50 minutes. Spoon the remaining sauce over the meatloaf. Bake for 15 minutes longer. Let stand for 10 minutes.

tip *If you don't have cooking spray, try parchment paper. The quickest way to line an 8- or 9-inch loaf pan is to cut **1** (5-inch) sheet of parchment and **1** (8- or 9-inch) sheet of parchment. Place these sheets in pan, criss-crossing at the center. Trim any excess parchment that extends above the edge of the pan.*

crispy chicken with asparagus sauce

prep 10 minutes | **cook** 20 minutes | **makes** 4 servings

1 **egg**
4 **skinless, boneless chicken breast halves (aobut 1 pound)**
½ **cup dry bread crumbs**
2 **tablespoons vegetable oil**
1 **can (10¾ ounces) Campbell's® Condensed Cream of Asparagus Soup**
⅓ **cup milk**
⅓ **cup water**
4 **cups hot cooked rice**
Grated Parmesan cheese

1. Beat the egg in a shallow dish with a fork or whisk. Dip the chicken into the egg. Coat the chicken with the bread crumbs.

2. Heat the oil in a 10-inch skillet over medium-high heat. Add the chicken and cook for 15 minutes or until well browned on both sides and cooked through. Remove the chicken from the skillet and keep warm.

3. Stir the soup, milk and water in the skillet and heat over medium heat until the mixture is hot and bubbling. Serve the chicken and sauce with the rice. Sprinkle with the cheese.

easy chicken molé

prep 15 minutes I **cook** 35 minutes I **makes** 6 servings

1 tablespoon vegetable oil

6 skinless, boneless chicken breasts halves (about 1½ pounds)

1 can (about 15 ounces) tomato sauce

½ cup Pace® Picante Sauce

1 tablespoon unsweetened cocoa powder

1 tablespoon packed brown sugar

1 teaspoon ground cumin

½ teaspoon ground cinnamon

¼ teaspoon garlic powder **or** 2 cloves garlic, minced

6 cups hot cooked rice, cooked without salt

1. Heat the oil in a 10-inch skillet over medium-high heat. Add the chicken in 2 batches and cook for 10 minutes or until well browned on both sides. Remove the chicken from the skillet.

2. Stir the tomato sauce, picante sauce, cocoa powder, brown sugar, cumin, cinnamon and garlic powder in the skillet and heat to a boil. Reduce the heat to low. Cook for 5 minutes. Return the chicken to the skillet. Cover and cook for 5 minutes or until the chicken is cooked through. Serve the chicken and sauce with the rice.

mexican lasagna

prep 25 minutes | **bake** 30 minutes | **stand** 10 minutes | **makes** 4 servings

- 1 **can (10¾ ounces) Campbell's® Healthy Request® Condensed Cream of Mushroom Soup**
- ½ **cup nonfat milk**
- ¾ **pound lean ground beef (80% lean)**
- ½ **cup chopped onion**
- 1 **tablespoon chili powder**
- 1 **can (10¾ ounces) Campbell's® Healthy Request® Condensed Tomato Soup**
- 4 **lasagna noodles, cooked without salt and drained**
- ½ **cup shredded reduced-fat Cheddar cheese (2 ounces)**

1. Stir the mushroom soup and milk in a small bowl until the mixture is smooth.

2. Cook the beef, onion and chili powder in a 3-quart saucepan over medium-high heat until the beef is well browned, stirring often to separate the meat. Pour off any fat.

3. Stir the tomato soup in the saucepan and cook until the mixture is hot and bubbling.

4. Layer **half** the beef mixture, **2** lasagna noodles and **half** the mushroom soup mixture in an 8-inch square baking dish, trimming the noodles to fit the dish, if needed. Repeat the layers. Sprinkle with the cheese.

5. Bake at 400°F. for 30 minutes or until the filling is hot and the cheese is melted. Let stand for 10 minutes before serving.

oven-fried chicken chimichangas

prep 20 minutes I **bake** 25 minutes I **makes** 6 servings

- ⅔ cup Pace® Picante Sauce
- 1 teaspoon ground cumin
- ½ teaspoon dried oregano leaves, crushed
- 1½ cups chopped cooked chicken
- 4 ounces shredded Cheddar cheese (about 1 cup)
- 2 green onions, chopped (about ¼ cup)
- 6 flour tortillas (8-inch)
- 2 tablespoons butter, melted
- Fresh cilantro leaves

1. Stir the picante sauce, cumin, oregano, chicken, cheese and onions in a medium bowl.

2. Place **about** ½ **cup** of the chicken mixture in the center of **each** tortilla. Fold the opposite sides over the filling. Roll up from the bottom and place seam-side down on a baking sheet. Brush with butter.

3. Bake at 400°F. for 25 minutes or until golden brown. Serve with additional picante sauce. Garnish with cilantro.

tip For 1½ *cups* chopped chicken, in a 2-quart saucepan over medium heat, in **4 cups** boiling water, cook ¾ **pound** boneless chicken breasts **or** thighs, cubed, for 5 minutes or until the chicken is cooked through. Drain and chop the chicken.

parties & entertaining

Entertaining should be as easy as it is fun.

pan-seared steaks with mushroom gravy

prep 5 minutes | **cook** 25 minutes | **makes** 4 servings

1 **boneless beef sirloin steak, cut into 4 pieces (about 1 pound)**

1 **tablespoon unsalted butter**

2 **cups sliced fresh mushrooms (about 6 ounces)**

1 **tablespoon all-purpose flour**

1 **cup Swanson® Beef Stock**

1. Season the steaks as desired. Cook the steaks in a 12-inch nonstick skillet over medium-high heat to desired doneness. Remove the steaks from the skillet. Do not pour off any fat.

2. Heat the butter in the skillet. Add the mushrooms and cook until tender. Stir in the flour and cook for 1 minute. Gradually stir in the stock. Cook and stir until the mixture boils and thickens. Serve the mushroom gravy with the steaks.

party & entertaining ideas

Entertaining should be as easy as it is fun. If you're planning a party, use these starting points as guidelines for how much food and drink to have on hand, and try out our tips for setting up a buffet. They'll help ensure that your event is as enjoyable for you as it will be for your guests.

- *Drinks:* Plan on your guests consuming about 1 drink per hour of the party. For ease, limit drink choices to 2 or 3 items (for instance, red and white wine plus bottled beer; or pitchers of margaritas or sangria and beer), plus a handful of non-alcoholic choices, like iced tea, sodas, and water. A 750-ml bottle of wine or champagne serves about 5 people.

- *Finger foods:* Plan an hors d'oeuvres party with 1 idea in mind—variety. Different textures, temperatures, and flavors will make the party come to life and give your guests lots of options. For a 2-hour appetizer-only party, plan on serving 5 or 6 different appetizers and allow for 2 pieces of each per person.

- *Buffet ideas:* Avoid buffet congestion by setting up multiple stations in different areas of the room. For example, use the main table for big items, then set up 2 smaller tables away from the big table for drinks and desserts.

fantastic cookie bars

thaw 40 minutes I **prep** 15 minutes I **bake** 30 minutes I **cool** 30 minutes I **makes** 48 pieces

 1 **package (17.3 ounces) Pepperidge Farm® Puff Pastry Sheets, thawed**
1½ **cups chopped pecans**
 1 **cup sweetened flaked coconut**
 1 **bag (12 ounces) semi-sweet chocolate pieces (about 2 cups)**
 1 **can (14 ounces) sweetened condensed milk**

1. Heat the oven to 400°F.

2. Unfold **1** pastry sheet on a lightly floured surface. Roll the pastry sheet into a 12-inch square. Place the pastry sheet onto a baking sheet. Brush the edges with water. Fold over the edges ½ inch on all sides, pressing firmly to form a rim. Prick the center of the pastry thoroughly with a fork. Repeat with the remaining pastry sheet.

3. Bake for 15 minutes, rotating the baking sheets between the top and bottom oven racks halfway through the baking time. Divide the pecans, coconut and chocolate between the pastry crusts. Drizzle **half** the condensed milk over **each**.

4. Bake for 15 minutes or until the pastries are golden brown, rotating the baking sheets between the top and bottom oven racks halfway through the baking time.

5. Let the pastries cool on the baking sheets on wire racks for 30 minutes. Cut **each** pastry into **24** bars.

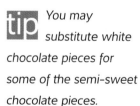 *You may substitute white chocolate pieces for some of the semi-sweet chocolate pieces.*

beef wellington

thaw 40 minutes I **prep** 15 minutes I **cook** 40 minutes I **chill** 1 hour I **bake** 25 minutes
makes 10 servings

1 **(2- to 2½-pound) beef tenderloin**
   Ground black pepper (optional)
1 **egg**
1 **tablespoon water**
1 **tablespoon butter**
2 **cups finely chopped mushrooms**
1 **medium onion, finely chopped (about ½ cup)**
½ **of a 17.3-ounce package Pepperidge Farm® Puff Pastry Sheets (1 sheet), thawed**

1. Heat the oven to 425°F. Place the beef into a lightly greased roasting pan. Season with the black pepper, if desired. Roast for 30 minutes or until a meat thermometer reads 130°F. Cover the pan and refrigerate for 1 hour.

2. Reheat the oven to 425°F. Beat the egg and water in a small bowl with a fork or whisk.

3. Heat the butter in a 10-inch skillet over medium-high heat. Add the mushrooms and onion and cook until the mushrooms are tender and all the liquid is evaporated, stirring often.

4. Unfold the pastry sheet on a lightly floured surface. Roll the pastry sheet into a rectangle 4 inches longer and 6 inches wider than the beef. Brush the pastry sheet with the egg mixture. Spoon the mushroom mixture onto the pastry sheet to within 1 inch of the edges. Place the beef in the center of the mushroom mixture. Fold the pastry over the beef and press to seal. Place seam-side down onto a baking sheet. Tuck the ends under to seal. Brush the pastry with the egg mixture.

5. Bake for 25 minutes or until the pastry is golden brown and a meat thermometer reads 140°F.

creamy dijon dressing

prep 5 minutes I **chill** 2 hours I **makes** 16 servings

1 can (10¾ ounces) Campbell's®
  Healthy Request® Condensed
  Cream of Celery Soup

½ cup reduced-calorie mayonnaise

¼ cup water

2 tablespoons vinegar

2 tablespoons Dijon-style mustard

½ teaspoon garlic powder

Stir the soup, mayonnaise, water, vinegar, mustard and garlic powder in a medium bowl. Cover and refrigerate for 2 hours. Stir the dressing before serving.

salsa-ranch dip

prep 5 minutes I **chill** 1 hour I **makes** 20 servings (2 ½ cups)

¾ cup Pace® Chunky Salsa

1 container (16 ounces) sour cream

1 package (1.0 ounce) ranch dip mix
  Tortilla chips *or* assorted cut-up
  fresh vegetables

Stir the salsa, sour cream and dip mix in a small bowl. Cover and refrigerate for 1 hour or until the mixture is chilled. Serve with the tortilla chips or vegetables for dipping.

roasted dijon & apple glazed turkey with fruited stuffing

prep 20 minutes | **roast** 5 hours | **stand** 10 minutes | **makes** 12 servings

3 cups Swanson® Chicken Stock

2 small Granny Smith apples, chopped (about 2 cups)

1 medium onion, chopped (about ½ cup)

1 package (12 ounces) Pepperidge Farm® Sage & Onion Stuffing

1 cup apple cider **or** juice

½ cup packed brown sugar

¼ cup coarse-grain Dijon-style mustard

1 (12- to 14-pound) turkey

2 tablespoons oil

2 cans (10½ ounces **each**) Campbell's® Turkey Gravy

1. Heat 2½ **cups** stock, apples and onion in a 3-quart saucepan over medium-high heat to a boil. Reduce the heat to low. Cover and cook for 5 minutes or until the onion is tender. Add the stuffing and stir lightly to coat.

2. Heat the remaining stock, cider, brown sugar and mustard in a 2-quart saucepan over medium-high heat to a boil. Reduce the heat to medium. Cook for 8 minutes or until the glaze is reduced by one-third.

3. Remove the package of the giblets and neck from the turkey cavity. Rinse the turkey with cold water and pat dry with a paper towel. Spoon the stuffing mixture lightly into the neck and body cavities. Fold the loose skin over the stuffing. Tie the ends of the drumsticks together. Spoon any of the remaining stuffing into a casserole. Cover and bake the stuffing alongside the turkey during the last 30 minutes of roasting or until the stuffing is heated through.

4. Place the turkey, breast-side up, on a rack in a shallow roasting pan. Brush the turkey with the oil.

5. Roast the turkey at 325°F. for 4½ to 5 hours or until cooked through. Baste occasionally with the glaze. Begin checking for doneness after 4 hours of roasting time. Remove the turkey from the pan and let it stand for 10 minutes before slicing.

6. Skim off the fat from the pan drippings. Stir the gravy into the roasting pan. Cook the mixture over medium heat until heated through, stirring occasionally. Serve with the turkey and stuffing.

company buffet layered salad

prep 35 minutes I **chill** 4 hours I **makes** 12 servings

- 1 can (10¾ ounces) Campbell's® Condensed Cream of Mushroom Soup (Regular **or** 98% Fat Free)
- 1 cup sour cream, plain yogurt **or** mayonnaise
- ¼ cup grated Parmesan Cheese
- 1 tablespoon grated onion
- 6 cups mixed salad greens, torn into bite-sized pieces
- 2 medium carrots, zucchini **or** cucumbers, thinly sliced
- 2 cups sliced mushrooms (about 6 ounces)
- 2 medium tomatoes, diced (about 2 cups)
- 4 green onions, sliced (about ½ cup)

    Sliced pitted ripe olives, parsley **or** chopped hard-cooked egg

1. Stir the soup, sour cream, cheese and onion in a small bowl.

2. Layer the salad greens, carrots, mushrooms and tomatoes in a clear 4-quart serving bowl. Spread the soup mixture over the salad. Cover and refrigerate for 4 hours. Sprinkle with the green onions and olives before serving.

 tip *Substitute Campbell's® Condensed Cream of Celery **or** Cream of Chicken Soup for the Cream of Mushroom Soup.*

challah

1 **can (10½ ounces) Campbell's® Condensed Chicken Broth**
1¼ **cups water**
2 **packages (¼ ounces *each*) active dry yeast**
4 **eggs**
¼ **cup vegetable oil**
1 **tablespoon salt**
1 **tablespoon sugar**
9 **cups all-purpose flour**

1. Heat the broth and water in a 1-quart saucepan over low heat until warm but not hot. Place the yeast into a large bowl. Add the broth mixture and stir until the yeast is dissolved.

2. Add **3** eggs, oil, salt and sugar to the bowl and beat with a fork or whisk. Stir in the flour. Place the dough on a lightly floured surface and knead until the dough is smooth.

3. Lightly grease a large bowl with butter or oil. Add the dough and turn to coat. **Cover** and let rise in a warm place for about 1½ hours or until the dough has doubled in size.

4. Beat the remaining egg in a small bowl with a fork or whisk.

5. Punch down the dough. Divide the dough into **6** pieces. Roll **each** into a 12-inch rope. Place **3** ropes side-by-side on a greased baking sheet. Begin to braid in the middle of the ropes and braid to one end. Turn the baking sheet around and braid from the middle to the other end. Repeat with the remaining ropes. Brush the loaves with the egg. **Cover** and let rise in a warm place for 1 hour or until the loaves are doubled in size.

6. Heat the oven to 350°F. Bake for 30 minutes or until the loaves are golden brown. Remove the loaves from the baking sheets and let cool on wire racks for 10 minutes.

chocolate pirouette-crusted cake

thaw 1 hour 30 minutes I **prep** 10 minutes I **makes** 8 servings

   1 **box (19.6 ounces) Pepperidge Farm® Chocolate Fudge 3 Layer Cake**
   ½ **of a 13.5-ounce canister Pepperidge Farm® Chocolate Hazelnut Pirouette® (about 18)**

1. Thaw the cake according to the package directions. Place the cake onto a serving dish.

2. Cut the wafers into 2½-inch-long pieces. Place the wafers upright, side-by-side, all around the edge of the cake, pressing them gently into the frosting. Place any remaining wafers on top of the cake.

 This cake can be prepared up to 2 days ahead and stored in the refrigerator.

bacon and cheddar puff pastry crisps

thaw 40 minutes I **prep** 20 minutes I **bake** 13 minutes I **cool** 10 minutes I **makes** 72 crisps

1 **package (17.3 ounces) Pepperidge Farm® Puff Pastry Sheets, thawed**

1 **cup finely shredded Cheddar cheese (about 4 ounces)**

1 **pound bacon, cooked and crumbled**

½ **cup prepared ranch salad dressing**

2 **tablespoons chopped fresh chives**

1. Heat the oven to 400°F.

2. Unfold **1** pastry sheet on a lightly floured surface. Roll the pastry sheet into a 12×12-inch square. Cut into **36** (2-inch) squares. Prick the pastry squares with a fork. Repeat with the remaining pastry sheet, making **72** squares in all. Place the squares onto baking sheets.

3. Bake for 8 minutes or until the pastries are golden brown. Using the back of a spoon, press down the centers of the hot pastries to make an indentation.

4. Spoon **about** ½ **teaspoon each** cheese and bacon onto **each** pastry. Bake for 5 minutes or until the cheese is melted. Remove the pastries from the baking sheets and let cool on wire racks for 10 minutes. Top with the dressing and chives.

herbed turkey breast

prep 10 minutes I **cook** 8 hours I **stand** 10 minutes I **makes** 8 servings

1 can (10¾ ounces) Campbell's® Condensed Cream of Mushroom Soup (Regular *or* 98% Fat Free)
½ cup water
1 (4½- to 5-pound) turkey breast
1 teaspoon poultry seasoning
1 tablespoon chopped fresh parsley
   Hot mashed potatoes

1. Stir the soup and water in a 3½- to 6-quart slow cooker. Rinse the turkey with cold water and pat it dry. Rub the turkey with the poultry seasoning and place it into the cooker. Sprinkle with the parsley.

2. Cover and cook on LOW for 8 to 9 hours* or until the turkey is cooked through. Let the turkey stand for 10 minutes before slicing. Serve with the soup mixture and mashed potatoes.

*Or on HIGH for 4 to 5 hours.

tip *If using a frozen turkey breast, thaw it before cooking.*

beefy taco dip

prep 5 minutes **| cook** 15 minutes **| makes** 2 servings

½ **pound ground beef**

1½ **teaspoons chili powder**

1 **cup Pace® Chunky Salsa**

½ **of an 8-ounce package cream cheese, cut into pieces**

½ **cup shredded Cheddar cheese**

Assorted Toppings (optional)

Sour cream (optional)

Tortilla chips

1. Cook the beef and chili powder in a 10-inch skillet over medium-high heat until the beef is well browned, stirring often. Pour off any fat.

2. Stir the salsa, cream cheese and Cheddar cheese in the skillet. Cook and stir until the cheese is melted. Sprinkle with the *Assorted Toppings* and top with the sour cream, if desired. Serve with the tortilla chips.

Assorted Toppings: Chopped tomatoes, sliced green onions, sliced pitted ripe olives.

stuffed pork roast with herb-seasoned artichoke & mushroom stuffing

prep 35 minutes | **cook** 45 minutes | **stand** 10 minutes | **makes** 12 servings

- ½ cup (1 stick) butter, cut into pieces
- 2 tablespoons olive oil
- 6 medium green onions, chopped (about ¾ cup)
- 1 tablespoon minced garlic
- 3 cups Swanson® Chicken Stock
- 2 cans (14 ounces *each*) artichoke hearts, drained and chopped
- 2 cans (14 ounces *each*) sliced mushrooms, drained
- 2 tablespoons chopped fresh parsley
- 1 teaspoon ground black pepper
- 1 package (14 ounces) Pepperidge Farm® Herb Seasoned Stuffing
- 1 (5- to 7-pound) center-cut boneless pork loin roast, butterflied
  Garlic powder

1. Heat the butter and oil in a 12-inch skillet over medium heat. Add the green onions and garlic and cook until the onions are tender. Stir in the stock, artichokes, mushrooms, parsley and black pepper and heat to a boil.

2. Remove the skillet from the heat. Add the stuffing and mix lightly.

3. Heat the oven to 400°F. Spoon **3 cups** stuffing mixture down the center of the pork. Fold the sides over the filling to form a roll. Tie the pork crosswise at 2-inch intervals with kitchen twine. (The remaining stuffing can be baked in a covered casserole during the last 15 minutes of roasting.)

4. Season the pork with additional black pepper and the garlic powder. Place the pork in a 17×11-inch roasting pan.

5. Roast for 45 minutes or until the pork is cooked through. Let the pork stand for 10 minutes. Remove the twine before slicing.

> **tip** *You can have the butcher butterfly the roast for you or do it yourself. To do it yourself, hold your knife horizontally and make a lengthwise cut about 1½ inches deep along the side of the roast (do not cut all the way through). Open the roast like a book. Pound the pork with a meat mallet to achieve an even thickness.*

classic standing rib roast

prep 15 minutes I **roast** 2 hours 20 minutes I **stand** 20 minutes I **makes** 8 servings

1 (7- to 8-pound) beef standing rib roast
¼ teaspoon ground black pepper
½ cup Swanson® Beef Stock (Regular **or** Unsalted)
3 tablespoons red wine

1. Heat the oven to 325°F. Season the beef with the black pepper. Place the beef into a roasting pan, rib-side down.

2. Roast for 2 hours 20 minutes for medium-rare or until desired doneness. Remove the beef to a cutting board and let stand for 20 minutes.

3. Spoon off any fat from the pan drippings. Stir the stock and wine, if desired, in the pan. Cook and stir over medium-high heat until the sauce is reduced slightly, scraping up the browned bits from the bottom of the pan. Season with additional black pepper, if desired. Serve the stock mixture with the beef.

herbed chèvre en croûte

thaw 40 minutes I **prep** 50 minutes I **bake** 20 minutes I **cool** 5 minutes I **makes** 8 servings

- 1 **egg**
- 1 **tablespoon water**
- ¼ **cup chopped fresh herbs (parsley *and* chives)**
- 1 **teaspoon cracked black pepper**
- 1 **package (8 to 10 ounces) soft mild goat cheese (chèvre)**
- ½ **of a 17.3-ounce package Pepperidge Farm® Puff Pastry Sheets (1 sheet), thawed**
  Salad Mesclun

1. Heat the oven to 375°F. Beat the egg and water in a small bowl with a fork.

2. Stir the herbs and black pepper on a plate. Coat the cheese with the herb mixture.

3. Unfold the pastry sheet on a lightly floured surface. With the short side facing you, place the cheese on the bottom third of the pastry sheet to within 1 inch of the edge. Starting at the short side, roll up like a jelly roll. Place the filled pastry seam-side down onto a baking sheet. Tuck the ends under to seal. Brush the pastry with the egg wash.

4. Bake for 20 minutes or until the pastry is golden brown. Let the pastry cool on the baking sheet on a wire rack for 5 minutes. Cut the pastry into **8** slices. Divide the *Salad Mesclun* among 8 plates. Top **each** with **1** slice cheese pastry.

> **tip** *Omit plain goat cheese, pepper and herbs. Substitute a soft mild goat cheese log with garlic and herbs.*

Salad Mesclun: Place *1* bag (about 9 ounces) gourmet salad mixed greens (arugula, frisée, mâche, oak leaf *and/or* radicchio) in a medium bowl. Beat *2 tablespoons* lemon juice, *1 tablespoon* grated lemon peel and *1 teaspoon* Dijon-style mustard in a small bowl. Gradually beat *3 tablespoons each* olive and canola oil into the juice mixture with a whisk. Season to taste. Toss the salad greens with dressing.

baked corn casserole

prep 10 minutes   I   **bake** 35 minutes   I   **makes** 6 servings

1   **can (10¾ ounces) Campbell's® Condensed Cream of Chicken Soup
      (Regular *or* 98% Fat Free)**

½   **cup milk**

2   **eggs**

1   **can (about 16 ounces) whole kernel corn, drained**

1   **package (about 8 ounces) corn muffin mix**

¼   **cup grated Parmesan cheese**

1   **can (2.8 ounces) French fried onions (about 1⅓ cups)**

1. Beat the soup, milk and eggs in a medium bowl with a fork or whisk. Stir in the corn, corn muffin mix, cheese and ⅔ **cup** onions. Pour the soup mixture into a 1½-quart casserole.

2. Bake at 350°F. for 30 minutes or until the mixture is hot.

3. Top with the remaining onions. Bake for 5 minutes or until the onions are golden brown.

basil skillet potatoes

prep 15 minutes | **cook** 15 minutes | **makes** 4 servings

1 **tablespoon butter**

1 **small onion, chopped (about ¼ cup)**

½ **teaspoon dried basil leaves, crushed**

1 **can (10¾ ounces) Campbell's® Condensed Cream of Celery Soup (Regular *or* 98% Fat Free)**

¼ **cup water**

½ **cup shredded Cheddar cheese (about 2 ounces)**

4 **medium potatoes (about 1¼ pounds), cooked and sliced ¼-inch thick**

1. Heat the butter in a 10-inch skillet over medium heat. Add the onion and basil and cook until the onion is tender.

2. Stir the soup, water and cheese in the skillet and heat until the cheese melts, stirring often. Add the potatoes and heat through.

apple-raisin stuffing

prep 25 minutes I **bake** 25 minutes I **makes** 4 servings

- ¼ **cup (½ stick) butter**
- 1 **stalk celery, chopped (about ½ cup)**
- 1 **small onion, chopped (about ¼ cup)**
- 1 **can (10½ ounces) Campbell's® Condensed Chicken Broth**
- 4 **cups Pepperidge Farm® Herb Seasoned Stuffing**
- 1 **medium apple, cored and chopped (about 1 cup)**
- ¼ **cup raisins**
- ¼ **teaspoon ground cinnamon**

1. Heat the butter in a 10-inch skillet over medium heat. Add the celery and onion and cook until tender, stirring occasionally. Add the broth and heat to a boil. Remove the skillet from the heat. Add the stuffing, apple, raisins and cinnamon and mix lightly. Spoon the stuffing mixture into a 1½-quart casserole.

2. Bake at 350°F. for 25 minutes or until the stuffing is hot.

double-apricot glazed ham

prep 15 minutes I **bake** 2 hours I **makes** 32 servings

- 1 **cup dried apricots**
- 1 **cup Swanson® Chicken Stock**
- ½ **cup packed brown sugar**
- 1 **fully-cooked whole boneless ham* (6 to 8 pounds)**
- 2 **tablespoons butter**
- ½ **cup finely chopped shallots**
- 2 **jars (12 ounces *each*) apricot preserves**
- ¼ **cup Dijon-style mustard**
- 2 **teaspoons grated orange zest**

*You can use a 3-pound fully-cooked half boneless ham for 16 servings. Prepare as directed above, but reduce the remaining ingredients in half and the cooking time to 1 hour or until the ham is heated through.

1. Place the apricots and stock into a microwave-safe measuring cup. Microwave on HIGH for 2 minutes. Let the mixture cool. Remove the apricots and cut into strips. Reserve the stock. Stir the apricots, brown sugar and ¼ **cup** reserved stock in a small bowl.

2. Place the ham into a roasting pan. Bake at 325°F. for 2 hours or until the ham is heated through. Brush with the apricot mixture during the last 30 minutes of baking and baste frequently with the pan drippings.

3. Heat the butter in a 10-inch skillet over medium heat. Add the shallots and cook until tender. Stir in the preserves, mustard, orange zest and remaining reserved stock and heat to a boil. Reduce the heat to low. Cook and stir for 10 minutes or until the stock mixture is slightly thickened.

4. Slice the ham and serve with the apricot sauce.

holiday brie en croûte

thaw 40 minutes I **prep** 15 minutes I **bake** 20 minutes I **stand** 45 minutes I **makes** 12 servings

- 1 **egg**
- 1 **tablespoon water**
- ½ **of a 17.3-ounce package Pepperidge Farm® Puff Pastry Sheets (1 sheet), thawed**
- ½ **cup apricot preserves *or* seedless raspberry jam**
- ⅓ **cup dried cranberries**
- ¼ **cup toasted sliced almonds**
- 1 **(13- to 16-ounce) Brie cheese round**
- 1 **package (13 ounces) Pepperidge Farm® Entertaining Quartet Distinctive Crackers**

1. Heat the oven to 400°F. Beat the egg and water in a small bowl with a fork.

2. Unfold the pastry sheet on a lightly floured surface. Roll the pastry sheet into a 14-inch square. Spread the preserves on the pastry to within 2 inches of the edge. Sprinkle with the cranberries and almonds. Place the cheese in the center of the pastry. Fold the pastry up over the cheese to cover. Trim the excess pastry and press to seal. Brush the seam with the egg mixture. Place seam-side down onto a baking sheet. Decorate with the pastry scraps, if desired. Brush with the egg mixture.

3. Bake for 20 minutes or until the pastry is golden brown. Let stand for 45 minutes. Serve with the crackers.

champagne-poached cornish game hens with artichokes, potatoes, spring onions and roasted garlic

prep 40 minutes I **cook** 20 minutes I **bake** 45 minutes I **makes** 2 servings

2 cups Swanson® Chicken Stock

1 cup champagne *or* other sparkling wine

½ cup black truffle juice

1 large leek, chopped (about 1 cup)

2 stalks celery, chopped (about 1 cup)

1 large carrot, chopped (about ½ cup)

2 cloves garlic, minced

2 sprigs fresh lemon thyme leaves

1 Cornish game hen (about 1½ pounds) *or* poussin (baby chicken)

2 artichoke hearts, cooked and sliced (about ½ cup)

¼ cup diced cooked potato

2 green onions, diagonally sliced (about ¼ cup)

6 cloves roasted garlic

1 tablespoon unsalted butter

1. Heat the stock, champagne, truffle juice, leek, celery, carrot, garlic and thyme in an oven-safe 4-quart saucepan over medium-high heat. Add the hen to the saucepan and heat to a boil. Place the saucepan in the oven.

2. Bake at 350°F. for 45 minutes or until the hen is cooked through. Remove the hen from the saucepan and keep warm.

3. Place the stock mixture into a blender or food processor. Cover and blend until the mixture is smooth. Pour the stock mixture through a sieve into the saucepan. Cook over medium-high heat until the mixture is reduced slightly.

4. Stir the artichokes, potato, green onions, roasted garlic and butter in the saucepan and cook until the mixture is hot and bubbling.

5. Cut the hen in half lengthwise. Place **each** half into a deep bowl. Spoon the vegetables and sauce over the hen halves.

veal spiedini

prep 30 minutes I **cook** 20 minutes I **makes** 6 servings

- ½ cup Italian-seasoned dry bread crumbs
- ¼ cup toasted pine nuts
- 6 slices prosciutto, cut into thirds
- 1¼ pounds veal scalloppine, cut into 18 pieces and pounded thin
- ¼ pound mozzarella cheese, cut into matchstick-thin strips
- ¼ cup olive oil
- 3 cups Prego® Traditional Italian Sauce *or* Heart Smart Traditional Italian Sauce
- 1 package (10 ounces) Pepperidge Farm® Mozzarella Garlic Bread
  Grated Parmesan cheese (optional)

1. Heat the oven to 400°F. Stir the bread crumbs and pine nuts in a small bowl.

2. Divide the prosciutto among the veal pieces. Top **each** with **1 tablespoon** bread crumb mixture. Divide the mozzarella cheese among the veal pieces. Roll up the veal pieces around the filling. Thread **3** veal rolls onto **each** of **6** (6-inch) skewers.

3. Heat the oil in a 12-inch skillet over medium heat. Add the skewers and cook for 3 minutes on each side. Pour the Italian sauce over the skewers. Reduce the heat to low. Cook for 15 minutes or until the veal is cooked through.

4. Meanwhile, bake the bread according to the package directions.

5. Cut the bread into 2-inch diagonal slices. Serve the bread with the veal and sauce. Sprinkle with the Parmesan cheese, if desired.

italian-style pot roast

prep 5 minutes | **cook** 2 hours | **makes** 8 servings

- 2 **tablespoons oil**
- 1 **boneless beef bottom round roast**
- 1 **jar (24 ounces) Prego® Traditional Italian Sauce**
- 6 **medium potatoes, cut into quarters**
- 6 **medium carrots, cut into 2-inch pieces**

1. Heat the oil in a 6-quart saucepot over medium-high heat. Add the roast and cook until browned on all sides. Pour off any fat.

2. Stir the Italian sauce in the saucepot. Heat to a boil. Reduce the heat to low. Cover and cook for 45 minutes.

3. Add the potatoes and carrots. Cover and cook for 1 hour or until the roast and vegetables are tender.

shortcut paella

prep 15 minutes | **cook** 25 minutes | **makes** 8 servings

- 1 tablespoon vegetable oil
- 2 cups **uncooked** regular long-grain white rice
- 4 cups Swanson® Chicken Stock, heated
- 1 cup Pace® Picante Sauce
- 1 teaspoon ground turmeric
- 1 package (16 ounces) turkey kielbasa, sliced
- 12 small frozen peeled, deveined, cooked shrimp, thawed
- 1 package (about 10 ounces) refrigerated fully-cooked chicken breast strips

1. Heat the oil in a 12-inch skillet over medium heat. Add the rice and cook for 30 seconds, stirring constantly. Stir the stock, picante sauce and turmeric in the skillet and heat to a boil. Reduce the heat to low. Cover and cook for 15 minutes.

2. Stir the kielbasa, shrimp and chicken in the skillet. Cover and cook for 5 minutes or until the rice is tender.

sausage-stuffed mushrooms

prep 25 minutes | **bake** 10 minutes | **makes** 24 appetizers

24 **medium mushrooms**

2 **tablespoons butter, melted**

¼ **pound bulk pork sausage**

1 **cup Pace® Picante Sauce**

½ **cup dry bread crumbs**

   Chopped fresh cilantro leaves *or* fresh parsley

1. Heat the oven to 425°F. Remove the stems from the mushrooms. Chop enough stems to make **1 cup**. Brush the mushroom caps with the butter and place top-side down in a shallow baking pan.

2. Cook the sausage and the chopped mushroom stems in a 10-inch skillet over medium-high heat until the sausage is well browned, stirring often to separate the meat. Pour off any fat.

3. Add ½ **cup** picante sauce and the bread crumbs to the skillet and mix lightly. Spoon **about 1 tablespoon** sausage mixture into **each** mushroom cap.

4. Bake for 10 minutes or until the mushrooms are hot. Top **each** with **1 teaspoon** picante sauce and sprinkle with the cilantro.

tips Cut a thin slice from the top of each mushroom cap to keep the caps from rolling in the pan.

To make ahead, prepare as directed above through Step 3. Cover and refrigerate the stuffed mushrooms up to 24 hours. Bake as directed in Step 4.

perfect bbq beef gravy & pot roast

prep 10 minutes | **cook** 2 hours 45 minutes | **makes** 8 servings

- 2 **tablespoons vegetable oil**
- 1 **boneless beef bottom round roast *or* beef chuck pot roast (about 4 pounds)**
- 2 **cans (10¼ ounces *each*) Campbell's® Beef Gravy**
- 2 **tablespoons barbecue sauce**
- 8 **medium carrots, peeled and cut into 2-inch pieces**

1. Heat the oil in a 4-quart saucepot. Add the beef and cook until well browned on all sides. Pour off any fat.

2. Add the gravy and barbecue sauce and heat to a boil. Reduce the heat to low. Cover and cook for 1 hour 30 minutes.

3. Add the carrots. Cover and cook for 1 hour or until the beef is fork-tender.

mozzarella cheese bread sticks

prep 15 minutes **I** **bake** 10 minutes **I** **makes** 24 servings

1 loaf (11¾ ounces) Pepperidge Farm®
Mozzarella Garlic Bread

1½ cups Prego® Traditional Italian Sauce *or*
Tomato Basil & Garlic Italian Sauce

1. Heat the oven to 400°F. Remove the bread from the bag. Carefully separate the bread halves with a fork. Place the **2** bread halves, cut-side up, onto a baking sheet.

2. Bake for 10 minutes or until the bread is heated through. Cut **each** bread half into **12** (1-inch) slices, making **24** in all. Serve with the Italian sauce for dipping.

chicken nachos

prep 10 minutes **I** **cook** 5 minutes **I** **makes** 6 servings

½ cup Pace® Picante Sauce

1 can (10¾ ounces) Campbell's®
Condensed Cheddar Cheese Soup

2 cans (4.5 ounces *each*) Swanson®
Premium White Chunk Chicken Breast
in Water, drained

1 bag (about 10 ounces) tortilla chips

Chopped tomato

Sliced green onions

Sliced pitted ripe olives

1. Heat the picante sauce, soup and chicken in a 1-quart saucepan over medium heat until the mixture is hot and bubbling, stirring often.

2. Place the chips on a platter. Spoon the chicken mixture over the chips. Top with the tomato, onions and olives.

stuffed clams

prep 20 minutes I **cook** 15 minutes I **bake** 20 minutes I **makes** 24 appetizers

24 cherrystone clams, scrubbed

2 slices bacon, diced

3 tablespoons butter

1 medium onion, chopped (about ½ cup)

¼ teaspoon garlic powder *or* 1 clove garlic, minced

1½ cups Pepperidge Farm® Herb Seasoned Stuffing

2 tablespoons grated Parmesan cheese

2 tablespoons chopped fresh parsley *or* 2 teaspoons dried parsley flakes

1. Heat the oven to 400°F.

2. Open the clams. Remove and discard the top shells. Arrange the clams in a 3-quart shallow baking dish.

3. Cook the bacon in a 10-inch skillet over medium-high heat until crisp. Remove the bacon from the skillet and drain on paper towels.

4. Add the butter, onion and garlic powder to the hot bacon drippings and cook until the onion is tender. Stir the stuffing, cheese, parsley and cooked bacon in the skillet and mix lightly. Divide the stuffing mixture evenly among the clams.

5. Bake for 20 minutes or until the clams are cooked through.

index

2-Bean Chili..167
2-Step Inside-Out Chicken
    Pot Pie...119
2-Step Skillet Chicken Broccoli
    Divan...27
3-Cheese Pasta Bake...............................74
7-Layer Meatless Tortilla Pie...............111
20-Minute Turkey & Rice.........................31
25-Minute Chicken & Noodles...........126

appetizers

Bacon and Cheddar Puff Pastry
    Crisps...296
Beefy Taco Dip...298
Buffalo Chicken Dip................................263
Chicken Nachos.......................................313
Festive Taco Nachos...............................243
Game-Winning Drumsticks...................201
Herbed Chèvre en Croûte.....................301
Holiday Brie en Croûte...........................306
Honey Mustard Chicken Bites.............235
Honey-Barbecued Ribs..........................141
Italian Dipping Sauce.............................237
Mini Tacos...239
Mozzarella Cheese Bread Sticks.......313
Pick-Your-Own-Topping Pizza
    Night..234
Salsa-Ranch Dip......................................291
Sausage Bites...72
Sausage-Stuffed Mushrooms..............311
Savory Stuffed Mushrooms...................273
Spinach-Cheese Swirls..........................251
Stuffed Clams...314
Summer Bruschetta................................212
Sweet Potato Dip....................................217
Apple-Raisin Stuffing..............................304
Asian Chicken with Peanuts.................116
Awesome Grilled Cheese
    Sandwiches..231
Bacon and Cheddar Puff Pastry
    Crisps...296
Bacon Horseradish Burgers.................255
Bacon Potato Chowder..........................164
Baked Apple Cranberry Stuffing.........202
Baked Corn Casserole...........................302
Baked Eyeballs Casserole.....................207
Baked Macaroni and Cheese...............228
Baked Pork Chops & Gravy.....................33
Baked Potatoes Olé...................................77
Balsamic Chicken with White Beans
    & Spinach..69
Bandito Baked Beans..............................267
Basil Skillet Potatoes.............................303

beef

2-Bean Chili..167
Bacon Horseradish Burgers.................255
Baked Potatoes Olé...................................77
Beef & Broccoli..73
Beef & Pasta...29
Beef Bourguignonne...............................254
Beef Enchiladas.......................................120
Beef 'n' Bean Bake....................................68
Beef Sirloin Steak with Baby
    Spinach..70
Beef Taco Bake...93
Beef Taco Skillet..32
Beef Teriyaki...61
Beef Wellington..290
Beefy Enchilada Skillet.............................39
Beefy Pasta Skillet.....................................80
Buffalo Burgers...89
Burgers Stroganoff..................................131
Burgundy Beef...259
Cheese Steak Pockets...........................119
Cheesy Enchilada Stack.........................272
Cheesy Jack Tacos..................................233
Cheesy Taco Meatloaf..............................68
Chili & Rice..179
Chili Mac..84
Classic Beef Stroganoff............................38
Classic Lasagna.......................................171
Classic Standing Rib Roast...................300
Creamy Beef Stroganoff........................122
Dripping Roast Beef Sandwiches
    with Melted Provolone......................79
Easy Spaghetti & Meatballs.................134
Easy Taco Tamale Pie...............................67
Fajita Beef Potato Topper.....................253
Family Spaghetti Pie.................................96
Festive Taco Nachos...............................243
French Onion Burgers...............................41
Good-for-You Stuffed Peppers.........136
Grilled Maui Burgers...............................261
Hamburger Pie...238
Hearty Lasagna Soup.............................246
Herb-Simmered Beef Stew...................205
Hidden Veggie Sloppy Joes..................247
Italian-Style Sloppy Joes......................144
Italian-Style Pot Roast...........................309
Lightened Up Beef & Vegetable
    Stir-Fry..175
Linguine with Savory Meat Sauce.....99
Meatloaf Casserole.................................170
Meatloaf with a Twist.............................194
Meatloaf with Roasted Garlic
    Potatoes..178
Mexican Lasagna.....................................284

Mexi-Mac...103
Mini Tacos...239
Mushroom Bacon Burgers...................146
Now & Later Baked Ziti..........................154
One-Dish Beef Stroganoff.......................53
Onion-Crusted Meatloaf with
    Roasted Potatoes............................265
Orange Beef Steak..................................190
Pan-Seared Steaks with
    Mushroom Gravy.............................288
Penne Bolognese-Style..........................157
Perfect BBQ Beef Gravy
    & Pot Roast.......................................312
Polynesian Burgers.................................143
Quick & Easy Dinner Nachos
    Supreme...40
Quick Barbecued Beef
    Sandwiches..57
Quick Skillet Ziti..61
Red Wine Braised Short Ribs
    with Smashed Fall Vegetables.......211
Shortcut Stuffed Peppers.......................42
Simple Salisbury Steak.........................180
Simply Delicious Meatloaf
    & Gravy..176
Sirloin, Pepper & Onion Skillet..........105
Slow Cooker Hearty Beef Stew.......184
Slow Cooker Veggie Beef Stew.......163
Slow-Cooked Taco Shredded
    Beef..118
Souper Sloppy Joes................................101
Spaghetti Bolognese..............................129
Spiced Pot Roast.....................................151
Teriyaki Burgers......................................110
Terrific Tacos...229
Thick & Hearty Two-Bean Chili.......218
Vegetable Beef Stew..............................214
Weekday Pot Roast
    & Vegetables....................................149

Beef & Broccoli..73
Beef & Pasta...29
Beef Bourguignonne...............................254
Beef Enchiladas.......................................120
Beef 'n' Bean Bake....................................68
Beef Sirloin Steak with Baby
    Spinach..70
Beef Taco Bake...93
Beef Taco Skillet..32
Beef Teriyaki...61
Beef Wellington..290
Beefy Enchilada Skillet.............................39
Beefy Pasta Skillet.....................................80
Beefy Taco Dip...298
Broccoli & Cheese Casserole................91
Broccoli & Cheese Stuffed Shells.......75

Broccoli & Garlic Penne Pasta 34
Broccoli & Noodles Supreme 81
Broccoli Chicken Potato Parmesan 232
Broccoli con Queso 28
Broccoli Fish Bake 145
Broth Simmered Rice 163
Buffalo Burgers 89
Buffalo Chicken Dip 263
Burgers Stroganoff 131
Burgundy Beef 259
Challah 294
Champagne-Poached Cornish Game
   Hens with Artichokes, Potatoes,
   Spring Onions and Roasted
   Garlic 307
Cheddar Broccoli Frittata 66
Cheddar Penne with Sausage
   & Peppers 83
Cheese Steak Pockets 119
Cheesy Broccoli 224
Cheesy Chicken Pizza 113
Cheesy Enchilada Stack 272
Cheesy Jack Tacos 233
Cheesy Taco Meatloaf 68

chicken
   2-Step Inside-Out Chicken
      Pot Pie 119
   2-Step Skillet Chicken Broccoli
      Divan 27
   25-Minute Chicken & Noodles 126
   Asian Chicken with Peanuts 116
   Balsamic Chicken with White
      Beans & Spinach 69
   Broccoli Chicken Potato
      Parmesan 232
   Champagne-Poached Cornish
      Game Hens with Artichokes,
      Potatoes, Spring Onions
      and Roasted Garlic 307
   Cheesy Chicken Pizza 113
   Chicken & Broccoli Alfredo 94
   Chicken & Shrimp Jambalaya 76
   Chicken & Stir-Fry Vegetable
      Pizza 121
   Chicken and Bean Burritos 37
   Chicken Cacciatore & Pasta
      Skillet 112
   Chicken Corn Chowder 181
   Chicken Creole with Chile
      Cream Sauce 267
   Chicken Crunch 124
   Chicken Fajitas 125
   Chicken Fusilli with Spinach
      & Asiago Cheese 117
   Chicken in Creamy Sun-Dried
      Tomato Sauce 274
   Chicken Nachos 313
   Chicken Pasta Salad Italiano 126

Chicken Picante Pizzas 236
Chicken Pizza Muffins 26
Chicken Pot Pie in a Shell 269
Chicken Quesadillas
   & Fiesta Rice 90
Chicken Seasoned Rice
   and Vegetable Casserole 64
Chicken Sorrento 92
Chicken Tetrazzini 54
Chicken Tortilla Soup 173
Chicken with Peas & Quinoa 261
Chicken with Savory
   Herbed Rice 132
Chicken with Wild Mushroom
   Cream Sauce 279
Citrus Chicken and Rice 203
Country Chicken Casserole 174
Creamy Chicken Quesadillas 65
Creamy Pesto Chicken
   & Bow Ties 35
Crispy Chicken with Asparagus
   Sauce 282
Crispy Italian Chicken 115
Crunchy Chicken and Gravy 133
Crunchy Chicken with
   Ham Sauce 128
Crunchy No-Fry Chicken 44
Curried Chicken Chowder 269
Dee's Curry Chicken 260
Easy Asian-Style Chicken & Rice 60
Easy Chicken & Cheese
   Enchiladas 85
Easy Chicken Molé 283
Easy Chicken Stroganoff 131
Fiesta Chicken & Rice Wraps 45
Game-Winning Drumsticks 201
Garlic Chicken, Vegetable
   & Rice Skillet 138
Golden Chicken & Autumn
   Vegetables 209
Honey Mustard Chicken Bites 235
Hot Chicken & Potato Salad 130
Lighter Chicken Cheesesteaks 50
Mediterranean Chicken
   Casserole 137
Mexican Chicken & Rice 150
Monterey Chicken Tortilla
   Casserole 142
One-Dish Chicken & Rice Bake 82
Oven-Fried Chicken
   Chimichangas 285
Oven-Roasted Chicken
   with Artichokes, Lemon
   and Tomato Sauce 277
Panhandle Pepperoni Chicken 252
Pan-Sautéed Chicken with
   Vegetables & Herbs 156
Picante Chicken & Rice Bake 155

Picnic Chicken Salad
   Sandwiches 226
Quick & Easy Chicken
   Quesadillas 43
Quick Chicken a la King 160
Quick Chicken Parmesan 48
Ranchero Enchilada Casserole 172
Salsa Chicken Soup 46
Savory Balsamic Herb Chicken 270
Savory Orange Chicken
   with Sage 258
Sensational Chicken Noodle
   Soup 185
Shortcut Chicken Cordon Bleu 58
Shortcut Paella 310
Simple Creamy Chicken Risotto ... 152
Sizzling Fajitas 135
Skillet Cheesy Chicken & Rice 183
Skillet Chicken & Rice 230
Slow Cooker Jambalaya 210
South of the Border Chicken
   & Bean Burritos 55
Spanish Chicken & Chorizo 268
Spicy Barbecued Chicken 187
Spicy Verde Chicken
   & Bean Chili 148
Whole Wheat Chicken Salad
   Sandwiches 107
Chicken & Broccoli Alfredo 94
Chicken & Shrimp Jambalaya 76
Chicken & Stir-Fry Vegetable Pizza ... 121
Chicken and Bean Burritos 37
Chicken Cacciatore & Pasta Skillet 112
Chicken Corn Chowder 181
Chicken Creole with Chile Cream
   Sauce 267
Chicken Crunch 124
Chicken Fajitas 125
Chicken Fusilli with Spinach
   & Asiago Cheese 117
Chicken in Creamy Sun-Dried
   Tomato Sauce 274
Chicken Nachos 313
Chicken Pasta Salad Italiano 126
Chicken Picante Pizzas 236
Chicken Pizza Muffins 26
Chicken Pot Pie in a Shell 269
Chicken Quesadillas & Fiesta Rice 90
Chicken Seasoned Rice
   and Vegetable Casserole 64
Chicken Sorrento 92
Chicken Tetrazzini 54
Chicken Tortilla Soup 173
Chicken with Peas & Quinoa 261
Chicken with Savory Herbed Rice 132
Chicken with Wild Mushroom
   Cream Sauce 279
Chili & Rice 179

Chili Mac..84

chilis & chowders
2-Bean Chili...................................... 167
Bacon Potato Chowder 164
Chicken Corn Chowder...................... 181
Chili & Rice 179
Curried Chicken Chowder.................. 269
Spicy Verde Chicken & Bean Chili .. 148
Thick & Hearty Two-Bean Chili 218
Vegetable Chili 106

Chocolate and Coconut Cream
Fondue.. 241
Chocolate Pirouette-Crusted Cake.....295
Chocolate Velvet Torte 177
Citrus Chicken and Rice 203
Classic Beef Stroganoff......................... 38
Classic Lasagna.................................. 171
Classic Standing Rib Roast................... 300
Classic Tuna Noodle Casserole............. 161
Company Buffet Layered Salad........... 293
Cookies 'n' Yogurt.............................. 242
Country Chicken Casserole 174
Cranberry Apple Bread Pudding 199
Creamy Beef Stroganoff...................... 122
Creamy Carrot Gingered Soup 168
Creamy Chicken Quesadillas................ 65
Creamy Dijon Dressing........................ 291
Creamy Pesto Chicken & Bow Ties 35
Crispy Chicken with Asparagus
Sauce... 282
Crispy Italian Chicken 115
Crunchy Chicken and Gravy................ 133
Crunchy Chicken with Ham Sauce..... 128
Crunchy No-Fry Chicken 44
Curried Chicken Chowder.................... 269
Dee's Curry Chicken............................. 260

desserts
Chocolate and Coconut Cream
Fondue 241
Chocolate Pirouette-Crusted
Cake.. 295
Chocolate Velvet Torte 177
Cookies 'n' Yogurt............................. 242
Cranberry Apple Bread Pudding 199
Fantastic Cookie Bars....................... 289
Graveyard Cupcakes.......................... 198
Sweet Potato Pie............................... 195
Tomato Soup Spice Cake 166
Dilled Tuna & Egg Sandwiches 77
Double-Apricot Glazed Ham 305
Dripping Roast Beef Sandwiches
with Melted Provolone 79
Easy Asian-Style Chicken & Rice........... 60
Easy Chicken & Cheese Enchiladas.....85
Easy Chicken Molé............................... 283
Easy Chicken Stroganoff...................... 131

Easy Mushroom Soup............................ 187
Easy Pasta Primavera............................. 78
Easy Spaghetti & Meatballs................. 134
Easy Taco Tamale Pie 67
Easy Turkey & Biscuits 139
Fajita Beef Potato Topper..................... 253
Family Spaghetti Pie............................. 96
Fantastic Cookie Bars........................... 289
Festive Taco Nachos............................. 243
Fiesta Chicken & Rice Wraps 45

fish & seafood
Broccoli Fish Bake 145
Chicken & Shrimp Jambalaya............. 76
Classic Tuna Noodle Casserole........ 161
Dilled Tuna & Egg Sandwiches............ 77
Fish & Vegetable Skillet...................... 36
Grilled Swordfish Steaks
with Citrus Salsa 49
Linguine with Easy Red Clam
Sauce... 264
Mediterranean Halibut
with Couscous................................ 276
Salmon with Cucumber-Dill
Cream Napoleons 280
Shortcut Paella 310
Slow Cooker Jambalaya.................... 210
Stuffed Clams................................... 314
Tuna & Pasta Cheddar Melt................ 30
Tuna Melts.. 225
Fish & Vegetable Skillet........................ 36
Florentine Turkey Meatloaf.................. 281
French Onion Burgers............................. 41
Game-Winning Drumsticks................... 201
Garden Vegetable Pizza....................... 244
Garlic Chicken, Vegetable & Rice
Skillet... 138
Garlic Potato Soup............................... 162
Glazed Pork Chops................................ 28
Golden Chicken & Autumn
Vegetables....................................... 209
Goldfish® Pizzas.................................. 227
Goldfish® Checkerboard
Sandwich.. 245
Good-for-You Stuffed Peppers............. 136
Graveyard Cupcakes............................ 198
Green Bean Casserole.......................... 165
Grilled Maui Burgers............................ 261
Grilled Swordfish Steaks
with Citrus Salsa................................. 49
Hamburger Pie..................................... 238
Hearty Lasagna Soup........................... 246
Hearty Old Fashioned Vegetable
Soup... 169
Herb Roasted Turkey............................ 191
Herbed Chèvre en Croûte.................... 301
Herbed Turkey Breast 297
Herb-Simmered Beef Stew................... 205

Hidden Veggie Sloppy Joes.................. 247
Holiday Brie en Croûte 306
Holiday Potato Pancakes...................... 208
Holiday Turkey with Cranberry
Pecan Stuffing.................................. 213
Honey Mustard Chicken Bites 235
Honey-Barbecued Ribs......................... 141
Hot Chicken & Potato Salad................. 130
Hot Sausage Casserole.......................... 97
Italian Dipping Sauce.......................... 237
Italian Sausage & Peppers
with Penne... 88
Italian-Style Pot Roast......................... 309
Italian-Style Skillet Pork Chops........... 86
Italian-Style Sloppy Joes..................... 144
Lasagna Primavera............................... 114
Lasagna Roll-Ups................................. 140
Layered Pasta, Veggie & Cheese
Skillet... 59
Lightened Up Beef & Vegetable
Stir-Fry... 175
Lighter Chicken Cheesesteaks.............. 50
Linguine with Easy Red Clam
Sauce.. 264
Linguine with Savory Meat Sauce 99
Mac & Cheese Veggie Bake 98
Meatloaf Casserole.............................. 170
Meatloaf with a Twist.......................... 194
Meatloaf with Roasted Garlic
Potatoes... 178
Mediterranean Chicken Casserole...... 137
Mediterranean Halibut with
Couscous.. 276
Mexican Beans and Rice 100
Mexican Chicken & Rice 150
Mexican Lasagna................................. 284
Mexican Pizza...................................... 104
Mexi-Mac.. 103
Mini Tacos... 239
Miracle Lasagna.................................. 120
Moist & Savory Stuffing 216
Monterey Chicken Tortilla
Casserole.. 142
Mozzarella Cheese Bread Sticks........... 313
Mushroom Bacon Burgers................... 146
Now & Later Baked Ziti 154
One-Dish Beef Stroganoff..................... 53
One-Dish Chicken & Rice Bake............. 82
Onion-Crusted Meatloaf
with Roasted Potatoes...................... 265
Orange Beef Steak 190
Oven-Fried Chicken Chimichangas....285
Oven-Roasted Chicken with
Artichokes, Lemon and Tomato
Sauce.. 277
Panhandle Pepperoni Chicken............. 252
Pan-Grilled Veggie & Cheese
Sandwiches.. 87

Pan-Sautéed Chicken with
  Vegetables & Herbs...............................156
Pan-Seared Steaks with Mushroom
  Gravy...288

pasta & pizza
  3-Cheese Pasta Bake..............................74
  25-Minute Chicken & Noodles.........126
  Baked Eyeballs Casserole...................207
  Baked Macaroni and Cheese.............228
  Beef & Pasta..29
  Beefy Pasta Skillet...................................80
  Broccoli & Cheese Stuffed Shells.......75
  Broccoli & Garlic Penne Pasta.............34
  Broccoli & Noodles Supreme................81
  Cheddar Penne with Sausage
    & Peppers...83
  Cheesy Chicken Pizza...........................113
  Chicken & Stir-Fry Vegetable
    Pizza...121
  Chicken Cacciatore & Pasta
    Skillet...112
  Chicken Fusilli with Spinach
    & Asiago Cheese.................................117
  Chicken Pasta Salad Italiano..............126
  Chicken Picante Pizzas.........................236
  Chicken Pizza Muffins.............................26
  Chili Mac..84
  Classic Lasagna.....................................171
  Classic Tuna Noodle Casserole.........161
  Creamy Pesto Chicken
    & Bow Ties...35
  Easy Pasta Primavera.............................78
  Easy Spaghetti & Meatballs...............134
  Family Spaghetti Pie..............................96
  Garden Vegetable Pizza......................244
  Goldfish® Pizzas.....................................227
  Italian Sausage & Peppers with
    Penne...88
  Lasagna Primavera................................114
  Lasagna Roll-Ups..................................140
  Layered Pasta, Veggie & Cheese
    Skillet...59
  Linguine with Easy Red Clam
    Sauce...264
  Linguine with Savory Meat Sauce.....99
  Mac & Cheese Veggie Bake.................98
  Mexican Lasagna..................................284
  Mexican Pizza..104
  Mexi-Mac..103
  Miracle Lasagna....................................120
  Now & Later Baked Ziti.......................154
  Pasta e Fagioli...71
  Penne Bolognese-Style........................157
  Picante Macaroni and Cheese..........255
  Pick-Your-Own-Topping Pizza
    Night..234
  Puff Pastry Vegetable Pizza...............102

Quick Skillet Ziti.......................................61
Simple Seasoned Ravioli........................56
Spaghetti Bolognese.............................129
Stuffed-Crust Sopressata Pizza
  with Lemony Arugula Salad...........256
Sun-Dried Tomato Bow Tie
  Pasta..127
Super Simple Nacho Pasta..................240
Tomato Walnut Pesto Penne..............197
Tuna & Pasta Cheddar Melt..................30
Pasta e Fagioli..71
Penne Bolognese-Style.........................157
Perfect BBQ Beef Gravy
  & Pot Roast..312
Picante Chicken & Rice Bake...............155
Picante Macaroni and Cheese............255
Pick-Your-Own-Topping Pizza
  Night..234
Picnic Chicken Salad Sandwiches......226
Pineapple-Picante Stir-Fried Pork
  & Cabbage..278
Polenta with Mushroom
  Vegetable Topping.............................275
Polynesian Burgers................................143

pork
  Baked Pork Chops & Gravy..................33
  Cheddar Penne with Sausage
    & Peppers...83
  Double-Apricot Glazed Ham.............305
  Glazed Pork Chops.................................28
  Honey-Barbecued Ribs........................141
  Hot Sausage Casserole.........................97
  Italian Sausage & Peppers
    with Penne...88
  Italian-Style Skillet Pork Chops..........86
  Pineapple-Picante Stir-Fried Pork
    & Cabbage..278
  Pork Chops & French Onion Rice....153
  Pork with Mushroom Dijon Sauce.....51
  Quick Bean & Rice Casserole...............80
  Sausage Bites..72
  Sausage-Stuffed Mushrooms............311
  Skillet Pork Chops Florentine..............47
  Slow Cooker Fall Harvest Pork
    Stew...204
  Slow Cooker Mole-Style Pulled
    Pork..266
  Slow-Cooked Pulled Pork
    Sandwiches..186
  Smothered Pork Chops...........................52
  Spanish Chicken & Chorizo...............268
  Stuffed Pork Roast with
    Herb-Seasoned Artichoke
    & Mushroom Stuffing........................299
  Tomato & Onion Pork Chops
    with Cannellini Beans.......................123
Pork Chops & French Onion Rice.......153

Pork with Mushroom Dijon Sauce........51
Power Breakfast Sandwiches...............229
Puff Pastry Vegetable Pizza................102
Quick & Easy Chicken Quesadillas........43
Quick & Easy Dinner Nachos
  Supreme...40
Quick Barbecued Beef Sandwiches.....57
Quick Bean & Rice Casserole................80
Quick Chicken a la King.......................160
Quick Chicken Parmesan........................48
Quick Skillet Ziti.......................................61
Ranchero Enchilada Casserole...........172
Ratatouille Soup.....................................198
Ratatouille Tart.......................................192
Red Wine Braised Short Ribs
  with Smashed Fall Vegetables.........211
Roasted Dijon & Apple Glazed
  Turkey with Fruited Stuffing............292
Roasted Garlic Mashed Potatoes........169
Roasted Orange Cranberry Sauce......194
Roasted Sweet Potato Soup................219
Roasted Tomato & Barley Soup..........182
Roasted Turkey Breast with Herbed
  au Jus..196
Root Vegetable Gratin..........................221
Salmon with Cucumber-Dill
  Cream Napoleons...............................280
Salsa Chicken Soup.................................46
Salsa-Ranch Dip.....................................291

sandwiches
  Awesome Grilled Cheese
    Sandwiches..231
  Cheese Steak Pockets.........................119
  Dilled Tuna & Egg Sandwiches...........77
  Dripping Roast Beef Sandwiches
    with Melted Provolone........................79
  Goldfish® Checkerboard
    Sandwich..245
  Lighter Chicken Cheesesteaks............50
  Pan-Grilled Veggie & Cheese
    Sandwiches..87
  Picnic Chicken Salad
    Sandwiches..226
  Power Breakfast Sandwiches.............229
  Quick Barbecued Beef
    Sandwiches..57
  Slow-Cooked Pulled Pork
    Sandwiches..186
  Tomato Soup & Grilled Cheese
    Sandwich..174
  Tuna Melts...225
  Turkey & Avocado Sandwiches...........46
  Whole Wheat Chicken Salad
    Sandwiches..107
Sausage Bites...72
Sausage-Stuffed Mushrooms..............311
Savory Balsamic Herb Chicken...........270

Savory Herb-Crusted Turkey
Pot Pie...220
Savory Orange Chicken with Sage....258
Savory Stuffed Mushrooms 273
Sensational Chicken Noodle Soup 185
Shortcut Chicken Cordon Bleu 58
Shortcut Paella...................................310
Shortcut Stuffed Peppers.........................42

side dishes

Apple-Raisin Stuffing............................304
Baked Apple Cranberry Stuffing......202
Baked Corn Casserole........................302
Baked Macaroni and Cheese............228
Bandito Baked Beans 267
Basil Skillet Potatoes..........................303
Broccoli & Cheese Casserole 91
Broccoli & Garlic Penne Pasta 34
Broccoli & Noodles Supreme................81
Broccoli con Queso...............................28
Broth Simmered Rice............................163
Challah...294
Cheddar Broccoli Frittata 66
Cheesy Broccoli..................................224
Company Buffet Layered Salad.......293
Creamy Dijon Dressing 291
Easy Pasta Primavera...........................78
Green Bean Casserole.........................165
Holiday Potato Pancakes....................208
Mac & Cheese Veggie Bake................98
Mexican Beans and Rice.....................100
Moist & Savory Stuffing 216
Polenta with Mushroom
Vegetable Topping........................275
Roasted Garlic Mashed Potatoes....169
Roasted Orange Cranberry Sauce..194
Root Vegetable Gratin.......................221
Spaghetti Squash Alfredo 147
Super Simple Nacho Pasta 240
Toasted Corn & Sage Harvest
Risotto..215
Twice-Baked Squash Medley 206

Simple Creamy Chicken Risotto 152
Simple Salisbury Steak............................180
Simple Seasoned Ravioli 56
Simply Delicious Meatloaf & Gravy....176
Sirloin, Pepper & Onion Skillet..............105
Sizzling Fajitas....................................135
Skillet Cheesy Chicken & Rice...........183
Skillet Chicken & Rice........................230
Skillet Pork Chops Florentine 47
Slow Cooker Fall Harvest Pork
Stew...204
Slow Cooker Hearty Beef Stew...........184
Slow Cooker Jambalaya......................210
Slow Cooker Mole-Style Pulled
Pork...266
Slow Cooker Veggie Beef Stew 163

Slow-Cooked Pulled Pork
Sandwiches..................................186
Slow-Cooked Taco Shredded Beef....118
Smothered Pork Chops...........................52
Souper Sloppy Joes.............................101

soups & stews

Chicken Tortilla Soup 173
Creamy Carrot Gingered Soup 168
Easy Mushroom Soup.........................187
Garlic Potato Soup.............................162
Hearty Lasagna Soup.........................246
Hearty Old Fashioned Vegetable
Soup..169
Herb-Simmered Beef Stew.................205
Pasta e Fajioli.......................................71
Ratatouille Soup.................................198
Roasted Sweet Potato Soup..............219
Roasted Tomato & Barley Soup.......182
Salsa Chicken Soup...............................46
Sensational Chicken Noodle
Soup..185
Slow Cooker Fall Harvest Pork
Stew...204
Slow Cooker Hearty Beef Stew.......184
Slow Cooker Veggie Beef Stew........163
Tomato Soup & Grilled Cheese
Sandwich.......................................174
Vegetable Beef Stew............................214

South of the Border Chicken
& Bean Burritos..............................55
Southwestern Turkey, Corn
and Chile Enchiladas.....................271
Spaghetti Bolognese..........................129
Spaghetti Squash Alfredo....................147
Spanish Chicken & Chorizo 268
Spiced Pot Roast.................................151
Spicy Barbecued Chicken...................187
Spicy Turkey, Corn and Zucchini
Skillet...200
Spicy Verde Chicken & Bean Chili......148
Spinach-Cheese Swirls........................251
Stuffed Clams.....................................314
Stuffed Pork Roast with
Herb-Seasoned Artichoke
& Mushroom Stuffing....................299
Stuffed-Crust Sopressata Pizza
with Lemony Arugula Salad...........256
Summer Bruschetta.............................212
Sun-Dried Tomato Bow Tie Pasta......127
Super Simple Nacho Pasta 240
Sweet Potato Dip...............................217
Sweet Potato Pie................................195

Teriyaki Burgers.................................110
Terrific Tacos......................................229
Thick & Hearty Two-Bean Chili........218
Toasted Corn & Sage Harvest
Risotto...215

Tomato & Onion Pork Chops
with Cannellini Beans....................123
Tomato Soup & Grilled Cheese
Sandwich.......................................174
Tomato Soup Spice Cake....................166
Tomato Walnut Pesto Penne..............197
Tuna & Pasta Cheddar Melt..................30
Tuna Melts..225

turkey

20-Minute Turkey & Rice 31
Easy Turkey & Biscuits........................139
Florentine Turkey Meatloaf................281
Herb Roasted Turkey...........................191
Herbed Turkey Breast 297
Holiday Turkey with Cranberry
Pecan Stuffing...............................213
Roasted Dijon & Apple Glazed
Turkey with Fruited Stuffing 292
Roasted Turkey Breast with Herbed
au Jus...196
Savory Herb-Crusted Turkey
Pot Pie...220
Shortcut Paella....................................310
Southwestern Turkey, Corn and
Chile Enchiladas............................271
Spicy Turkey, Corn and Zucchini
Skillet...200
Turkey & Avocado Sandwiches...........46
Zesty Turkey Burgers..........................257

Turkey & Avocado Sandwiches...........46
Twice-Baked Squash Medley 206

veal

Veal Spiedini......................................308

Veal Spiedini......................................308
Vegetable Beef Stew...........................214
Vegetable Chili...................................106

vegetarian dishes

7-Layer Meatless Tortilla Pie............111
Broccoli & Cheese Stuffed Shells 75
Lasagna Primavera 114
Lasagna Roll-Ups...............................140
Layered Pasta, Veggie & Cheese
Skillet...59
Miracle Lasagna.................................120
Ratatouille Tart..................................192
Tomato Walnut Pesto Penne.............197
Vegetable Chili..................................106
Wild Mushroom Ragoût in Puff
Pastry Shells..................................262

Weekday Pot Roast & Vegetables......149
Whole Wheat Chicken Salad
Sandwiches...................................107
Wild Mushroom Ragoût in Puff
Pastry Shells..................................262
Zesty Turkey Burgers..........................257

VOLUME MEASUREMENTS (dry)

¹/₈ teaspoon = 0.5 mL
¹/₄ teaspoon = 1 mL
¹/₂ teaspoon = 2 mL
³/₄ teaspoon = 4 mL
1 teaspoon = 5 mL
1 tablespoon = 15 mL
2 tablespoons = 30 mL
¹/₄ cup = 60 mL
¹/₃ cup = 75 mL
¹/₂ cup = 125 mL
²/₃ cup = 150 mL
³/₄ cup = 175 mL
1 cup = 250 mL
2 cups = 1 pint = 500 mL
3 cups = 750 mL
4 cups = 1 quart = 1 L

VOLUME MEASUREMENTS (fluid)

1 fluid ounce (2 tablespoons) = 30 mL
4 fluid ounces (¹/₂ cup) = 125 mL
8 fluid ounces (1 cup) = 250 mL
12 fluid ounces (1¹/₂ cups) = 375 mL
16 fluid ounces (2 cups) = 500 mL

WEIGHTS (mass)

¹/₂ ounce = 15 g
1 ounce = 30 g
3 ounces = 90 g
4 ounces = 120 g
8 ounces = 225 g
10 ounces = 285 g
12 ounces = 360 g
16 ounces = 1 pound = 450 g

DIMENSIONS

¹/₁₆ inch = 2 mm
¹/₈ inch = 3 mm
¹/₄ inch = 6 mm
¹/₂ inch = 1.5 cm
³/₄ inch = 2 cm
1 inch = 2.5 cm

OVEN TEMPERATURES

250°F = 120°C
275°F = 140°C
300°F = 150°C
325°F = 160°C
350°F = 180°C
375°F = 190°C
400°F = 200°C
425°F = 220°C
450°F = 230°C

BAKING PAN AND DISH EQUIVALENTS

Utensil	Size in Inches	Size in Centimeters	Volume	Metric Volume
Baking or Cake Pan (square or rectangular)	8×8×2	20×20×5	8 cups	2 L
	9×9×2	23×23×5	10 cups	2.5 L
	13×9×2	33×23×5	12 cups	3 L
Loaf Pan	8¹/₂×4¹/₂×2¹/₂	21×11×6	6 cups	1.5 L
	9×9×3	23×13×7	8 cups	2 L
Round Layer Cake Pan	8×1¹/₂	20×4	4 cups	1 L
	9×1¹/₂	23×4	5 cups	1.25 L
Pie Plate	8×1¹/₂	20×4	4 cups	1 L
	9×1¹/₂	23×4	5 cups	1.25 L
Baking Dish or Casserole			1 quart/4 cups	1 L
			1¹/₂ quart/6 cups	1.5 L
			2 quart/8 cups	2 L
			3 quart/12 cups	3 L